INTELLIGENT SYSTEMS IN BUSINESS:

INTEGRATING THE TECHNOLOGY

edited by

J. Jeffrey Richardson
Marjorie J. DeFries

Center for Applied Artificial Intelligence
Graduate School of Business Administration
University of Colorado at Boulder

 ABLEX PUBLISHING CORPORATION
NORWOOD, NEW JERSEY

Printed in the United States of America

Library of Congress Cataloging-in-Publication Data

Intelligent systems in business : integrating the technology / edited
  by Jeffrey Richardson and Marjorie J. DeFries.
       p. cm.
    "Edited papers and transcripts from An International Forum:
  Increasing Management Productivity with Intelligent Systems, held
  August 29–31, 1988, In Snowmass/Aspen, Colorado, and sponsored by
  the Center for Applied Artifical Intelligence, Graduate School of
  Business Administration, University of Colorado"—Pref.
    Includes bibliographical references.
    ISBN 0-89391-550-5
    1. Business—Data processing Congresses.   2. Management—Data
  processing—Congresses.   3. Artificial intelligence—Congresses.
  4. Expert systems (Computer science)—Congresses.   I. Richardson,
  Jeffrey.   II. DeFries, Marjorie J.   III. International Forum:
  Increasing Management Productivity with Intelligent Systems (1988 :
  Snowmass, Colo. and Aspen, Colo.)   IV. University of Colorado,
  Boulder. Center for Applied Artificial Intelligence.
  HD30.2.I555   1990
  650'.0285'63–dc20   90–260
                                                                        CIP

Ablex Publishing Corporation
355 Chestnut Street
Norwood, New Jersey 07648

To Edward S. Safford

Contents

22

Preface

When business managers begin to contemplate the value of applying an artificial intelligence system within their own company, sources of information have been mostly technical. Managers, however, are not usually technicians, and they need nontechnical advice—preferably advice from others with some experience using these new systems. Why projects were started, how they were justified, what difficulties were encountered, and the results achieved are among the valuable lessons learned.

This book will help fill the need managers have for nontechnical descriptions of successful business uses of artificial intelligence. It is most important to inform managers about the value of this new technology—for they set the agenda for change. Formerly, AI systems were stand-alone systems, while the trend today and into the future is *integration* of these valuable systems with conventional computer databases and applications. This is an important message woven into every chapter of this book and one that managers need to hear.

We have prepared this book to help managers learn, not about techniques, but about applications of intelligent systems to the business problems of today. It is our hope that as more managers see how intelligent systems are paying off for others, they will see how they may begin to utilize these valuable tools in their own business.

The contents of this book are edited papers and transcripts from *An International Forum: Increasing Management Productivity with Intelligent Systems*, held August 29–31, 1988, in Snowmass/Aspen, Colorado, and sponsored by the Center for Applied Artificial Intelligence, Graduate School of Business Administration, University of Colorado at Boulder.

Business men and women don't need to "publish or perish," as is the case for university faculty. Thus, most AI literature stems from academia and is technical. Reports from the field of the hard-fought battle to apply AI technology to corporate enterprise are few. It is for this reason that we believe this collection of essays about corporate implementation of AI technology is an especially valuable record.

J. Jeffrey Richardson
Marjorie J. DeFries

Boulder, Colorado
May 17, 1989

Acknowledgments

This book is the proceedings of an August 1988 forum "Increasing Management Productivity with Intelligent Systems" held in Snowmass/Aspen, Colorado. The forum was sponsored by the Center for Applied Artificial Intelligence, a unit of the Graduate School of Business Administration, University of Colorado at Boulder. The planning took well over a year and involved an effort on the part of many people. As members of the planning team, we would like to express our appreciation to all those who contributed to this effort but especially those mentioned below.

Our most heartfelt thanks go to Edward Safford, who as Forum Chairman committed himself to the success of the forum and graciously donated his business acumen, energy, and an enormous amount of his time without compensation to the Graduate School of Business Administration for over a year. In recognition of his generous gift to the University, this book has been dedicated to him.

Our special appreciation, also, goes to Dean Edward Johnson of the Graduate School of Business Administration, who made the initial request that the Center for Applied AI sponsor a forum. He provided the necessary support of the effort and offered words of encouragement during the long months of planning.

As forum coordinator, Melissa Eiles used her superb organizational and management skills to coordinate all the activities with a great deal of professionalism. No better coordinator could have been provided us and we extend to her our very special thanks.

The preparation of the forum papers into chapters for this book involved many hours of work on the part of the editors but also on the part of Lucile Zellar, Center secretary. Our sincere appreciation to Lucy for the hours she devoted to the manuscript preparation and author contact.

Thanks go also to Bruce Johnson, Thea Turner, and Timothy Smith who served as session moderators at the forum. Additionally, we extend our appreciation to Center staff and School of Business students who served in many capacities during the forum and without whose help the forum would not have been possible.

Finally, Marc Jalbert and Mary Little, Center graduate assistants in Spring 1987, deserve special mention. Their early joint effort provided the feasibility assessment and basic design for the forum. Their initial hard work culminates with the publication of this book.

J. Jeffrey Richardson
Marjorie J. DeFries
Coeditors

Contributors and Editors

Craig S. Atkinson
Chemical Bank

While employed by Chemical Bank, New York City, Mr. Atkinson was vice president of the Information and Technology Management Division, Advanced Technology Department, which serves as the focal point for knowledge-based systems and provides education, consulting, and joint development throughout the bank. Previously employed by Chase Manhattan Bank and the Securities Industry Automation Corporation, he has held various management positions in the planning, operations, control, and administration of large-scale computer and communications systems.

Craig Atkinson is currently vice president of Research and Development within the Strategic Technology and Research Group of Manufacturers Hanover Trust Company. Mr. Atkinson is a former director of the Association of Data Communication Users, a member of the Associations of Information Systems Professionals, and a member of the American Association of Artificial Intelligence. He is a founding member of the Society for the Management of AI Resources and Technology—Financial Services.

Stephen P. Barba
Balsams Grand Resort Hotel

Stephen Barba is president and managing director of the Balsams Grand Resort Hotel located in Dixville Notch, New Hampshire. He began his continuous association with the hotel in 1959 while working as a caddy, and in 1971 he and a friend began to manage the hotel. Since 1976 he and his three partners (the maintenance superintendent, the executive chef, and the general manager) have leased and profitably operated the 15,000-acre resort.

Among Mr. Barba's credits are the following: director from 1973–1987 of the New Hampshire Travel Council; member since 1979 of the New Hampshire Select Committee for Joint Promotional Program—Matching Grants; member since 1980 of the American Hotel and Motel Association Resort Committee; President from 1983–1985 of the New Hampshire Golf Association; President from 1985–1986 of Ski the White Mountains; and President from 1984–1985 of the New Hampshire Hospitality Association. Mr. Barba was designated Innkeeper of the Year, 1980–1981.

Bert L. Bivens
Lockheed Aeronautical Systems Company

Bert Bivens is an Information Systems Specialist at Lockheed Aeronautical Systems Company in Burbank, California. Employed by Lockheed Corporation since 1956 in the fields of scientific computing and information technology, he has worked on many projects using computers to assist in the process of aircraft design.

Mr. Bivens was instrumental in establishing an Artificial Intelligence Center at Lockheed's facility in Southern California and in initiating a number of expert systems at that facility. Among these systems are Medical Charge and Evaluation Control (MEDCHEC) used to audit group medical insurance claims and Composite Orientation and Stacking Expert Reasoner (Composer) developed to assist structural engineers in developing aircraft parts from composite materials.

Richard L. Blumenthal
U S WEST Advanced Technologies

Richard Blumenthal is a member of the technical staff of the Advanced Systems Research Department, U S WEST Advanced Technologies, Englewood, Colorado. He is a principal researcher responsible for the formation, design, and prototype development of research projects in the areas of knowledge acquisition and representation, automated model building, and parallel distributed processing.

Prior to joining U S WEST, Mr. Blumenthal was a member of the technical staff in the Knowledge Systems Research Department of AT&T Bell Laboratories.

Mr. Blumenthal is a member of the board of directors of the Rocky Mountain Society for Artificial Intelligence and has served as editor and tutorial chairman for the annual Rocky Mountain Conference on Artificial Intelligence. Additionally, Mr. Blumenthal is a member of both the American Association of Artificial Intelligence and of the IEEE Computer Society. He is author of various published articles on expert systems and artificial intelligence.

Barbara L. Braden
Bull HN

Barbara Braden is director of Advanced Technologies Corporate Information Services of Bull HN, Inc., Waltham, Massachusetts. Previously Dr. Braden was responsible for the development and application of new technologies for the Customer Services Division, which developed several knowledge-based systems to advise and assist the field engineer. One set of systems can be accessed remotely from the field at any time. Another set of systems assists personnel of the Technical Assistance Center to support the field engineer and customers at any location.

Prior to working with expert systems, Dr. Braden held positions in marketing and internal business systems.

Joe K. Carter
Arthur Andersen and Company

Joe Carter is a partner in the Chicago-based Artificial Intelligence Group of Arthur Andersen and Company. The group he heads provides training, technology tracking, methodology, project management, and technical support to Artificial Intelligence groups in Arthur Andersen's offices worldwide.

Since joining the firm in 1977, Mr. Carter has designed and implemented computerized business systems in construction companies, utilities, insurance companies, retail and wholesale distributors, manufacturing companies, and not-for-profit institutions. His recent projects using AI technology include life and automobile insurance underwriting, financial analysis, and manufacturing production scheduling.

Marjorie J. DeFries
Volume Coeditor
University of Colorado at Boulder

Marjorie DeFries is the coordinator of the Center for Applied Artificial Intelligence, University of Colorado at Boulder. In this capacity, one of her major responsibilities is managing the administration of the Colorado Institute for Artificial Intelligence, a state university-industry research consortium. Ms. DeFries served on the planning committee for the forum and was involved in every aspect of the conference. The writing and production of conference materials was one of her major responsibilities.

Prior to joining the Center, Ms. DeFries was employed in the publication industry as well as in management, administration, and public relations in university, national laboratory, and government settings.

Laurie Dowell
Texas Instruments, Inc.

Laurie Dowell is methods supervisor for the Microwave Technology and Products Division of the Defense Systems and Electronics Group at Texas Instruments. When Ms. Dowell joined Texas Instruments in 1984, she was responsible for capital equipment justification. In 1985 she was assigned the job of knowledge engineer for the Capital Investment Expert System, and in 1987 she began supervising expert system development.

Robert A. Dwinnell
5thGen Technology Inc.

Robert A. Dwinnell is chief scientist for 5thGen Technology Inc., Long Lake, Minnesota. He has worked for over 20 years in many different areas of computer technology, including computer hardware design, magnetic recording, peripheral systems design, firmware development, and electrical computer-aided design.

For the last six years Mr. Dwinnell has been working with the application of AI programming technology to planning problems with an emphasis on manufacturing planning.

David W. Erbach
Great-West Life Assurance Co.

David Erbach is information systems consultant for Great-West Life Assurance Co., Winnipeg, Canada. His former positions included responsibility for software, database, and telecommunication architectures; internal education; and application software development. For the last two years he has directed expert systems development for Great-West Life.

Dr. Erbach received his Ph.D. from Cambridge University and is a former faculty member of the University of Wisconsin-Madison. He has been an invited speaker at a number of executive and technical conferences in North America and Europe.

Jack Gary
Texas Instruments, Inc.

Jack Gary has been employed by Texas Instruments since 1984 and is currently serving as a manufacturing manager in the Microwave Technology/Products Division of the Defense Systems and Electronics Group. He is responsible for the fabrication of semirigid coaxial cables, acoustical surface wave devices, and thin film networks.

In past assignments, Mr. Gary has been responsible for Capital Procurement and Industrial Engineering. He has published three papers concerning artificial intelligence and manufacturing strategies.

Michael P. Gelhausen
Andersen Consulting

Michael Gelhausen is a partner in Andersen Consulting's Dallas office with responsibility for the firm's worldwide Transportation Industry Team. With 11 years of systems and consulting experience, he specializes in transportation and logistics work and is also responsible for the Artificial Intelligence activities of the Southwest Region.

As a member of the Artificial Intelligence team of Andersen Consulting, Mr. Gelhausen is responsible for coordinating area and firmwide training and production in the various areas of artificial intelligence. Included in these functions are expert systems maintenance diagnostics, materials routing, finite scheduling, transportation scheduling, and materials transfer accounting applications.

W. T. Illingworth
Texas Instruments, Inc.

W. T. Illingworth is engineering manager of Texas Instruments, Dallas, Texas, and a member of the Group Technical Staff. He has been with Texas Instruments since 1956 and is currently serving as manager of Artificial Intelligence Applications for Microwave Manufacturing in the Defense Systems and Electronics Group. In this role he is responsible for new artificial intelligence concepts including productivity improvement programs employing expert systems and neural networks.

Mr. Illingworth has held managerial positions in industrial engineering, plant mechanization, and product line automations at several sites for Texas Instruments. He has published 12 papers and has several patents.

Kristina M. Johnson
University of Colorado at Boulder

Kristina Johnson is associate professor, Department of Electrical and Computer Engineering, Optoelectronic Computing Systems Center, University of Colorado at Boulder. She is an innovator in applying optoelectronics and engineering to the needs of business.

Dr. Johnson received her doctorate from Stanford University in 1984; was a NATO post-doctoral fellow at Trinity College, Dublin, Ireland, 1984–1985; has been a visiting scientist at IBM Research Laboratories in San Jose, California; and was named Presidential Young Investigator by the National Science Foundation in 1985. A member of six professional organizations, Dr. Johnson has over 20 publications and two patent-pending inventions to her credit.

Julie Wallin Kaewert
Digital Equipment Corporation

Julie Kaewert is an AI business consultant at Digital's corporate AI Technology Center in Marlborough, Massachusetts. Ms. Kaewert is an advocate of the integration of AI techniques with existing systems and offers proof of the success of this approach in the form of Digital's own AI achievements.

She is knowledgeable about expert system applications in a variety of industries worldwide and tracks expert system products and developments in the U.S., Australia, Japan, and Europe. Her responsibilities include product marketing, product strategy, and competitive analysis.

Before joining Digital Ms. Kaewert worked as a journalist and consultant in London and gained a background in DEC systems from the user's point of view. She is author of *A Strategic Guide to Implementing Expert Systems*, published by United Kingdom consultancy Systems Dynamics Ltd. Ms. Kaewert has experience with a variety of expert system development tools and has completed Digital's Intelligent Systems Technology Training Program in knowledge engineering.

J. Kenneth Klitz
IBM

J. Kenneth Klitz is program manager, Systems Integration Division, International Business Machines, Boulder, Colorado. Currently he is responsible for providing artificial intelligence solutions to IBM customers and is implementing a transporation expert system that solves problems of distribution.

Previously Mr. Klitz managed the IBM Corporate Manufacturing Modeling Center of Competency and was IBM manager of a resource planning organization for a manufacturing and laboratory installation. As senior scientist at IIASA, Laxenburg, Austria, he was involved in modeling global energy resource requirements and alternatives. Mr. Klitz has also served as assistant director of a U.S. Presidential commission on resource availability and environmental impacts.

Mike Kranzdorf
University of Colorado at Boulder

Mike Kranzdorf is president of Oblio, Inc., a consulting firm specializing in computer animation and simulation. Mr. Kranzdorf received his BS degree in electrical engineering from Tufts University in 1983 and his M.S. degree in electrical engineering from the University of Colorado in 1988.

As a professional research assistant at the Optoelectronic Computing Systems Center (OCS), Mr. Kranzdorf has published papers in the fields of artificial neural networks and their optical implementations. His current interests include connectionist networks, appropriate interfaces for computer simulations, and three-dimensional graphic design and animation. He is the author of an introductory connectionist simulator for the Macintosh called Mactivation, which has been distributed in over 15 countries.

Ed Mahler
E.I DuPont de Nemours & Co.

Ed Mahler is program manager, Artificial Intelligence, Information Systems Department, E.I. DuPont de Nemours & Co., Wilmington, Delaware. During his employment with DuPont he has held numerous managerial positions in research and manufacturing. During a five-year assignment in Corporate Strategic Planning, he served as liaison for emerging technologies and founded the Corporate Artificial Intelligence Task Force. In his current position he is responsible for implementing DuPont's artificial intelligence program worldwide.

DuPont is a widely recognized leader in the application of expert systems with about 100 systems in routine use and several hundred more in field testing. Highly oriented toward business needs and early economic benefits, DuPont's strategic plan for implementing artificial intelligence focuses on these three key elements of success: understanding business opportunities, technology, and resourcing options. DuPont's approach has yielded an average 1,500 percent return on total cash effort and serves as a model for implementing other emerging technologies.

Nelson Marquina
Coopers & Lybrand

Nelson Marquina is a partner in Coopers & Lybrand's Management Consulting Practice, New York. He has over 15 years of experience in electronic data and information processing, decision support systems, statistical modeling, and computer simulation. He has directed projects in areas of factory automation, statistical process control, manufacturing productivity improvement, expert systems for decision support, and embedded knowledge-based software systems.

Prior to his employment with Coopers & Lybrand, Dr. Marquina was an assistant professor of Industrial and Systems Engineering at the University of Houston and an associate professor of Electrical Engineering at the University of Rhode Island. He was employed by General Electric as head of the AI Laboratory at the Advanced Technology Laboratories.

Dr. Marquina has chaired national conferences and technical sessions in expert systems, quality assurance, autonomous systems, automated planning, robotics, and computer vision. He is a member of the editorial board of the journal *Expert Systems: Planning/Implementation/Integration.*

Dr. Marquina received his doctorate in systems engineering from the University of Houston, Houston, Texas.

Claude McMillan
Management Robotics

Claude McMillan is the president of Management Robotics, Inc., Boulder, Colorado. He is a pioneer in the application of artificial intelligence and operations research to the problems of scheduling, especially personnel scheduling.

Dr. McMillan received his doctorate in business administration from Ohio State University in 1955. At the University of Colorado at Boulder he was professor of management science and professor of computer science from 1965 to 1987, director of the Information Sciences/Genetic Resources Program from 1977 to 1980, and co-director of the Center for Applied Artificial Intelligence from 1984 to 1986. He has been involved in consulting in business and government since 1955. Dr. McMillan is a renowned lecturer, member, and officer of many professional organizations, and the author of many published articles and books.

Hon. D. Bruce Merrifield
United States Department of Commerce

Dr. Bruce Merrifield was appointed by President Ronald Reagan in 1982 as assistant secretary for Productivity, Technology, and Innovation, United States Department of Commerce, Washington, D.C. Dr. Merrifield is responsible for examining the effect of government policies on private sector productivity growth with a view to eliminating barriers and stimulating productivity through cooperative research and development consortia and through transfer of federally developed technology into the private sector. His responsibilities also include the assessment of the competitive position of U.S. industries in world markets as a guide for federal policy options in critical areas. He is responsible for coordinating patent policy and metric conversion activities and for preparing studies of strategic resources. He is a leader in stimulating productivity with intelligent systems and other innovations.

Dr. Merrifield was vice president of Technology and Venture Management for the Continental Group before he joined the Commerce Department. He has been a director, vice president, and president-elect of the Industrial Research

Institute and is a former trustee of the American Management Association and chairman of its Research and Development Council. Currently he is a member of the Directors of Industrial Research and a fellow of the American Association of Sigma Xi and the American Chemical Society.

A graduate of Princeton University, Dr. Merrifield earned M.S. and Ph.D. degrees in physical organic chemistry from the University of Chicago.

Felix J. Nidzgorski
Information Builders, Inc.

Felix Nidzgorski is national sales manager for LEVEL5, a product of Information Builders, Inc. For the past 16 years he has been involved in leading edge computers and software with such companies as Tandem Computers and Dun and Bradstreet.

Mr. Nidzgorski has published many articles on expert systems and the practical use of computer systems to solve business requirements.

J. Jeffrey Richardson
Volume Coeditor
University of Colorado at Boulder

J. Jeffrey Richardson is director of the Center for Applied Artificial Intelligence, Graduate School of Business Administration, University of Colorado, Boulder, Colorado. He also heads the Colorado Institute for Artificial Intelligence, a statewide university/industry consortium dedicated to enhancing the technology and human resources foundation for AI in Colorado.

Dr. Richardson's principal research interest is in AI applications, specifically in equipment maintenance and in training. Dr. Richardson is an expert in the systems engineering approach to AI applications in machine diagnosis and is editor of the two principal reference volumes in this field. He is editor of a book on the foundations of intelligent tutoring systems and is actively building intelligent tutoring systems.

Dr. Richardson spent five years as Research Scientist at the Denver Research Institute, University of Denver. One of his major research achievements while there was the development of a prototype Maintainer's Associate for the Air Force. This is a portable, computer-based, job-aid maintenance that technicians use in troubleshooting equipment. The evaluation of this prototype helped establish guidelines for the functional specifications of such systems.

Additional research conducted by Dr. Richardson includes work in task analysis, problem-solving instruction, and computer-managed instruction.

Dr. Richardson received his doctorate in mathematics education at the University of Colorado at Boulder. In addition to a number of published articles, Dr. Richardson is the author of FactMaster, a published computer program for elementary school mathematics that implements many of the tenets of intelligent tutoring in the area of number fact mastery.

Ron Roberts
Federal Express Company

Ron Roberts is business applications advisor, Federal Express Company, Memphis, Tennessee. Responsible for the introduction and use of artificial intelligence and expert systems throughout Federal Express, he is working currently in the formation of a Knowledge Systems Development Group in the Information and Telecommunications Division.

In his 16 years with Federal Express Mr. Roberts has held numerous professional and management positions in operations and staff support functions.

Tom Sargent
Texas Instruments, Inc.

Tom Sargent joined Texas Instruments in May, 1984, as an industrial engineer supporting the start up of the Advanced Microwave Module Factory for Microwave Technology Products Business Development. Since November 1985 Mr. Sargent has been assigned as a knowledge engineer for the Capital Expert System.

Donald K. Stratton
Fireman's Fund Insurance Company

Donald Stratton has been project development manager of Fireman's Fund Insurance Company for eight years. In 1986 he was active in an effort to apply expert system technology to the underwriting automobile business, an effort that established the potential of expert systems in that area. Subsequently he has headed a very successful project to implement expert systems for 130 underwriters nationwide and to enhance the functionality and scope of the initial system.

Prior to his involvement with expert systems, Mr. Stratton managed a variety of application development projects using structured methodologies and prototypes on both the PC and the mainframe.

Perry W. Thorndyke
FMC Corporation

Perry Thorndyke is currently program manager of corporate Strategic Programs at FMC Corporation in Santa Clara, California. Between August 1984 and February 1989 he served as director of the FMC Artificial Intelligence Center. In this position he directed the company's 35 AI scientists in research and development operations comprising research, exploratory and applied development, and technology transfer to FMC operating divisions. Dr. Thorndyke was the principal architect of the AI Center's technology strategy, of its growth from 5 to 35 scientists, of the formal training program to develop AI professionals, of FMC's equity investment in and strategic affiliation with Teknowledge, and of the corporate-wide program to disseminate knowledge systems software and training.

Between 1981 and 1984 Dr. Thorndyke was director and general manager of the Knowledge Systems Branch of Perceptronics, Inc. Prior to joining Perceptronics, he served as a computer scientist in the Information Sciences Department of the Rand Corporation. In both positions he played a principal role in organizational and business development of the company's AI capabilities. Dr. Thorndyke has also held research positions in AI at Bolt, Beranek, & Newman, Inc.; SRI International; and Xerox Palo Alto Research Center.

Dr. Thorndyke holds a B.A. Degree in computer and information sciences from Yale University and a Ph.D. degree in cognitive psychology from Stanford University. He has served on the faculty of UCLA and is currently on the advisory board of the *Spang-Robinson Artificial Intelligence Report*. He has authored or coauthored over 40 articles and reports in the areas of distributed AI, knowledge-based systems, planning, instruction, and human cognition.

Winston J. Wade
U S WEST Advanced Technologies

Winston Wade has been president of U S WEST Advanced Technologies Division, Englewood, Colorado, since 1985. Since his employment with the Bell System in 1962, he has held numerous supervisory and leadership positions. Under Mr. Wade's direction, U S WEST Advanced Technologies has become a leader in software research and applications. U S WEST has recently committed to build a large research and development facility, including its research unit in software and systems.

Mr. Wade serves on the board of directors of Bellcore, Computer Technology Associates, and Ameritas. He is a member of the Institute of Electrical and Electronic Engineers and is a Trustee of the University of Nebraska Foundation.

Dennis H. West
Motorola Corporation

Dennis West is manager of Service Technology, Field Service Division, Motorola Corporation, Dallas, Texas. He has over 30 years of experience in the computer industry and is involved in the long-range planning of service and support requirements for Motorola. He implemented the expert system "Helpdesk" designed to service products related to hardware and software. This system was installed in one of Motorola's National Technical Support Centers in 1988.

Mr. West is a member of Motorola's Corporate Artificial Intelligence Committee.

Foreword

The examples presented in this book give us a glimpse of a quiet revolution taking place in industry. The striking thing is that this revolution is having a profound effect on the few visionary companies who have ventured into the new realm of this, the knowledge revolution, and are transforming their companies with a new kind of computer program, the expert system, that automates routine decision making.

The chapters in this book clearly point toward the new era in computing, the use of these machines as knowledge partners—beyond effective data logging and personal productivity tools. Cost-effective tools have finally arrived in the marketplace to enable automation of routine analysis and decision making. Striking in the breadth of applications spanning business functions and industries, these stories depict visionary climbers using new technology to reap bottom-line results. The climbers frequently encountered a series of barriers such as communications difficulties, hardware anomalies, the press of current operations, and internal politics. But they persevered with innovative solutions like "Sneakernet" for data transfer and others equally focused on solving the business problem.

Let me tidy up a few definitions from the first two paragraphs and, I hope, create a template for viewing the chapters in this book. First, expert systems: *An expert system is a computer program for capturing valuable knowledge and delivering it at the point of decision making.* Fundamental to understanding expert systems is understanding the difference among data, information, and knowledge. Transactions create *data* whether it be a sensor on the factory floor measuring some variable, a phone call, or an entry into a corporate order system. From our viewpoint, then, transaction processing creates data. Data is mind-deadening for us to deal with so we select, sort, and summarize data into *information*. This selecting, sorting, and summarizing process, known as information processing or decision support systems, usually arranges data into the three forms most often used in industry: text, tables, and graphics. We as humans revel in our domain of *knowledge processing*, the *analysis* of information to make decisions. In many ways an expert system mimics our reasoning process, that is, applying our knowledge to analyze some information to make a decision. Analogous to storing data in a data base, expert systems store knowledge in a knowledge base—both, naturally, for later use, frequently at some other place. Just as the record is the storage unit for data bases, a simple if/then rule is the storage unit for knowledge bases. (This is a gross oversimplification on my part, as several other storage units for knowledge do exist but the dominant form being used in industry today is the simple rule.)

So much for the 50,000-foot view of the enabling technology. The real point is the bottom-line impact of adding this new technology for transferring knowledge to the points of decision making. Enjoy these success stories, learn of the impact you could have on your business, and launch a successful program at your place.

E. G. Mahler
E. I. DuPont de Nemours & Company

part I
Introduction

1
Introduction*

J. Jeffrey Richardson

Center for Applied
Artificial Intelligence

This chapter serves as introduction to this book, which contains business testimonials of successful expert systems applications. Since the focus of the book is nontechnical and the viewpoint largely managerial, this introduction begins by providing background on the technology of artificial intelligence and expert systems. Subsequently, the chapter integrates and synthesizes material from the remainder of the book on business applications of expert systems focusing on the benefits, applications, problem selection criteria, costs, development strategies, integration, and maintenance of expert systems. The chapter closes with a look into the future of expert systems.

BACKGROUND

To a great extent, business enterprise depends on the successful exploitation of technology. Growth in business stems from the exploitation of new technology. Many companies are now starting to take advantage of a new technology that is the subject of this book: artificial intelligence and especially expert systems. The purpose of this book is to share the experiences of 17 companies who have begun to utilize intelligent systems in their business practices. Chapter 2 makes the case that future business competitiveness critically depends on successfully exploiting the power of intelligent systems. Each of the 17 corporate applications chapters describes how a corporation turned to expert systems in an attempt to improve its strategic advantage and competitiveness. This chapter is intended to introduce the reader to the technology of artificial intelligence and expert systems and to draw together and highlight the main points and common themes of the chapters, especially with regard to suggestions about how to manage the incorporation of this new technology into business practice.

Natural Intelligence

A book about artificial intelligence (AI) ought to start out with a good definition of AI: *AI is the attempt to emulate intelligent behavior on computers.* But this

---

3

just begs the question of what intelligent behavior is, which is the discipline addressed by cognitive psychology.

One major attribute of intelligent behavior is the ability to use and understand language. It has proven to be very difficult to develop a detailed and satisfactory theory of language understanding. To illustrate the difficulty, suppose you read that "San Antonio is under ten feet of water." Does this mean that San Antonio lies completely under water, like the mythical lost city of Atlantis, with the tips of even the tallest buildings below the surface? Obviously, the meaning of language is not intrinsic in the words of a sentence alone; context, prior knowledge, and common sense play a role too. For context to play a role, the hearer must have a mental representation or model of the situation. Thus, processing language and memory are closely linked.

Memory is the second attribute of intelligence—the ability to store and retrieve relevant experiences. Representation is a key issue in the study of memory, that is, what kind of formal structures store our knowledge and memories or at least what kind of structures can help explain the phenomenon of memory. Knowledge representation is one of the most mature areas of cognitive psychology and is heavily exploited by expert systems technology.

The third attribute of intelligence is problem solving—achieving a goal in new and novel situations. Cognitive psychology has been quite successful in describing and formalizing problem solving behavior. The theories developed have common-sense appeal and emphasize such mechanisms as "divide and conquer," "working backward from the goal," "trial and error," and the use of patterns or schema. Such problem-solving models play an important role in expert systems technology.

Once achieved, the path to the solution can be stored in memory for later use, illustrating a fourth attribute of intelligence—learning. In this sense, learning is an inevitable consequence of problem solving. While knowledge representation and problem solving have been exploited in expert systems technology, it has proven far more difficult to develop "machine learning." Hence, in this regard, expert systems do not replicate human behavior very well; people learn from experience, but expert systems (on the whole) do not.

Of course, intelligent behavior also means being able to perceive and act—to use our senses (to hear, see, touch, or smell) and to move, grasp, or manipulate. Thus, intelligence can be summarized by these six attributes: language processing, memory, problem solving, learning, perception, and motor control.

Artificial Intelligence

Having described intelligence, we may now turn to *artificial* intelligence. As stated above, AI is the study of replicating intelligent behavior on the computer—the above six attributes of intelligent behavior.

How do AI researchers learn how to replicate these things? One key approach is to use ourselves as models—to recreate in computers our own image of intelligence. In fact, we are our best and only model of intelligent beings. But AI is a pragmatic science. Any way of achieving the goal will do, even though the "natural" way (determined through self-study) often proves the best.

The game of chess illustrates how there can be differences between "natural" and "artificial" intelligence. The game is a set of moves and countermoves. Suppose you have 30 moves at your disposal. For each of these, your opponent may counter with, say, another 30 moves. Thus, as you look forward into the sequence of possible moves and countermoves, the possibilities grow by a factor of 30 at each step. An examination of a sequence of 10 moves and countermoves yields 590 trillion possibilities!

The basic AI approach to chess is based on an examination of as many potential moves as possible. This strategy is modified to reduce the number of overall moves that need to be examined. This is done by cutting off further examination of the moves that follow after a move predicted to lead to unsatisfactory results.

The human strategy, however, is quite different. Studies of chess experts (De Groot, 1965) have shown that they do not examine millions or even thousands of moves. They *recognize* the five or ten moves that are best at the outset and spend their time analyzing these few moves. That is, they draw heavily on their experience, memory, and knowledge of the game.

That "knowledge" plays a role in human play of chess is easily demonstrated (Chase & Simon, 1973). Show a midgame board to a novice and an expert chess player, give them a recall test, and the expert outperforms the novice. Then show a random arrangement of the same pieces (not in a midgame configuration). Then novice and expert perform the same. Evidently, the expert is able to use information about the *meaningful* arrangement of pieces to aid in recall.

The point here is that AI does not and need not always use human approaches in emulating intelligence.

Principles of AI. Several principles of intelligence have emerged in the over 30 years of research in the field of AI. These principles (Reddy, 1988) help illustrate what AI programs are:

First, *search makes up for lack of knowledge.* The chess example above amply illustrates this: The computer method compensates for its lack of knowledge of chess by considering (searching) a vastly greater number of alternative moves.

Conversely, the second principle states, *knowledge compensates for limited search capability.* If you cannot efficiently search through millions of possibilities, knowing a set of good solutions will get the job done. In the early days of AI, it was thought that general purpose reasoning strategies could account for all intelligent behavior. But it was found that without the aid of knowledge, there are too many possible paths to try out, not only in chess, but in any reasoning task (the so-called "combinatorial explosion"). When trying out all possibilities, there is not enough time available to arrive at satisfactory solutions. The advent of knowledge-based systems characterizes the more recent years of AI and the realization, captured by the second principle, that, intelligence stems not from the ability to reason alone but from the possession of large amounts of specific knowledge. Knowledge *is* power.

The third principle quantifies how much knowledge is needed in expert performance: 50,000 or so "chunks." An example of a chunk of knowledge would be a midgame board position the chess expert recognizes. Knowledge is specific, technical, and usually nontransferrable from one task to another: masons "know" how to lay brick; surgeons "know" how to operate. Expert-level performance in any field requires acquisition of massive amounts of knowledge. At rates of acquisition commensurate with satisfactory performance in most professional training and education programs, professional expertise—from tennis to theology—can take up to 10 years to acquire.

A fourth principle is perhaps the most important, for it answers the question, What is new about AI? The principle is the *physical symbol system hypothesis*, and its answer to the question is: AI is *not* new—at least not any newer than computers. This hypothesis states that given any set of symbols, the ability to make comparisons of one symbol against another, the ability to compose symbols of others (as words are composed of letters), and the ability to store and retrieve these into a memory are *the necessary and sufficient conditions for intelligence*. An ordinary computer has all these attributes. In fact, these attributes are a good functional definition of what a computer does.

The implications of the physical symbol system hypothesis are vast. First, since your PC has these "necessary and sufficient" conditions for intelligence, the principle claims that the difference between your intelligence and the computer's is not a matter of *kind*—both you and it are presumed to have the same physical symbol systems. It is simply a matter of *degree*—presumably you manipulate vastly more symbols than the PC does. A second, far-reaching implication of this hypothesis is that symbol manipulation is the universal basis of intelligence. Thus, human, machine, and Martian intelligence are fundamentally equivalent.

As a footnote before moving on from the physical symbol hypothesis, it must be mentioned that all AI researchers do not subscribe to the view that symbol manipulation is the *only* way to achieve intelligence. Indeed, recent activity in artificial neural networks (described in Chapter 5) demonstrates the achievement of intelligent behavior from *patterns of activity* of collections of very simple "neuron-like" processors, each of which, in and of itself, does not represent a symbol.

Is AI new? AI is not any newer than computers; in fact, it's a lot *older*. The dream of "creating man in his own image" is probably as old as the quest for immortality. Even Hebrew folklore speaks of the Golem, an artificial human being endowed with life. What is new with AI is the exploitation of the *essence* of the computer—the capability to carry out computations which we specify. The advent of computers makes possible 1 to 10 millionfold increases in the speed of computation carried out by hand. Such scale-of-magnitude increases in the *quantity* of computation engender a *qualitative* change in the nature of computation. AI is the attempt to apply this explosion in quantitative computing power to qualitatively new kinds of computational objectives. Instead of using computers for tasks formerly "computed" by hand (such as payroll or inventory), AI scientists have striven to use computers for computational tasks more qualitatively similar to those involved in intelligent behavior. AI provides *techniques* for accomplishing this broader utilization of computers. In fact, artificial intelligence has generated many techniques with which we are all familiar, for example, the mouse, bit-mapped displays (that show images and not just text) and icons. Even the older advances of time-sharing or interpreters were first developed in AI labs. These techniques suggest an alternative definition for AI—*AI is an attempt to make computers easier to use.*

Is AI a fad? To answer this, ask, "Are computers a fad?" Of course not! Computers are becoming more and more a part of everyday life. The days of "one person/one computer" are not very far off. Computing power is getting cheaper every year; computers are becoming smaller and faster. There is no end in sight to the trend. In fact, new and fundamentally more powerful architectures for computing machines based not on electronics but on optics are now being developed (see Chapter 5).

As computers become pervasive and the need to interact with them becomes universal, we *cannot* fashion *ourselves* into *their* image—it has to be the other way around: the more powerful computers become, the more it becomes necessary for us to learn how to *make them in our own image*—and this is the definition of AI this introduction began with: replicating intelligent behavior in computers.

BUSINESS APPLICATIONS OF EXPERT SYSTEMS

Of all AI techniques, the one that has the greatest practical importance today is the expert system. An expert system is a program that replicates skilled (or expert) behavior. What led to the development of the expert system was the realization that intelligence derives from knowledge (the second principle of intelligence above). The more you know, the easier it is to be smart. Learning is hard; reasoning is hard—in both natural and artificial intelligence. Applying what we already know is easier.

Chapter 15 discusses several other AI techniques that are of interest to that company besides expert systems. A theme in that chapter is that there are other practical AI techniques besides expert systems. Speech recognition, advanced user interfaces, and advanced software technology are three areas discussed. However, in terms of fielded, practical, cost-effective applications of AI to date, the expert system reigns supreme.

Expert Systems

The key to the success of expert systems was that the expertise AI researchers attempted to capture was in technical, narrow, and clearly circumscribed domains. Expert systems are feasible because they are not built to solve general problems requiring common sense. Expertise is specialized by nature. As a problem becomes more and more specialized, it gets smaller and smaller, until it becomes tractable. Solving the world's problems is too big a task, but making a small contribution is something we each can do. Similarly, "managing the enterprise" is too big a job for expert systems, but "controlling capital expenditure authorizations" is feasible; diagnosing and prescribing in medicine is too general, but diagnosing infectious blood diseases is feasible; exploring for oil is too general, but interpreting oil exploration logs is feasible.

Because knowledge is specialized, it is necessarily localized—nontransferrable. The specific knowledge of capital authorizations is of little use in insurance underwriting. The specific diagnostic knowledge of medical science is of little use in electronics troubleshooting. Thus, most expert systems will be developed to solve problems local to specific organizations—where most specialized knowledge resides. That is, expert systems are fundamentally "grass roots" in nature—tailored to address a problem of a particular nature.

Expert systems guidance advises us to avoid *at all costs* problems that involve common sense—that kind of general knowledge we all share—in favor of problems that involve technical expertise. The narrow focus of expert systems is a two-edged sword: It permits success, but it assures failure when the expert system is exposed to problems on the periphery or outside of its realm of expertise, a phenomenon sometimes called the "knowledge cliff." It is ironic that AI's first success, expert systems, deals with the latest human intellectual achievements—knowledge of technical fields—and not the early and more fundamental intelligent behaviors of language, perception, or motion.

After the first few expert systems were developed (in the early 1970s) the knowledge they embodied was stripped out, leaving a "shell" to be filled with other knowledge. These expert systems shells are like any computer application package—word processors, spreadsheets, data bases: They are interfaces to the computer that do not require programming. Expert system shells are simply *rule interpreters*, sometimes called by the fancy name of "inference engines." These shells take knowledge often represented as 50, 500, or even 5000 IF-THEN rules, and chain the rules together. An example of a rule from Chapter 10 is:

IF   the cost of an item is greater or equal to 1000, AND the useful life is greater or equal to 2 years, AND the item is not software,

THEN   it is 100% definite the item is capitalized.

In forward chaining, the reasoning is forward—from IFs to THENs. If a certain collection of facts enables some IFs to be true, then their THENs become true too and their conclusions are added to the body of facts. Then the cycle is repeated. Now that the collection of facts is enlarged, additional THENs may be triggered yielding additional conclusions, and so on.

In backward chaining, the reasoning is backward—from THENs to IFs. The THEN is often taken as a goal. The object is to find out how the goal can be concluded as true. It will be true, so backward reasoning dictates, if all its IFs are true. So a new goal is established to prove each of the IFs is true. The process repeats as we look to see what rules' THENs would conclude the sought after IF, and so on, until known facts are found to trigger the sequence forward, concluding the goal.

The details of forward and backward chaining are less important than the fact that having a shell means that programmers no longer need to specify how rules are "linked." Any FORTRAN program is also a collection of IF-THEN rules, but the order in which these are interpreted—that is—program control, is intertwined in an inseparable mass of code with the rules themselves. Expert system shells separate control from knowledge. That's what's new.

Domain of Applications

Expert systems have, by now, been applied in virtually hundreds of settings. Feigenbaum, McCorduck, and Nii (1988) lists 139 expert systems in use by the commercial sector in such categories as agriculture, commutations, computers, construction, utilities, finance, manufacturing, mining, geology, medicine, science, and transportation. A list of manufacturing applications (*AI Week*, 1988) includes equipment repair and maintenance, process diagnosis, process planning, process control and optimization, production planning, work scheduling, electrical and electronic testing, and many other applications. Chapter 12 illustrates how expert systems applications span the manufacturing process continuum—from design, to production planning, to production control. Chapter 13 reports how expert systems are proving useful in all aspects of the business enterprise: engineering, sales, service, manufacturing, and distribution.

As of 1987, expert systems applications have made modest (about 10 percent) penetration across the board in most major financial applications: financial planning, real estate, accounting, corporate treasuries, brokerages, merchant banking, money managers, consumer finance companies, savings and loans, commercial banks, and especially insurers. Cognitive Systems, Inc. projects virtual saturation (100 percent of firms) by shortly after 1992 (Blanchard, 1989). Chapter 9 reports the result of a similar 1987 market analysis of financial applications and presents two case studies.

Technical knowledge is not limited to engineering and financial domains. Chapter 22 describes how expert systems were found useful in solving the difficult problem of providing quality customer service at The Balsams Grand Resort Hotel. Table 1.1 summarizes the expert systems discussed in this book.

The human impact of expert systems (and of AI) is worth noting before leaving this applications section. Some may ask, "Will expert systems replace humans?" The resounding answer from the applications reported in this book is "No!" The goal of building expert systems is to help people work "smarter," not to replace them. The thrust is to *augment* human intelligence, not to *replace* it. In cases where expert systems do perform what humans formerly did (as in wellhead configuration tasks at FMC or VAX computer configuration tasks at Digital), the freed human labor resource is absorbed by even more demanding tasks. That is, human productivity and the appropriate use of human labor is increased.

Decision Criteria of Candidate Applications

Knowing the potential benefit of expert systems and of their extremely broad range of application, an important question becomes, What decision criteria determine a good application? Fortunately, this issue was examined early on by Waterman (1986) and more recently by Slagle and Wick (1988). Both analyses are roughly equivalent and compatible and are incorporated together with lessons from this book's chapters in this section.

The decision criteria examine the task, the development project, and organizational context. The task should, of course, be a problem. That is, most successful applications of expert systems technology were responses to a problem, not the other way around. Often, expert systems successfully solve problems traditional information technology cannot—expert systems fill an "applications void," as described in Chapter 16, of problems once considered too complex for conventional solutions. Both Chapters 12 and 13 describe expert systems that were successful in solving problems where traditional software approaches had failed.

The single most important concern for appropriate tasks is whether expertise is unavailable or in short supply. Problems may stem from the difficulty of transferring expertise from one individual to another, a requirement for expertise distributed over a wide geographical area (service technicians in different regions), or the need for vigilant and alert expertise over an extended period of time (process control). The problem may also stem from a general shortage of skilled personnel (due to growth in business or scarcity of labor). An interesting

Table 1.1. Expert Systems Described in this Volume

US WEST	SALAD—System for Analog Link and Diagnosis
	INDUS—Internal Document Understanding System
	BACH—Basic Account Code Handler
	GNMS—Generic Network Modeling System
Fireman's	Automobile Workbench
Coopers & Lybrand	ExperTax
	REINSURANCE
TI	Capital Expert System
Lockheed	MEDCHEC—Medical Charge Evaluation and Control
	COMPOSER—Composites Orientation and Stacking Expert Reasoner
	ATEX—Aircraft Technician's Expert System
	MSCST—Manufacturing Science of Complex Shape Thermoplastics
FMC	design—wellhead configuration
	production planning—carrageenan blending
	production control—controlling a phosphorus plant
	integrated—computer-integrated gaging
Digital	APES—Automatically Produced Engineering Schematics
	XSEL—Expert Selling Assistant
	AI SPEAR—prognosticate on equipment error logs
	XFL—Expert Floor Layouts
	XCOM—Expert Configuration System
	MOC—Manufacturing Operations Consultant
	CAN BUILD—inventory re-utilization
	performance analyzer—management decision support
	DELPHI—quality control in manufacturing
	IMACS—shop floor control
	INET—national dispatch router
IBM	cargo loading expert system
Andersen Consulting	ship scheduler
	TRA—truck routing assistant
	micro-dispatch assistant
	AM/DS—aircraft maintenance/diagnostics system
	in-air maintenance debrief
MRI	SuperSched—employee scheduling
BULL HN	PAGE-X—high speed printer diagnosis
	ISC—intelligent software configurator
	PERMAID—diagnose disk subsystems
Motorola	field service planner
The Balsams Grand Resort Hotel	hotel management

example cited in Chapter 12 is the need to have human expertise control a phosphorus plant. The natural cycle or periodicity of control in that plant is 24 or 48 hours, whereas the natural cycle for the human operators is the 8-hour work shift. Using expert systems, the rhythms of human expertise and of the job were better matched.

The task itself should be knowledge-intensive (symbolic in nature, cognitive, with knowledge easily partitioned into categories), heuristic (based on "rules of thumb" that are useful, general advice but not infallible), and subjective. Experts who can perform the task and who agree on and can justify or explain solutions should exist. It should *not* be natural language-intensive, and it should not require common sense, an optimal solution, or creativity. While not needing a real-time response has formerly been a criteria, expert system shells specialized for real-time performance do now exist, and customization to optimize for speed is always an option.

With respect to development, it is helpful if the system can be built incrementally and iteratively (e.g., rapid prototyping). Chapter 9 describes FFAST, a tool used to facilitate rapid prototyping. In general, iterative and incremental development is a hallmark of the expert systems development strategy.

Verification and validation of the system require the availability of test cases. If a similar expert system has been built before, this is a good indication of feasibility, but it should not deter an appropriate novel or innovative application. There is always a first in any application area.

In terms of the system's interaction with its users, it is preferable that sequences of questions follow an intelligent pattern and that the system explain its reasoning upon request. Indeed, this is one of the major attributes of expert systems; they are the first class of computer programs to have a limited ability to explain their reasoning.

Organizationally, smooth insertion into the workplace is a requirement. Many of the applications chapters that follow indicate that a major cost involved in an expert system project is interfacing with the user and with the work environment (including other, mainstream hardware/software systems).

Benefits

Expert systems "owners"—many of whom are represented in the following chapters—report two distinct main benefits of expert systems. One is increased productivity, an enhancement in the *efficiency* of existing operations. This benefit often translates to cost of labor savings.

However, the predominant benefit in expert systems applications is *effectiveness* gain. Using the automobile insurance example in Chapter 7, one benefit reported was a decrease in the time it takes to write a policy. But the greater benefit resulted from better underwriting practice, reducible to avoiding underwriting bad risks and avoiding not underwriting good ones. A similar example may be drawn from the Chapter 12, where the efficiency gains in wellhead design (reduction in the time required to get the job done) are dwarfed by the effectiveness gains (reduction in errors in wellhead configuration). It has been estimated (Feigenbaum et al., 1988) that the value of the effectiveness gains exceeds the efficiency gains by as much as five to one.

The utility of expert systems in training and orientation is another benefit. Learning on-the-job is facilitated when what is to be learned has already been codified and can be presented to the trainee in the context of actual job performance. For example, the Fireman's Fund expert system has a training mode in which underwriters are asked to make their underwriting determination before the expert system reveals its own. The beauty of expert systems is that they not only reach a conclusion but can offer a rudimentary explanation justifying the conclusion. These explanations, usually a recapitulation of the sequence of rules employed, may help develop understanding.

Another benefit is consistency. Consistency in product quality of a commodity chemical plant is cited as a benefit Chapter 12. Consistency in the application of insurance underwriting policy, as described Chapter 7, helped turn a loss into a profit. The "activation" of knowledge formerly lying dormant as text—by recasting it as expert system rules—represents a major opportunity for benefit. The Capital Expert System reported in Chapter 10 illustrates what can be done in this area. By providing a central repository for corporate expertise, expert systems provide both consistency and continuity in the application of the policies and procedures corporate productivity and profitability are based upon.

As real and concrete as these benefits are, one must be on guard against the "superhuman fallacy." That is, expert systems are not magical—they will not be able to solve problems that people cannot solve. In a sense, human performance provides an upper bound of expert system performance. Often expert systems achieve much better than the average human performance. Chapter 12 cites the 80/20 rule (which suggests that 80 percent of the work gets done by 20 percent of the people) and the hope that, with expert systems, the majority 80 percent of the people can share that superior competence of the minority 20 percent.

Costs

Costs can be broken down into three areas: knowledge acquisition, user interface, and systems integration. While one might suspect that an expert systems' greatest cost factor would be knowledge, the experience of developers suggests that these three cost areas may be roughly equal.

Thus, a significant cost of an expert systems project is cost of acquiring its knowledge base. Expert systems organize and interpret specialized, technical knowledge. To get a feel for the cost of knowledge acquisition, it will take about as much effort (i.e., cost) explicitly to develop formerly implicit knowledge for a hardcopy manual as for an expert system. That is, when the knowledge has not yet been made explicit, the major cost of explicating the knowledge is roughly equivalent for expert systems as for other codified forms of expertise—manuals, training, traditional management information systems. We all know such costs are substantial. Once the knowledge is explicated, however, there are the vast efficiency and effectiveness gains as mentioned above to be obtained by *interpreting* this knowledge electronically. In knowledge acquisition, there are opportunity costs as well. Because the time of a committed subject matter expert must be dedicated to every expert system project, that expert becomes otherwise unavailable for his or her former tasks. Therefore, opportunity costs can be high (if this expert performs an otherwise essential function in the firm) and must be considered in the overall estimate of the costs of the project.

Expert systems and computer science studies suggest that roughly half the cost of a computer application is involved in the user interface—getting information from the user and providing information to the user. This important cost area should not be overlooked when budgeting an expert systems project.

The third main cost area in expert systems is systems integration. The issue of integration was initially raised by attempts to apply expert systems in "real world" settings. Laboratory prototypes never had to grapple with this issue. But as elaborated below, this has become the one predominate issue in expert systems applications work. Integrating an expert systems application into its information processing environment may account for as much as half the project's cost. Integration incurs costs in two areas. The first area is the obvious infrastructure of hardware, software, telecommunications, database integration. The second area is in overcoming the institutional resistance to change. Organizationally, integrating expert systems into a company is not a neat and tidy affair, as further discussed below, and requires the cooperation of management.

Payoffs

The same cost/benefit analysis is required of an expert systems project as is required for any information technology project. Most of the projects reported in this book were based on sound business cases—the projects reported in Chapter 12 and 15, respectively, explicitly mention this. Furthermore, the payoff projections of these analyses were borne out: Time and time again in the chapters that follow, the return on investment for expert systems development costs is reported to follow within days or months of installation For example, Lockheed's MEDCHEC paid back cost of investment in "approximately five months"; Digital's Can Build "paid back 60 times its cost within its first quarter of use."

Not all endeavors succeed; not all expert systems projects will pay off. People talk about their successes, not their failures; therefore, the expert systems literature (including this book) focuses on what people are proud to share. In achieving the successes reflected in the chapters of this book, however, there were many lessons learned that serve to guide future efforts—to minimize chances of failure and maximize chances of success. The "lessons learned" reviewed in this chapter and reported in the remainder of the book, while they by no means guarantee the success of an expert systems project, do point out concerns which, if attended to, will increase the probability of success.

Project Initiation

Leadership from the top has played a large role in the introduction of expert systems technology into corporations. American Express's successful Authorizer's Assistant expert system was initiated due to a challenge and funding from the CEO to become more involved in high risk R&D. FMC's development of a corporate AI group stemmed from the CEO's interest in the technology, coupled with proposals from technical staff. Chapter 6 describes how the management sponsor of the foreign exchange expert system was the chief technology officer in the corporation, who reported directly to the president of the bank. Initiative from technologists has also played a role in starting expert system projects. Texas Instruments' Capital Expert System was begun without funding until enough of a system was developed (covertly) to interest management.

A recurrent theme is that the technology should follow the problem and not the other way around. Thus, since it is the responsibility of management to identify and resolve business problems, it follows that, primarily, it is management who should be aware of and, when appropriate, supportive of expert systems' solutions to identified business problems. Expert systems projects need management champions.

Different environments confront attempts to initiate projects. At Digital, there is an extensive record of success for expert systems projects. At Federal Express, the planning and development of their first project is just underway. Digital probably views expert systems as less risky because of their track record of success. To reduce risk, Federal Express (see Chapter 17) is employing an incremental development strategy—where a collection of small projects will lead to comprehensive system. Upon reflection, this is exactly what Digital has done—each new project has led to a more and more comprehensive network of knowledge-based systems.

The Development Team

An expert system project team consists of far more players than the "techies" who will do the programming. On the nontechnical side, besides having its own project manager, the project will need a champion (discussed in the previous section) and management representatives of the user and the systems communities (to be discussed in the following section). The remainder of this section focuses on the technical knowledge engineering talent needed in an expert systems project.

The technical team can be subdivided in two, the subject matter expert and the knowledge engineer. Since the expert system seeks to replicate expert performance, a person or group of persons with the requisite expertise needs to be a part of the project team. It is important that the expert(s) be articulate—able to express in words how they do their job. A large part of project effort will be spent in developing a rapport between the subject matter expert and knowledge engineer. While the experts may have difficulty at first in articulating their knowledge, as the knowledge engineer begins to codify the knowledge, the expert's expressiveness is stimulated by the emerging rule base and feedback questions asked by the knowledge engineer. Now there are examples to react to; there are obvious omissions; there is something the knowledge engineer did not get quite right or did not quite understand; there is a noticed contradiction. Often (but not always), this partnership is so close that the expert becomes knowledge engineer or the knowledge engineer becomes the expert. As the relationship develops, the tendency is for each party to become more sensitive to and knowledgeable of the needs, methods, knowledge, capabilities, limitations and point of view of the other.

The advent of expert system shells (Intellicorp's KEE, Inference Corporation's ART, Teknowledge's M.1 and S.1, Carnegie Group's Knowledge Craft, IBM's ESE and Knowledge Tool, plus literally scores of others for all hardware environments) has theoretically made it possible for nonprogrammers to do the work of building expert systems. But, in the place of programmers, a new job has developed: the knowledge engineer, the person who is to act as intermediary between the subject matter (domain) expert and the shell. The knowledge engineer teases out knowledge from the domain expert in a process called "knowledge acquisition." Other sources of knowledge tapped include tables, manuals, textbooks, databases, and any other source of documentation on the subject. One would like to eliminate the requirement for the knowledge engineer and have the subject matter expert develop the rule base directly. However, this is usually not possible. The shells are not powerful enough to support this. Domain experts are usually not computer experts and may not even be computer literate.

An ultimate goal of knowledge acquisition would be to eliminate the need not only for a *knowledge engineer* but for a *domain expert* as well! For example, in the realm of equipment diagnosis, there is a desire to develop diagnostic expertise directly from device specifications. In a sense (de Kleer, 1985), "knowledge is evil" in that knowledge costs a lot to get, and one always wants to avoid cost.

Since the state of the art currently requires skilled knowledge engineers with programming expertise, the organization that develops the expert system will have to possess these talents. To the extent that such talents exist or can be developed in-house, the home organization can develop the expert system. Such skills would be present in the typical information systems support group of a large company or high technology firm. Digital and Boeing are two prime examples of corporations that have instituted formal in-house AI training and education programs to help successful transfer of expert systems technology throughout the company. Many companies (for example, FMC and Chemical Bank) maintain centralized AI development groups. These groups develop expert systems in such a way that the business units will be able to do the maintenance.

An often preferable approach, however, is to contract out the work of expert systems development to AI consulting houses. Chapter 17 states that effort will be augmented by contracted assistance from a qualified external supplier. This is coupled, however, with the intent eventually to eliminate dependence on third-party support. The AI firms that developed the commercial shells also provide development services. Some of the major AI consulting firms include Texas Instruments, Carnegie Group, Teknowledge, Inference Corp., Intellicorp (see Feigenbaum et al., 1988; and Waterman, 1986). While these consulting companies had origins in the academic community where AI research was conducted in relative isolation from the realities of business-oriented data processing, their practice is now well attuned to the requirements for integration posed by real business applications. AI work is now also being done by traditional systems integration firms such as Andersen Consulting, Coopers & Lybrand, and IBM. Representative consulting work being conducted by all three of these firms is reported in this book.

Integrating the Technology

The key to expert systems success is in integrating this new technology within its overall cultural, organizational, work place, and information systems environment. Virtually every chapter in this book stresses this point—lessons learned in the heat of battle. This theme is *so pervasive* in the reports contained in this book, we decided to subtitle the book "Integrating the Technology." Chapter 4 is dedicated to this theme and advises businesses to make AI systems compatible with traditional computing, embed AI programs so they run in the same hardware and software environment as conventional programs, provide for the access of corporate data resident on conventional data bases, address the entire business problem, use expert systems technology if appropriate, not to default to conventional data processing, and assure adequate performance.

Chapter 9 emphasizes a development methodology for building expert systems that allows a company to move an expert system from the prototype to the actual implementation stage. Probably the most important step toward integration lies in the requirements definition phase where a real business problem is identified.

The overall market direction for AI is toward "mainstreaming." Business managers do not want to have to buy special purpose AI workstations to build expert systems. First, these cost money, and sufficient computing capacity may already be at hand. Second, even if special hardware is bought, it often ends up being "stand-alone" (precisely because it is special purpose) and needs to be integrated with the remainder of the enterprise's hardware. Often, due to AI hardware's specialized nature, this integration is costly and difficult, if not impossible. The recent availability of AI shells on PCs, mainframes, and UNIX workstations is making AI more accessible and its adoption more feasible.

A typical expert system may be only a part of the overall solution to a specific information processing problem. Chapter 17's analyses indicate that knowledge-based systems development will represent only a relatively small percentage of the total development effort. Chapter 7 contains five basic modules, only one of which involves expert systems technology. Since complete solutions involve a mix of information processing and organizational strategies, expert systems have to be "team players" along with communications, computer graphics, conventional databases and transaction processing. Part of Chapter 16 reviews the historical development of the information technology with which expert systems must now be integrated.

Examples of the imperative to integrate expert systems applications with the enterprise's database systems abound in the applications chapters. Chapter 13 illustrates just how far integration can go. Digital's Knowledge Network integrates marketing and sales, order administration, engineering, manufacturing planning, manufacturing production, distribution, and customer service. The initial seed of this concept was the famous configurator for new VAX computer orders, the XCON expert system. XCON naturally led to the development and integration of the other Knowledge Network expert systems, including XSEL (expert sales assistant) and XFL (floor layout composer). Digital's Knowledge Network depends on access to a great variety of preexisting, standard corporate databases. In Chapter 6, a project developed by Chemical Bank in late 1986 and early 1987 is described where, due to the then-current state of the art, integration issues were consciously avoided. But integration was still required and was solved by a manual exchange of computer tapes between systems, a strategy affectionately named "Sneakernet." Chapter 11 describes the MEDCHEC expert system for medical insurance claims auditing. Not only did MEDCHEC need access to all claims data entered into databases each working day by a group of claims processors, but it notes that access to history files was also crucial for making good judgments about the validity of current claims.

Fundamentally, an *expert* system is an *information* system, and, as such, it is subject to the historical constraints on information flow that develop in organizations. A complaint about management information systems in general is that they may further institutionalize and calcify ineffective communications strategies: departmental territoriality, authoritarian hierarchies, or overspecialization (Strassman, 1988). When a new information product is introduced, including expert systems, this larger context should be recognized. An expert system's installation may impact the status quo and engender reorganization of the channels of information in ways and at levels that go beyond the function of the expert system itself.

A case in point from Chapter 7 indicates that experience in installing the Automobile Workbench expert system at Fireman's immediately raised the issue of the informational separation of application processing from application approval. A system written to bridge these two activities naturally suggested that these activities no longer be treated as separate. Chapter 12 describes how an expert system initially designed to help configure custom products (an engineering function) could be of great use to the sales function when used as a point-of-sale entry system. Digital's Can Build, described in Chapter 13, was first developed to salvage unused inventory. Its success in its intended application, however, led to a growing influence of this program which now synchronizes and manages all inventory across the corporation.

It is imperative that end-users be "in on the takeoff so they will be in on the landing." User input is needed early to make the appropriate problem selection. Their involvement is needed throughout the project to see that the problem goal is kept clearly in focus and appropriately addressed. Their feedback is critically needed in developing and fine-tuning the user interface. A commonly cited statistic in information systems development is that the user interface involves as much as half of the code (and therefore cost) of an information system. In the PAGE-X expert system for troubleshooting high speed printers described in Chapter 19, almost 65 percent of the expert system's rule base was devoted to the human-computer interface. In fact, with that system it was discovered that the acceptable solution required three user interfaces—one each for beginner, intermediate, and advanced troubleshooter.

Business's information systems people are also stakeholders in most expert systems projects. They probably support the hardware on which the expert system will run, and, almost certainly, they manage the databases and communications systems interfaced to the expert system. Thus, an expert systems project will likely incur costs for the information systems department. As the old saying goes, "It takes two to Tango," and if the expert systems people need to integrate, they will need, as a willing and cooperative dancing partner, the information systems department.

Maintenance

We may add to our "knowledge is power" and "knowledge is evil" epithets that "knowledge is perishable." Yesterday's news is no news; and yesterday's knowledge (policy, procedure, strategy, standards, etc.) is no knowledge—or worse, *mis*information. Organizations change, contexts change, rules change. Consequently, any expert system developed is never finished; to remain useful it must be constantly maintained.

Fortunately, a key attribute of expert systems is the modularization of control (the inference engine) and knowledge (the rules). So expert systems are easier to maintain than traditional computer programming. Chapters 6, 9, 12, and 19, respectively, all emphasize the importance of placing maintenance responsibility in the end-user organization's hands; they have the stake in the system to motivate maintenance, and they have the most current and accurate knowledge to incorporate in the system.

Chapter 8 presents several considerations regarding planning for maintenance—including the issues of version control (how do you assure everyone begins using updates simultaneously and that some are not left using "yesterday's news") and the issue of being able to reconstruct the rationale for any given rule, perhaps even one written years ago. There is a need, in realistic systems, to have an audit trail of past decisions.

The Future for Expert Systems

Business applications. The thrust of this book is that employing expert systems for practical business applications is technically feasible and economically desirable. The 17 corporations who report successful applications in this book are pioneers in this field; they are among the first enterprises to apply expert systems to increase productivity and profitability. Their success and the lessons they have learned will make it easier for others to follow. Commensurate with these users' successes, expert systems shell vendors have become much more aware of the requirements for the successful adoption of their technology. "Integrate the technology!" is the imperative of the late 1980s; the challenge has been stated and met. In the future, it is likely that wherever there is a shortage of technical expertise, expert systems applications will be developed to fill the need.

The need for expertise is broad and pervasive. Our era is known as the "information age." We characterize over half of the industrialized work force as "knowledge workers." These perceptions indicate the pervasiveness and importance of expertise and specialized technical knowledge in modern economies. Because expertise is becoming so important and because expert systems can augment expertise where needed, the future of business applications of expert systems seems bright. The hundreds of examples of business applications of expert systems cited in the later 1980s seems bound to be replaced by thousands or tens of thousands of examples by the mid-1990s. The millions of dollars in productivity gains stemming from the aggregate of today's use of expert systems is bound to translate into billions of dollars productivity gains in the 1990s and therefore play a key role in increasing the productivity and competitiveness of those firms and those nations aggressively employing this new information technology.

Commodity expert systems. Beyond specialized, technical expertise, will the future provide us with a variety of "commodity" expert systems sold to mass markets? The critical key to success in limiting the scope of the knowledge in business applications of expert systems suggests that "knowledge bases" with the breadth to have mass market appeal would be difficult if not impossible to construct. For the same reason expert systems should not involve common sense; having expert systems that deal with common situations may be too difficult to build. There are, however, narrowly circumscribed domains of knowledge of general importance that may be amenable to expert systems treatment and mass marketing—for example, algebra tutoring, first aid, and income tax preparation. But an idea for such a seemingly specific area as automobile maintenance is not viable since most automobiles have subtle differences in construction. Such a maintenance expert system would have to be deployed for specific makes and models, placing us squarely back into the custom market.

Commodity AI. As one looks beyond expert systems to the field of AI in general, perhaps the greatest opportunity in the future is precisely "commodity" applications in the fields of perception and motor control. These aspects of AI have proven to be the most difficult and intractable—precisely because they are so general. The tasks of natural language understanding, speech understanding, robotics, and machine vision involve the subtleties of language, sensory perception, vast background knowledge, and common sense.

Given the relentless trend toward increased computing power, some progress toward the practical solutions of these problems may well be made in the future. In perhaps 10 or 20 years we may see the beginnings of such commodity applications of AI as self-piloting cars, voice-activated typewriters, or home robots. These will, with all plausibility, come to fruition in time.

But today, practical applications of AI are limited to expert systems, where specialized, localized, and technical knowledge is brought to bear on problems of economic importance to business and industry.

REFERENCES

AI Week, 5(3). (1988, February). Areas of application for expert systems, p. 11.

Blanchard, D. (1989). Expert systems on Wall Street. *AI Week, 6* (7), 16.

Chase, W., & Simon, H. (1973). The mind's eye in chess. In W.G. Chase (Ed.), *Visual information processing.* New York: Academic Press.

De Groot, A. (1965). *Thought and choice in chess.* The Hague: Mouton.

de Kleer, J. (1985). AI approaches to troubleshooting. In J. Richardson (Ed.), *Artificial intelligence in maintenance.* Park Ridge, NJ: Noyes Publications.

Feigenbaum, E., McCorduck, P., & Nii, P. (1988). *The rise of the expert company.* New York: Times Books.

Reddy, R. (1988). Foundations and grand challenges of artificial intelligence. *AI Magazine, 9* (4), 9–23.

Slagle, J., & Wick, M. (1988). A method for evaluating candidate expert system applications. *AI Magazine, 9* (4), 44–53.

Strassmann, P. (1988, March). Information strategist. *Inc.*, pp. 27–40.

Waterman, D. (1986). *A guide to expert systems*. Reading, MA: Addison-Wesley.

part II
Economic Overview

2

Industrial Competitiveness: The Role of Intelligent Systems

D. Bruce Merrifield

U.S. Department of Commerce

This is an overview of the global marketplace that is and will be developing in response to the major forces of change existing in the world today. In this environment of continuous change, excess capacity worldwide is causing the decline, loss of competitiveness, and the rapid restructuring of basic industries. In addition, rapidly advancing technology is collapsing product and process life cycles and causing obsolescence of existing facilities long before their useful lives can be realized. The urgency for continuous generation of knowledge-intensive new products derives from these major forces of change. The author calls for the removal by government of bureaucratic procedures and the high cost of capital that act as barriers to progress, together with formation of international strategic alliances that pool limited resources and skills, increase market potential for new developments, and shorten time to commercialization. He sees a new industrial revolution coming about through shared flexible computer integrated manufacturing (FCIM) facilities that aggregate the manufacturing function for the first time in history as a service function. Whoever has the human capital, skills, and resources to develop new products will have the comparative advantage in the global marketplace. A major factor in comparative advantage will be advanced software. To achieve competitiveness today, the author includes as a third factor the computer-aided life-long reskilling of the adult workforce involving interactive software.

PERSPECTIVE

When we stepped out of our front door this morning we stepped out into the global marketplace, which today is beset with massive forces of change. In fact, management today, by definition, is the management of continuous change. Classical economic theory predicts that production tends to move to zones of comparative advantage. Moreover, the classical factors of comparative advantage traditionally have included access to arable land, natural resources, low-cost labor, nearby markets, and capital. Even small advantages that result from these

25

factors often have been the margin of industrial competitiveness. But today these classical factors have become secondary; the primary factors that overwhelm them are innovation, automation, sophisticated skills, and strategic management, all of which are heavily dependent upon intelligent software systems that drive them. These "value-added" factors now are dominant in the global marketplace, and we must clearly understand that production will no longer move to zones of cheap natural resources or labor but flexible facilities will be shared in many places but driven by knowledge-intensive programming. Therefore, it is clear that the software revolution will be a dominant factor required for comparative advantage.

More specifically, an explosion of technology over the last 30 years has generated about 90 percent of all scientific knowledge. This advanced technology, in turn, has spawned a tidal wave of entrepreneurial new business development that is restructuring both U.S. and world economies. Continuous computer-aided design of leading-edge, next-generation technology is combining with flexible computer integrated manufacturing (FCIM) systems to generate a historically unprecedented expansion of the global economy, creating new wealth, that will steadily raise the quality of life of almost all nations. Survival now boils down to "innovate, automate, or evaporate" and to lifelong computer-aided reskilling of an adult workforce that is required to design, develop, manage, and operate sophisticated intelligent systems.

DRIVING FORCES

An urgency exists for continuous generation of such knowledge-intensive new products, processes, and services and the FCIM systems to make them. This urgency derives from major forces of change that are causing the decline, the loss of competitiveness, and the rapid restructuring of basic industries. Many of these older industries have been a dominant focus of commercial activity for most of the 20th century (e.g., mining, agriculture, steel, aluminum commodity petrochemicals, textiles, and shipbuilding). However, now major forces of change are compelling these industries to restructure, while creating a myriad of new businesses. Some of these forces follow below.

Instantaneous Industrialization

One of the major forces of change in today's hypercompetitive global marketplace is the emergence of the newly industrializing countries using what I call the "strategy of instantaneous industrialization." Any rice paddy in the world now can be transformed in 6 to 12 months by one of the international construction firms to a current state-of-the-art, turnkey manufacturing facility operated by two-dollar-an-hour labor. Until recently, developed nations, which represent only about 12 percent of the world's population, have had a total command of the global economy, but now the rest of the world is entering these markets. Facilities in developing nations are underpricing similar facilities in developed nations by 20 to 30 percent, putting heavy downside pressure on prices and profits. This rice-paddy syndrome is very important: It's going to accelerate with major effects on our existing industries. Also, it is a disinflationary process that tends to destroy the industries involved as it produces a glut of production capacity worldwide. This phenomenon is occurring at an accelerated rate in South Korea, Taiwan, Brazil, Mexico, Indonesia, Malaysia, Singapore, India, and China. These nations comprise much of the lesser developed world population, which has 88 percent of the world's total population.

However, developing countries are not able to develop "next generation" technology as we in the developed nations can, but they can copy anything that currently exists. This strategy eventually results in tremendous national debts for the countries that invest in already obsolescing technology. Instead, collaborative efforts, or strategic alliances, with developed nation companies can be much more fruitful. Fifty-fifty, win-win joint ventures to develop new products and processes now are needed.

The Targeted Industry Strategy

The Japanese first developed this strategy, which has been copied by other developed nations. It is based on the Boston Consulting Group (BCG) learning curve theory (see Figure 2.1) for which Japan was an early disciple. It assembles vertically integrated consortia that, with heavy government subsidies, are designed to capture market share with predatory pricing.

The BCG learning curve predicts that every doubling of cumulative sales volume decreases costs of production by 15 to 20 percent as economies of scale and increased productivity result. Traditionally, however, the typical field manager leaves his price where he started, as the top line of Figure 2.1 shows, because his bonus is based on profits, which are increasing nicely as he moves from 1 to 2 to 3, down the cost-experience curve. What he is doing, of course, is trading market share for short-term profits and frequently after he has lost about half the market, prices collapse. The BCG said two things about this: First, prices should have been brought down with the cost as shown by the dotted line. As a result, a company could have captured the whole market and maintained it for a much longer period of time. But, there is a second strategy: Price may be forwarded all the way down to number 4, way below cost. That requires an initial negative cash flow but results in driving all competitors out of business. Prices then can be raised to just below the entry point of a new competitor. However, not even a big company in this country can do that, but a nation can, and the

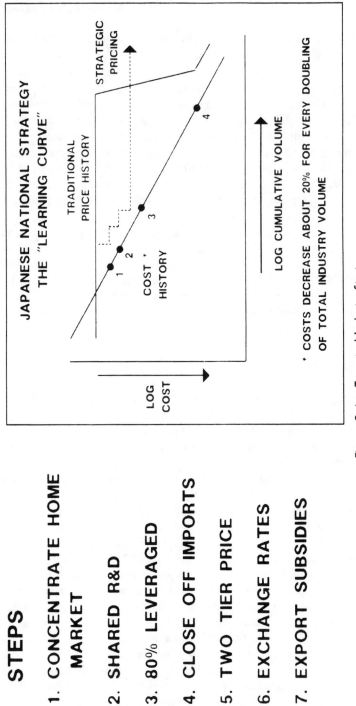

STEPS

1. CONCENTRATE HOME MARKET
2. SHARED R&D
3. 80% LEVERAGED
4. CLOSE OFF IMPORTS
5. TWO TIER PRICE
6. EXCHANGE RATES
7. EXPORT SUBSIDIES

Figure 2.1. Targeted Industry Strategy

Japanese understood this and developed an embellishment of the BCG learning curve, which we call the targeted industry strategy.

The targeted industry strategy has seven steps, as noted on the left of Figure 2.1:

Step 1. Concentrate the targeted business to a few players in the home market.

Step 2. Share process manufacturing improvements among the few players to avoid redundant efforts. Begin with the world's best technology focused primarily on manufacturing engineering improvements and quality production.

Step 3. Leverage the resulting manufacturing investments (70 to 80 percent) with very low cost of capital (2 to 3 percent).

Step 4. Close off imports into the home market to protect the new home market and prevent competition.

Step 5. Use "two-tier pricing" in a captive home market by charging domestic buyers more than export customers (now called "dumping").

Step 6. Manipulate the exchange rate to undervalue the currency.

Step 7. Eliminate the domestic value-added tax for exports (another 10 to 15 percent subsidy).

Unfortunately, there are two fallacies in this concept. First, there is the assumption that after the big negative cash flow of capital, the company remains in business long enough to recover the investment. With 3- to 5-year life cycles for many businesses, this assumption will not necessarily be borne out. The second assumption is that no other nation will use the same concept. However, when everyone around the world copies the same strategy, then excess capacity destroys the industry. The Japanese are having to write-off major investments in some commodity areas—steel, aluminum, commodity, petrochemicals, ship-building, textiles—where they are operating at 50 percent or less in many of them. We must remember that much of that development involved leveraged assets and the Japanese national debt now is about 100 percent of their gross national product as compared with our debt of 41 percent of GNP.

So this strategy is both destructive and also disinflationary, leading to excess world capacity in many basic industries. It has been used all over the world. For example, the European airbus industry has run a $12 billion negative cash flow on the A-300 and the A-310, another $4 billion on the A-320, and now they are talking about another $4 billion or so on the A-330 and 340. Since they are only halfway to break even on the first one, they will never break even because there aren't that many aircraft to be sold. Underpricing true costs tends to destroy the whole industry. Instead, we must collaborate together to build, develop, and expand the global economy instead of carving the pie into smaller and smaller pieces as these two strategies do.

The Technology Explosion

A third major force of change has resulted from the technology explosion that has collapsed industry life cycles. For example, in electronics, life cycles already have collapsed to 3-to-5 years. Rarely will life cycles exceed 5-to-10 years in most other industries, with facilities and equipment becoming obsolete long before their useful lives can be realized or the investments amortized.

About 90 percent of what we know in the sciences has been generated just in the last 30 years and will double again in the next 15. Moreover, about 90 percent of all scientists and engineers who have ever lived now are living and working. Their numbers will double again worldwide over the next two decades as all nations increasingly participate in this entrepreneurial technology-driven process of new business formation. This process is dramatically shown in Figure 2.2, which begins at the dawn of civilization 10,000 years ago and proceeds to the present day.

Only about 5 percent of the world's population live in the U.S., but 15 years ago we were generating about 75 percent of the world's technology. Our share now is down to about 55 percent, and in another decade it will only be a third, not because we're generating less, but because the other 95 percent of the world

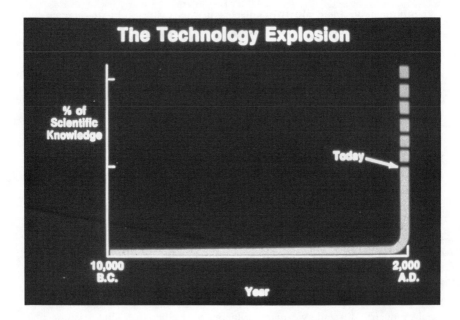

Figure 2.2.   The Technology Explosion

will be participating more fully. Everybody now understands that technology is the engine that drives all world economies, and they intend to participate.

But the point is that this explosion of knowledge has opened up historically unprecedented opportunities to develop new businesses and create new ideas, new concepts, and to expand the global economy for the first time in history to the point where all of us can benefit from this process. Industrial survival increasingly will depend upon effective participation in this process. Of course, one of the mechanisms for doing this is through strategic alliances, collaborative efforts on an international scale. George Berry, the former dean of the Harvard Medical School, has pointed out that this period in which we are now living one day will be recognized as the second great divide in human history—the first being the emergence of civilization 10,000 years ago.

THE PROCESS OF INNOVATION

Let me talk a little about the process of innovation, because it is so important to understand this. Innovation starts with an idea in a basic research laboratory and is followed by a few technical feasibility checks. If it looks good, it progresses into a series of development stages where variable studies are run, which define some limits. Then the next step is to scale it up to a preprototype or pilot plant stage to get some engineering data. If it still looks good, it is scaled up to an interim manufacturing facility to get feedback from the marketplace before going full-scale commercial. Of course, this is just a technical track, and in parallel with this is a marketing, a legal, a financial, and a production engineering track. Milestones at each stage have to be met before you move on. Management of innovation is a very sophisticated process. We know how to do it better than anyone in the world if we just get our act together, get some of the barriers out of the way, and provide incentives for this process.

Simplistically, think of innovation as a three-stage process. The first two boxes shown in Figure 2.3 are the invention, and that's where our universities and our government laboratories are currently spending about $15 billion a year in basic research. The U.S. expenditure is about 10 times more than any other nation spends or can spend. It probably has cost this country about a trillion dollars over 40 years to build our academic capability. No other nation has that in place, no other nation can replicate it in any reasonable period of time—a permanent and enduring advantage—and I would like to see that $15 billion of primarily federally funded research go to $30 billion over the next decade. That is the seed corn that produces thousands of new products and processes them downstream. But the next three boxes are the translation of that early knowledge into something useful. And that is where about 90 percent of the cost and the risk and the time is involved. That is where industry has to be operative.

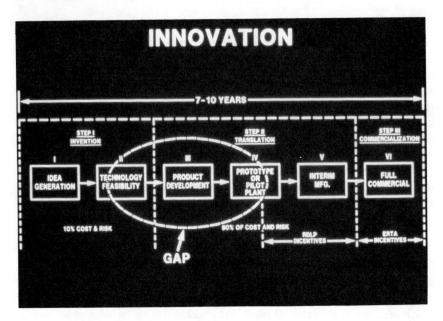

Figure 2.3. Innovation

Barriers to the Translational Process

Industry cannot do the basic research; universities and government laboratories cannot do this translational process effectively. But, unfortunately, there are a lot of barriers to translation here in the United States and a lack of incentives, so we have not been capitalizing very well on the basic research we have been doing. In fact, for many decades we have just been publishing that information, letting everybody in the world use it. However, the Technology Transfer Act of 1980, 1984, and 1986 now provide that our universities, our government laboratories, and any contractor doing federal research can now own the commercial rights to their efforts, and either use or patent them and license them to someone else. And so, for the first time, we are going to be capturing that basic knowledge. These Acts are landmark legislation and represent the biggest act of privatization of federal assets ever made, releasing literally tens of billions of dollars of fundamental work that has previously been bottled up by bureaucratic procedures in Washington.

However, there have been a number of barriers other than the bureaucratic ones. One has been the high cost of capital in this country, 3 to 4 times as high as in Japan—a major deterrent to investment, innovation, and automation. We need to bring that down very urgently if we are going to mobilize our capabilities more effectively. The antitrust laws are another barrier: These are 100-year-old laws that were designed for a slow-moving, domestic scene, and now are basically anticompetitive in a rapidly changing global marketplace. Unnecessarily restrictive liability and regulatory legislation also needs to be selectively modified.

In the three and one-half years since passage of the Cooperative R&D Act, we have started up 126 major consortia involving over 1,000 companies. This form of collaborative effort pools resources and skills, multiplies the capabilities, and accelerates the development process. Of course, there are many regulatory barriers that still need selective modification to be less anticompetitive. Also, we need specific incentives for innovation and also for automation, where flexible computer integrated manufacturing facilities will be required. I address this subject below.

To provide incentives for the translation stages, the only thing I have been able to come up with so far is the R&D Limited Partnership, which is based on a 1954 tax law (would you believe that it has been around all that time?). The U.S. Department of Commerce brought out guidelines in late 1982, and since then about $4 1/2 billion of private sector funding has been developed, most of which (80 percent) has gone into small new, startup businesses. We really have a remarkable thing going on here in the United States: It is a bottom-up entrepreneurial revolution that the Europeans call the American Miracle. We are now creating between 600,000 to 700,000 new small businesses every year in this country. Less than 10 percent of that number fail each year, and that is where 90 percent of the 18 million new jobs have been created between 1980 and 1988.

I would like to address the myth that has circulated recently that the United States is deindustrializing. Manufacturing as a percentage of a rising GNP has been 22–24 percent for 40 years, and now it is actually rising. In fact, about a third of these new startup businesses are manufacturing businesses. So if anything, manufacturing is increasing. What is happening, however, is that the direct labor content in manufacturing businesses will decline as we automate further, while the increased formation of new businesses will create many support or service jobs in maintenance, construction, marketing, distribution, legal, financial, communications, and clerical categories. About 75 percent of our economy now is in the support or service function area, driven by the manufacturing function.

The Need for Strategic Alliance

Competitive advantage and therefore industrial competitiveness increasingly will depend upon continuous generation of leading edge next-generation technology and upon flexible computer integrated manufacturing (FCIM) facilities to make an everchanging mix of new products. International strategic alliances that pool limited resources and skills can multiply the market potential for a new development, shorten the time to commercialization, and avoid the destructive effects of "targeted industry" and "instantaneous industrialization" strategies. Moreover, these strategies no longer will be effective as product and process life cycles continue to collapse to a few years. For example, let us look briefly at the traditional four-stage S-Curve life cycle (Figure 2.4) for products and processes. Sales growth starts out slowly, then accelerates and finally tails off with time, but basically this S-curve has four stages: the initial stage is the original invention where, for example, Apple Computer first demonstrates that there is a market for personal computers. The second stage is where many other companies swarm into that market with new versions of that original invention. This second stage is a period of very dynamic and rapid new product development. But later in this stage, a dominant design usually emerges that tends to freeze out further major innovations, and ushers in a third stage of process improvement. This stage involves optimization of the variables and automation of the systems. Finally, in Stage Four the consolidation of the market begins with a few large companies doing technical service, and the next S curve involving next generation technology is beginning.

This S-curve life cycle will progressively be shortened to the first two stages as intelligent systems-stimulated innovation and flexible automation tend to eliminate the last two stages. The destructive "targeted industry" and "instantaneous industrialization" strategies have been focused on Stages III and IV but collapsing life cycles may rarely allow a Stage III product or process to exist for long. Therefore, these strategies no longer will be viable and industrial competitiveness increasingly will depend on continual generation of leading edge next-generation systems and upon flexible automated systems to make them. International strategic alliances increasingly will be attractive to pool resources, skills, and risk, and to multiply the market potential for such new developments with limited life cycles.

The New Industrial Revolution

Shared flexible computer-integrated manufacturing facilities now are being developed in multiple locations throughout the United States. They are being focused primarily on small and medium-sized supplier companies that are not competitive with offshore production and alone do not have sufficient skills or resources to automate their operations. Figure 2.5 illustrates how the concept for the first time aggregates the manufacturing function.

In shared facilities of this type, individual companies from the same or different industries may "buy time" as needed to make one or a thousand of a kind for just-in-time delivery. Economies of scale approaching those of a dedicated single-product facility can be achieved, together with quality control and re-

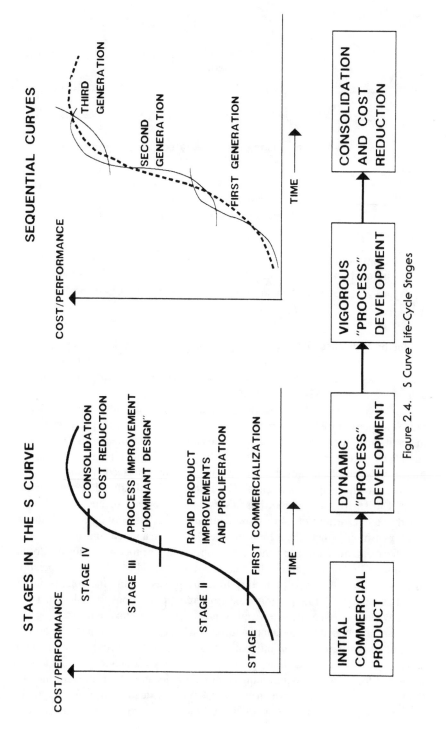

Figure 2.4. S Curve Life-Cycle Stages

35

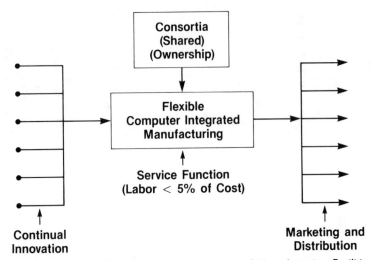

Figure 2.5.   Shared Flexible Computer-Integrated Manufacturing Facilities

producibility needed for global competition. FCIM facilities also can provide rapid entry into the market for new or modified products. These shared facilities realize costs of labor of less than 5 percent of the direct cost of manufacturing, and some of them are down around one percent or less.

Sematech is one of the consortiums we have formed that involves 14 different big companies pooling resources and skills to develop a 16 megabit, then a 64 megabit, mass memory chip and a flexible automated manufacturing facility that can all be shared by those companies. Many other big-company consortia also may follow this lead, but the primary focus is on our second- and third-tier suppliers to the major contractors. For example, in Meadville, Pennsylvania, about 130 small machine-tool businesses were going out of business. We put together a consortium of 24 of those companies that are pooling $15 million of their own money to build a four-module flexible manufacturing facility—one each for metal machining, plastics extrusion, ceramics processing, and electronic assembly. Once in operation, the National Tooling and Machining Association intends to clone that type of facility in many places around the country. Such facilities can be satellite programmed from remote locations to make what you want, where you want it, when you want it, for just-in-time delivery.

This is a new concept in manufacturing that can be replicated not only around the United States, but on an international scale as well. Once developed, these software-driven FCIM facilities can be cloned through strategic alliances around the world for satellite programming from remote locations. As a result, international trade will become primarily capital flows instead of transfer of goods.

Currently, we are working with about 45 locations around the United States.

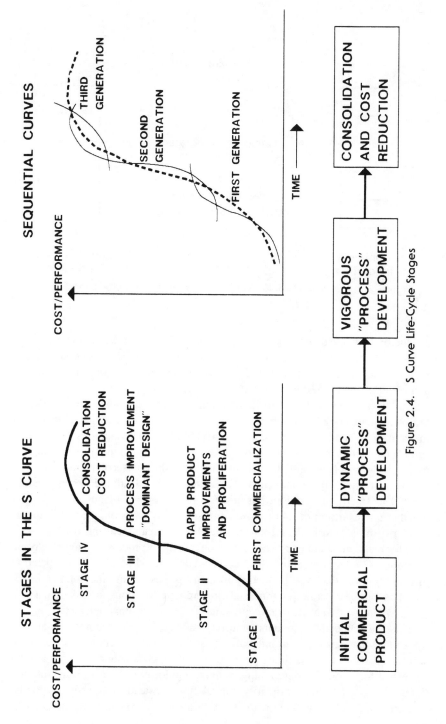

Figure 2.4. S Curve Life-Cycle Stages

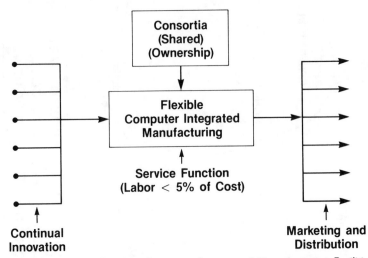

Figure 2.5.   Shared Flexible Computer-Integrated Manufacturing Facilities

producibility needed for global competition. FCIM facilities also can provide rapid entry into the market for new or modified products. These shared facilities realize costs of labor of less than 5 percent of the direct cost of manufacturing, and some of them are down around one percent or less.

Sematech is one of the consortiums we have formed that involves 14 different big companies pooling resources and skills to develop a 16 megabit, then a 64 megabit, mass memory chip and a flexible automated manufacturing facility that can all be shared by those companies. Many other big-company consortia also may follow this lead, but the primary focus is on our second- and third-tier suppliers to the major contractors. For example, in Meadville, Pennsylvania, about 130 small machine-tool businesses were going out of business. We put together a consortium of 24 of those companies that are pooling $15 million of their own money to build a four-module flexible manufacturing facility—one each for metal machining, plastics extrusion, ceramics processing, and electronic assembly. Once in operation, the National Tooling and Machining Association intends to clone that type of facility in many places around the country. Such facilities can be satellite programmed from remote locations to make what you want, where you want it, when you want it, for just-in-time delivery.

This is a new concept in manufacturing that can be replicated not only around the United States, but on an international scale as well. Once developed, these software-driven FCIM facilities can be cloned through strategic alliances around the world for satellite programming from remote locations. As a result, international trade will become primarily capital flows instead of transfer of goods.

Currently, we are working with about 45 locations around the United States.

Most of them involve universities because we see these facilities as hands-on teaching facilities for the engineers, the technicians, and the business school people who need to know how to run and operate them. Shared international flexible manufacturing will obviate or mitigate low-cost labor differentials, and other classical factors of comparative advantage. Comparative advantage, instead, primarily will be a function of value-added knowledge-intensive technology. Those nations that have the human capital and the skills and resources to develop new things will have the dominant advantage in the global marketplace. Manufacturing, in this context, essentially becomes a service function, for the first time in history, driven by expert systems software.

Lifelong Continuous Reskilling

Industrial competitiveness, then, increasingly will involve a combination of collaborative development of next-generation technology, flexible computer-integrated manufacturing systems, and lifelong continuous reskilling of the adult workforce. The accelerating pace of new technology development and the corresponding collapse of product and process life cycles now also has led to an increasingly rapid obsolescence of skills. Any set of skills can be obsolescent in 5-to-10 years, creating an urgent need for an effective process of lifelong adult education. A remarkable opportunity exists to address this problem. It involves the use of computer interactive videodisc educational systems, perhaps the most important potential contribution to education since the invention of the printing press in the 15th century.

An IBM program "Writing to Read" was tested on about 2,000 kindergarten and first-grade students in about 200 schools. It demonstrated a 100-to-500 percent greater rate of learning and up to 75 percent retention, versus 15 percent in a normal school classroom. It is color-blind, of course. Just as you might expect, the minorities do just as well as the others. This is a stunning statement, though, because it says that the opportunity now exists to eliminate functional illiteracy and entrenched poverty in our inner cities, using these seductive systems as the "modern textbook." A major new industry will emerge for the interactive software systems that will be needed to exploit this educational concept, not only for restructure of the school curricula, but also for lifelong adult work force reskilling.

The Government Role

Many political, economic, and social barriers exist throughout the world to rapid exploitation of what has emerged as a historically unprecedented opportunity to expand the global economy and raise the quality of life of all nations. Our problem here in the United States is to continue to remove unnecessary barriers—such as the antitrust laws, counterproductive regulatory barriers, and the high cost of U.S. capital—and to incentivize the process of innovation and automation. Collaborative efforts among companies on an international scale will be one of our priority initiatives. Collaborative efforts can expand the global marketplace, multiply the market for a given new development with a short life cycle, and of course provide access to technology wherever it is being developed, building human capital in the process. We now can systematically raise the quality of life of every nation in the world.

The governmental role must not be one that attempts to manage or direct the creative entrepreneurial process involved but rather must be one that proactively removes unnecessary barriers, and provides effective incentives for innovation and automation as well as for lifelong continuous "upskilling" of the adult work force now required to design, develop, manage, and operate these systems. I see the government role as one that is a proactive agent of change that catalyzes collaborative efforts that increasingly will be necessary to be operative in the remarkable global marketplace we now share.

SUMMARY

Major forces of change now will continually restructure and expand the global economy. The United States has incomparable resources and capabilities not only to recapture and maintain industrial leadership in almost any industry but also to lead the rest of the world to historically unprecedented growth and quality of life. The language of growth will be expert systems and artificial intelligence.

part III
Corporate Overview

3

Intelligent Business Solutions: The Corporation Today and Tomorrow

Winston Wade

U S WEST Advanced Technologies

This is a chapter by the president of the research and development subsidiary of a company leading in the application of intelligent systems for business today—U S WEST. In this chapter, the author provides a sweeping view of the current and future uses for artificial intelligence within his own company and stimulates the reader to imagine such uses in his or her own. Noting that the demand in industry for artificial intelligence and expert systems is increasing dramatically, the author points out the reasons for this trend—the tremendous value for a company because they allow people to work faster and smarter; increase productivity by allowing the machines to make decisions for us; help solve day-to-day business problems. Applications within U S WEST already in use or planned for the future that serve as witness to these benefits include: speech recognition, knowledge representation, troubleshooting, diagnostics, strategic planning, network modeling, and pattern recognition.

As president of U S WEST Advanced Technologies, I am pleased to be included in this volume on business applications of artificial intelligence. Artificial Intelligence, and in particular expert systems technology, is one of U S WEST's most promising research priorities. We are making great progress here.

Although the primary topic of this book is applications of artificial intelligence technology, much of what follows relates more to business and less to technology. It is how technology can help our businesses grow that makes it important. In another context, I might discuss the importance of basic and applied research to the advancement of science and human understanding. The subject, however, of this book is management productivity; a business issue with critical ramifications for every company, employee, and manager in the country.

Most business people, I am sure, can appreciate the importance of productivity in meeting competitive challenges and in meeting customer needs. A New York Stock Exchange study indicates that increased productivity derives from more capital, from better capital, but most important of all, from *working smarter* with the capital at hand. I will discuss how artificial intelligence can help you work smarter with your human and financial capital.

I will discuss how artificial intelligence can have an impact on your business productivity. How these technologies can help you distinguish your company in the marketplace. How these technologies can help you produce more work with the same resources and increase the profit potential of your organization. But do not forget that technology, as flashy and exciting as it is, is a tool of the trade, not the reason for the business.

Other chapters in this book give a good idea of what intelligent systems are, and what, realistically, they are not. There are limits to artificial intelligence that have become accepted after 30 years of academic and industry research and experimentation.

Human cognition, the brain, language, creativity, intuition—all of these components in human decision making are studied in relation to intelligent systems. Yet while they are far better understood than they were a generation ago, there remain many mysteries. We cannot explain, for instance, how Chinese acrobats make split-second decisions that enable them to keep their balance. We cannot tell a computer what it is like to ride a bicycle. Such things involve intuition, gut-level feeling, reaction from experience. Call it what you will, we still cannot explain it.

Through 30 years of scientific study we have come to appreciate our decision making faculties with renewed fascination and awe. No one knows precisely how we make decisions. We just know we have to and that we do. Humans are weirdly but wonderfully complex creatures, and it is now clear that the natural abilities we possess will not be duplicated by hardware and software, nor replaced by them.

I used to wonder whether the distinctive intellectual gifts that enabled an Albert Einstein to formulate the theory of relativity could ever be captured on an intelligent system. I do not believe they ever completely could be. People, without a doubt, shall remain the prime corporate asset, because people make all the real decisions. In the research and development work we do, people are our *only* assets. Technology is, after all, people with knowledge.

Yet some of the rudimentary work decisions we have to make to keep our companies moving forward can be passed on to machines, and we can be freed to do other things with our time. In seeking over the years to build logic machines that might approximate what people can do, we have done right to shoot for the stars.

There is a great need for intelligent systems in business right now, particularly where internal organization, troubleshooting, and interpersonal communication are concerned. And this need will grow in the future.

Let me quote you some observations from a recent issue of *The Futurist* (Cetron, M. J. et al., 1988):

By 2001 artificial intelligence will be almost universally used by companies and government agencies to help assimilate data and solve problems.

By 2001 expert systems will be in universal use in such areas as manufacturing, energy prospecting, automotive diagnostics, medicine, insurance underwriting, law enforcement [and my addition to that list, telecommunications—Ed.].

In the next few years the demand for expert systems will increase dramatically. Industry leaders predict the expert systems market will grow from $225 million at present to more than $800 million by 1991.

It is imperative that businesses today increase their productivity. In every business—not just telecommunications—there are global competitive challenges and marketplace demands affecting our work. We are being challenged to move forward, and at an astounding pace.

The shelf life of high technology today is short and getting shorter. To quote Cetron et al. (1988) again:

> The interval between ideas, invention, innovation and imitation, in other words the time between basic research and application, is decreasing daily. Successful products will have to move from technology to the marketplace very rapidly.

Artificial Intelligence will drive companies to meet such challenges and demands by allowing people to work faster and work smarter. It can help companies be more proactive, more active, and more reactive than ever before.

Proactivity. Also called focused foresight, this means using machines to anticipate trends and patterns that will affect our business. It means tracking customers' tastes and trends to anticipate market demands before they appear. It means teaching machines to make more decisions for us so we can make even better decisions ourselves.

Activity. Machines have always increased worker activity, and artificial intelligence will free people's time so they can do more creative problem solving. If routine decisions can be handled by an expert system, the senior workers can spend their time on advanced challenges.

Reactivity. The quicker a company can know and react to customer demands, or react to problems in its automated systems, the stronger, more competitive that company will be, and the more value it will provide in the marketplace.

This new level of competitiveness will create new opportunities, making business a more efficient engine of progress and growth. Increasing worker productivity. Meeting marketplace demand faster. Managing the global competitive challenges. All of these are realistic benefits of artificial intelligence technologies.

At U S WEST, we are implementing these technologies right now. U S WEST Advanced Technologies is the research, development, and technology planning arm of U S WEST. Formed in 1985, the Advanced Technologies unit provides

S WEST companies with new technologies that aim to increase the overall profitability of U S WEST, and, more significantly, to meet the changing needs of U S WEST companies and their customers. Stated differently, we leverage technology to create solutions for customers. There is nothing artificial about this.

Expert systems research is high on our priority list because these systems have practical and attainable value for business. Other priority projects include speech technology and knowledge representation.

Our expert systems work is helping solve problems in our day-to-day business operations. We have developed prototypes that diagnose problems in switching systems, or help isolate troubles in large private networks.

The immediate goal of our speech technology project is to get machines to recognize spoken words. For now, we are working on the small vocabulary of numbers zero through nine when they are spoken over the telephone. Eventually, we hope to contribute to the certain myriad benefits that stand to come about as machines become capable of understanding spoken languages.

In our knowledge representation project, we are looking for ways to facilitate document understanding and mail routing. There are many corporate possibilities here as well that will save time and money.

Above and beyond our own research efforts, U S WEST Advanced Technologies has entered a strategic partnership with the Carnegie Group, a company founded in 1984 by several computer scientists from Carnegie Mellon University. The Carnegie Group is an industry leader in providing knowledge-based solutions for complex problems in manufacturing, engineering, and related information processing.

One of the many noteworthy Carnegie projects is TestBench™, a troubleshooting system for guiding technicians through fixing a machine failure or a production process problem. This and other Carnegie products and systems can increase manufacturing efficiency, productivity, product quality, and customer satisfaction. And it is customer satisfaction that is a primary driver for our research and development efforts. One thing is certain, if artificial intelligence is to have any payoff in telecommunications, or any industry for that matter, it will have to meet customer needs.

At U S WEST our present focus is expert systems, so let me discuss in more detail our work in that area. Our research in expert systems aims first at capturing, and then leveraging human knowledge to increase productivity and profits. The goal? Better business decisions.

How can we capture human knowledge, or expertise? How close can we get to taking an Einstein and turning his experience and his method of decision making into code? Could we code the experience and split-second decision making processes of Chinese acrobats?

Human intelligence and intuition are complex and likely undefinable abilities. Without being able to define, truly, how we make decisions, we are limited in any effort to duplicate these processes. But we are not trying to duplicate them. We are working to enhance our gift for making decisions by extending its usefulness with machines. We are trying to work smarter.

When computers were first introduced, they were lauded because they could free people from day-to-day tasks like long calculations, or number crunching. With artificial intelligence, computers are able to handle day-to-day decision making which until now has kept people on a leash.

There is an astronomical difference between the two. Expert systems compute with knowledge, not just numbers; with "rules of thumb," not repetitive instructions. A plain computer is nothing more than an abacus fueled with electricity. An expert system is more like the person using the abacus; it can make recommendations and take action, not just take instructions.

Artificial Intelligence enhances the decisions we make in the telecommunications industry. In our society today there exists a large and very complex telecommunications network: sophisticated switches, information transmission systems. Everything from telephones to computers to satellites is linked into this growing worldwide network. This indispensable network is used by all of us to communicate ideas that are critical to our daily lives. It forms the underpinning of any business, but like anything else, it can always be improved.

Thousands of capable people are required to plan, engineer, install, administer, maintain, and operate today's vast telecommunications system. And it is here, on the people side, that artificial intelligence is improving telecommunications. By helping us leverage the people we have, we can do more with less; we can accomplish greater tasks with fewer people. At U S WEST, expert systems are being used in network operations to extend productivity—of both personnel and capital—and improve customer service.

Simply stated, a lot can go wrong with the telecommunications network that exists today. And when something fouls up, someone has to go fix it. Enter diagnostics—or troubleshooting. Toward better handling of potential billing difficulties, for instance, U S WEST is developing a special diagnostician. It is an expert system that helps technicians interpret messages and alarms within our billing information system.

The diagnostic expert system monitors streams of information coming from our automatic billing systems. The expert system has been programmed to recognize unusual types of data flows and interpret messages from other computers. If the expert system sees a problem, it informs a human technician, gives an analysis of the problem and a likely source.

What values does this expert system provide? Well, we have to track the usage of ll million customer lines all at the same time. This translates into billions of dollars of billing information each year. If the billing information is inaccurate, we could over- or underbill our customers for their calls. Even a few minutes of faulty data from our billing systems could mean millions of dollars of lost revenue. So anything we can use to minimize those errors is important.

We are also in the process of developing a System for Analog Link and Diagnostics, which we call SALAD. This expert system finds and examines faults in telecommunications links. Because it takes more time to find network link failures than it does to fix them, we are letting machines do the finding and people do the fixing. With SALAD an error is detected the moment it emerges, if not before.

With both the diagnostic expert system and SALAD, we have a computer that contains everything there is to know about a certain aspect of our network. Plus, we have software that reacts with logical recommendations of what to do if any part of that network malfunctions.

By loading a computer with what is essentially a perfectly detailed understanding of one facet of the network, and factoring in an expert's logical reaction for anything that might go wrong, we have an indispensable asset: a machine that thinks. These systems continually monitor, diagnose, and assess everything that goes on within their environment. Moreover, the systems remember all actions performed and continually update themselves. In this sense, they not only think, but they learn. Having these systems in place helps free individuals to do more productive and creative tasks, which is a better use for both our people and our money.

We are building a knowledge-based system called the Strategic Planner's Assistant, which will be used by U S WEST's Strategic Planning group. This system harnesses data about key markets, and combines it with how our in-house experts think. We are pushing the current boundaries of expert systems with this internal application.

If we are considering expanding our services in Aspen, Colorado, for example, the strategic planner's assistant will provide a thorough "What If?" analysis for this market. Our planners can understand well in advance of any major expenditure what would happen if we did offer more services in Aspen. It will look at population growth, demographics, and current services being provided by U S WEST, compare these with other markets, recommend whether we should expand our services in Aspen, and give us various alternatives if we should not.

The system will not only outline the logical implications of a given action or a sequence of actions, it will explain why a given outcome can be anticipated. And it will tell how it reached that decision. The machine will reason based on the information it contains—information we have compiled in the course of business. And it will do this faster while analyzing more information than a human strategic planner alone could handle.

Our generic network modeling system is another internal application in development. U S WEST covers 14 states, and in those states there is a constant need for improved communication networks. This expert system is essentially a canvas that enables an individual to draw a complete communications network—every line, link, and transmitter—from square one.

When you take the time to think about the thousands of switches and trunks involved in voice or data communication, you can image the complexity and the level of expertise required when making an addition to the network. The generic network modeling system shares this experience with a relative novice, and enables a less experienced worker to produce flow charts showing exactly how electronic communication—data, voice, or video—would flow over the network, if it were created.

In creating a communications network, there are not only technological nightmares to deal with but also regulatory ones. The generic network modeling system would tell us whether a connection is possible in a given location, and also whether it is legal given the everchanging regulatory climate of our industry.

The value to U S WEST of both the strategic planner's assistant and the generic network modeling system, and I use these as only two of many possible examples, is at least threefold.

First, a less experienced worker can share in the knowledge contained in the system and handle decisions previously reserved for the company elite. Plus, this knowledge can be distributed wherever necessary; it is portable.

Second, the experts or more experienced workers are free to do more creative problem solving, handle more advanced challenges—in the same day.

Third, and this is important, these systems can be viewed as profit producers. Company training costs will diminish. Fatigue will not be so much of a factor that cuts into productivity—machines do not get tired. A knowledge reservoir will grow as the system does and learns more things.

More can be gained from personnel resources and capital resources alike. And this is the most direct route to greater competitiveness and increased productivity. By giving ourselves more time to do things, we serve more people better. It is the role of technology—in the context of artificial intelligence—to interact with humans charged with making decisions so we can meet the needs of customers and managers; of business owners or shareholders; of buyers and investors.

Other U S WEST Artificial Intelligence research efforts underscore our commitment to moving these products into the commercial marketplace as fast as we can.

Your company may eventually have use for Internal Document Understanding System (INDUS), a research application. How much of what you do not need crosses your desk every day? INDUS will read and understand your company's internal documents well enough to control memoranda distributed via electronic mail and make sure you get only the information you really need. Extraneous information will be rejected and not take up your valuable time.

Your company may also have a use for Basic Account Code Handler (BACH). This U S WEST application will go on-line in 1988 to help our accounting department code expenses properly. If your company is anything like ours, you have hundreds of account codes and require staffs of people to assign and code bills and expenses. BACH will act as an assistant to this staff.

Using a pattern recognition and key-word matching system, BACH will either code an expense directly, or walk the technician through a classification process that will assign the bill to the proper account. The artificial intelligence benefits are not only the coding capability but an interface that recognizes hundreds of key words and account types that speed input and processing.

At present, an expert system tells the expert what to do in a given situation; it facilitates an expert's decision making. In the not-too-distant future, expert systems are expected to react autonomously to a situation. Expert systems will actually "reason." The system will monitor its own internal state. It will develop an institutional memory. It will monitor its own external environment, factoring in such things as air temperature, moisture levels, and noise. In short, the machine will have some degree of self-awareness.

Not long from now, various separate technologies currently being developed will come together, further improving our quality of life—and the quality of our business—dramatically. Work in pattern recognition, computer vision, general problem solving, natural language processing, speech synthesis, expert systems, neural networks, and machine learning will change the corporation by leaps and bounds.

Where will telecommunications be when these technologies eventually come together? Simply stated, your business communication will be far easier and far more fluid than it is today. Corporations are becoming more spread out geographically. U S WEST, for instance, operates in 14 states and internationally. Through artificial intelligence and expert systems, we are working to reduce this distance using technology. We want to make communications an interpersonal art once again.

Here is one likely scenario, a hypothetical office setting 10 years from now, where artificial intelligence and expert systems are in support. This example is called the "Telecollaboration Project" and U S WEST began work in earnest on this project in 1988.

Let us say it is the year 1999. My office is in Boulder, Colorado. Your office is in Chicago. Both locations have knowledge-based and expert systems that control everything that impacts our business day—office lighting, temperature, telephone calls, your meeting schedule, your filing needs, corporate expenditures, security, inventory counting, banking tasks—let your imagination go. Imagine that the many basic but "real world" decisions you make every day are now handled autonomously by machines—at least the decisions you want to relinquish.

Let us say, then, that at a given moment in your business day you need to communicate with me. One wall in your office is a huge video screen, as is mine. Both of our offices have undetectable video cameras that allow us to appear to each other visually. You need to talk with me, so you approach the video wall, and call out my name. Because of work in speech recognition, the intelligent systems you have in place will understand this voice command. All you will have to do is say my name. If I am available, the system will bring my office into yours, and your office into mine, instantaneously. We will have an in-person meeting, perhaps over lunch.

If you cannot get through to me, my intelligent assistant—a machine—will work you into my schedule, tell your machine when it is a good time to reach me. And, say at 10:00 a.m. the next day, the machine automatically will try to put us together again. Of course, if it is an emergency, there are means to override whatever action the machines take on our behalf.

Though extremely simplified, I am sure your imagination and your familiarity with James Bond movies lets you understand what I am talking about. All of this is made possible with expert systems that control our respective office environments and allow us to use the existing telecommunications network. When merged with the technologies of voice, data, and video communications, these expert systems enable us to communicate over thousands of miles, to access and share information in virtually any form desired—textually, visually, graphically—to meet our needs of the moment.

CONCLUSION

Of all the technologies offered by artificial intelligence, expert systems provide the greatest immediate promise for business. Expert systems capture the knowledge of your company's best and brightest. They leverage that knowledge for the benefit of the entire organization. The result: What used to be the sole domain of one individual or an elite group can be shared widely. And, by classifying not only what the experts know but also how they reason, others using the system can be enlightened.

Expert systems can contain a vast reservoir of experience, strategies, procedures, and policies—all of which may enhance your company's employee training capability. A novice using an expert system may learn from the wealth of information contained in the system simply by using it. A whole new bent for the concept of on-the-job training.

Any industry can benefit from knowledge-based and expert systems. Within this book, you will read of applications in the financial, transportation, heavy manufacturing, and telecommunications industries. But despite the many benefits of expert systems, they are *not* the panaceas of the modern age. They can only do what we enable them to do. Expert systems will never have a flash of brilliance or a gut-level instinctive hunch. Moreover, if the knowledge or rules-of-thumb loaded into the system are flawed, the recommendations and decisions that come out will be just as erroneous. Expert systems are today's technologies; nothing more. Chinese acrobats will still put on a great show.

With that in mind, probe the productivity potential of artificial intelligence to its depths. As you read this book, seek out new ways to leverage your experts' knowledge. Empower your employees with systems that make every worker a decision point, a point that adds value. Dream up new ways to add value to the lives of your customers by being ready with a new product the moment they want it. In short, get to work figuring ways to make your operation productive to its highest degree. If you can do that, you will dominate your industry or market. You will be the competition that others are concerned about. And most important, you will be the supplier or vendor of choice for your customers. That is what we plan to be at U S WEST.

REFERENCES

Cetron, M. J. et al. (1988, July-August). Long-term trends affecting the United States. *The Futurist, XXII* (4), 29–40.

part IV
Data Processing Overview

4

Integrating AI Technology and Traditional Data Processing: Putting the Technology To Work

Joe K. Carter

Arthur Andersen and Company

Practical and economic payoff from AI is critically dependent on integrating AI technology with traditional database processing. Through integration, AI is seen as one of several powerful new tools that are revolutionizing what can be done to automate information processing in business. Several examples are provided showing how complex, low to medium transaction volume problems that have previously defied computerization are now being addressed with integrated AI technology. The chapter concludes with guidelines which stress the need to integrate AI applications with the traditional MIS computing environment by choosing AI software that is compatible with traditional software environments, by embedding AI applications in traditional software environments, by using AI approaches when appropriate, by designing for adequate performance, and, most importantly, by integrating with the business itself through addressing a genuine business problem.

INTRODUCTION

My topic is integrating artificial intelligence technology into traditional data processing. Over the past couple of years I have come to the conclusion that the artificial intelligence business is very similar to the real estate business in that it has three critical success factors. In real estate those are, in this order, location, location, and location. In the AI business the three critical success factors are, as you can guess, integration, integration, and integration, in that order. What we have found and what we have observed in putting these systems in over the past several years is that by and large the systems that are successful are the ones that are integrated into the organizational fabric and information-processing environment in which they are operating. The ones that are not successful are the ones that are stand alone and not integrated. We believe, therefore, that such integration is very important. This presentation is about how at Arthur Andersen we are going about trying to achieve this integration and what our general thoughts are on the topic.

A PRACTICAL VIEW OF ARTIFICIAL INTELLIGENCE

I want to ask exactly what it is that we are integrating when we talk about integrating AI. Are we integrating artificial intelligence? Are we integrating expert systems knowledge? Is it something more, something less, something in between, or something that we cannot imagine? It's a very difficult question to answer, partly because of the newness of the technology and the lack of any historical perspective that would provide us with guidelines to integration. It is also difficult because of definition problems with the terms "artificial intelligence," "expert systems," and "knowledge-based system."

I heard about some research recently into the true meaning of intelligence that illustrates very well the difficulty of defining that term. The organization doing this research decided they were going to get to the bottom of the question once and for all, and, given its importance, they assigned their most senior scientist to it. He spent several months conducting his research. At the end of that period he gathered all his colleagues together and held up in front of them the artificially intelligent artifact that he had chosen as the subject of his research. He said, "Gentlemen, this is a thermos bottle. It keeps hot stuff hot, and it keeps cold stuff cold. My question is, how does it know?"

As a result of research like that into that question, I decided to avoid the issue as much as possible and concentrate on figuring out how to make the technology that we are using, whatever we call it, solve complex business problems. That is the vein in which my remarks are going to be directed.

Another difficulty in defining intelligent systems, as I mentioned earlier, is the lack of perspective, because we have been dealing with this technology for such a short period of time in comparison with the overall scheme of information systems. In order to provide an idea of where the technology is in relation to integration and where it might be going, I want to use an analogy with another artificial technology that we are very familiar with—artificial flight. According to Leonardo da Vinci's work of around the 1500s, the original goal of artificial flight as a field of study was to fly by the flapping of wings. Da Vinci's idea was that we should study nature, study wing flapping and feathers, in ignorance of more abstract concepts like lift and propulsion. This line of reasoning leads to a contraption like the one in Figure 4.1—something very much like a bird in flight; da Vinci filled several notebooks with drawings like this.

As a result of that line of thinking, do we all now travel on DC-10s or 747s that flap their wings and have feathers? Yes? No. We don't. And the reason for that is that after da Vinci, technology took a turn different than what we had originally expected it to take. We integrated some other technologies with the

Figure 4.1.   Goal of Artificial Flight: "To fly by the flapping of wings"

original concept of artificial flight that had absolutely nothing to do with the original concept, and we only took a subset of the original concept of artificial flight. A very similar thing is happening in artificial intelligence.

Recently, scientists in the United States did create a machine that flies by flapping its wings. It looks like a pterodactyl. But the earlier and successful approach to artificial flight was the Wright Brothers' decision to ignore feathers and wing flapping and concentrate on the essential components of the technology, the ideas of lift and propulsion. Thus, they generated the Wright biplane and the first flight of man.

Then followed commercialization and the advance into some areas of technology, such as jet and rocket engines, that did not have anything at all to do with the original ideas that da Vinci and others had. Very similar things are going to happen, I predict, in artificial intelligence. The original conception of artificial intelligence, even as recently as 1987, is that it is the field of study whose goal is to understand minds by building them. This idea is that we have got some sort of a biological machine that is able to be creative, to learn, to be curious, and to do things like knowledge representation and inference. The idea is that we are going to be able to take that biological machine that does all these things, the human brain, and recreate it as an electronic machine.

I predict that the goal of creating an artificial mind will not take the 400 years it took us to realize commercial flight. Sometime in the 21st century some scientist will have invented a machine that actually does think as we think, analogously to the pterodactyl that flies by flapping wings. But this will not be a momentous event, just as the pterodactyl was not a momentous event, because in the meantime we shall have integrated AI with some other technologies that have little to do with the original conception of artificial intelligence.

Here is what I think is going to happen and is, in fact, already happening. We have taken a small component of the original concept of artificial intelligence. We have ignored, at least for the time being in the commercial setting, things like creativity, curiosity, and learning. There are people working on these attributes of intelligence—perfectly good research objectives which may move into the realm of commercial viability at some point. But for now, the primary commercial concern is on only two components of artificial intelligence—knowledge representation, the ability to store knowledge in a form that a computer can use, and inferencing, the ability to take that knowledge once it is stored and draw new conclusions from it.

Practicalities in Applying AI

We have been very successful in developing systems that represent knowledge and draw inferences, simulating elements of human reasoning in which humans are highly competent, areas of reasoning characterized by skilled performance and expertise. However, even here there are some glitches, as illustrated by a recent article in the *Wall Street Journal*. It was entitled "An electronic clone of a skilled engineer is very hard to create." We already knew that, but that has not stopped us from creating them, and we have been very successful in creating them. But the more telling thing was buried in the text of the article where it said that with Mr. Kelly, the expert in this case, handy, there was not a lot of demand for his electronic counterpart. The implication is that for many expert systems directed at replacing experts, there is no economic justification for their being built. If there is an expert around being paid $50,000 a year, there is no reason to spend $250,000 or a million dollars on an expert system to replace him.

We have gotten a little bit smarter in the academic setting and in the commercial setting. We have determined that rather than replacing experts or simulating experts, a more effective way to employ this new technology would be to support aspects of reasoning in which humans are weak. This line of reasoning leads to the realization that what we need to provide is decision-assist capabilities. We call these knowledge-based systems because they are not so much expert systems in that they replace an expert as they are systems which process knowledge.

Again, the allusion to "flying by flapping wings" is not strict. Knowledge-based systems process knowledge in ways that may not match a human expert's approach. For example, experts, and humans in general, tend to be inconsistent; they have difficulty assimilating large bodies of unfamiliar knowledge quickly, and they tend to forget. Indeed, even the smartest individuals among us have difficulty making a decision based on more than about seven variables. So in integrating artificial intelligence into the broader context of information technology, we have taken a little bit of artificial intelligence technology, a little bit of object-oriented programming, and a little bit of human-computer interface technology to create a composite that is a major and striking advance in information technology. We have increased computerized decision-assist capabilities by using AI together with things outside of the original realm of AI. When combined with AI, the composite provides significant value. For example, since we do have the situation that experts and people in general have difficulty thinking of more than seven variables at a time, we build systems using advanced human-computer interface techniques and object-oriented programming techniques with some expert system capability that help people reduce problems to a manageable size.

This point is illustrated by Figure 4.2, a depiction of the gate area in an airline operation. Around each gate are the airplanes it serves. Previously, experts using their own mental faculties were able to do a good job of, say, scheduling or handling seven airplanes. But with this type of interface, they can handle many

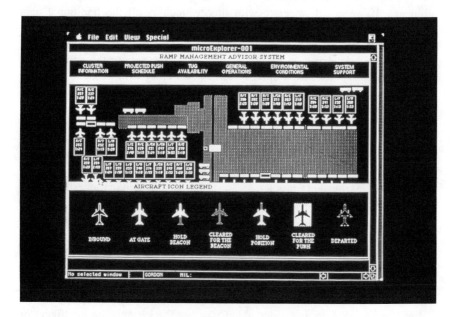

Figure 4.2. Airport Gates

more. The system provides them with the capability to see the status of all airplanes interactively and dynamically. As a new airplane comes in, it shows up on the screen. As the status of the airplanes change, the colors of the icons change to show what the new status is. If the controller gets bored or distracted, or simply makes an error, such as sending one of the smaller planes out too close to the backwash of a larger plane, the system will use its expert system capabilities to flag this situation and inform the controller. The expert can now keep track of 30 to 40 airplanes at the same time.

The decision-assist capabilities demonstrated by the gate controller example are very exciting. The expert system capability underneath is also very exciting. But, as a data processing professional, the thing that is really exciting is the rapidity with which we are able to develop systems like this. This system admittedly is not yet complete, but to provide the functionality that it currently has only took about six labor weeks to implement. To have done that using conventional data processing technology without the advanced human-computer interface capabilities, without object-oriented programming, and without the underlying inferencing and knowledge representation techniques, I think—if we could have done it at all—it would have taken us six months.

As we get data processing people like myself involved with this technology and we see that we can develop systems quickly and rapidly, we question limiting the use of this technology for what we consider to be expert system problems. If we could integrate with this technology all the traditional data processing capabilities and general information processing capabilities, such as database interfaces, access to corporate DB2 databases, other relational databases, and IMS databases, if we could get enough transactions through it, if we could generate reports and do things such as data entry with it, then we would have a very good way to develop systems, any system. It doesn't have to be an expert system.

The next phase is beyond knowledge-based systems, what I consider the next generation of information processing systems—integrated AI and knowledgebase technology with traditional data processing capability. In doing this we get a very cost-effective way to build flexible and maintainable information systems to address complex business problems. So, to answer my original question: Yes, we are integrating artificial intelligence technology; however, we are only integrating a small component of it. Yes, we are integrating knowledge-based systems and we are integrating expert systems as a subcomponent of knowledgebased systems. But, the most exciting thing is the ability to integrate both expert systems capabilities and knowledge-based systems capabilities together with conventional data processing capabilities to provide very cost effective, very flexible, maintainable solutions to business problems.

Let's get away from questions about whether the systems are intelligent or not. What I want to do is get you to start thinking about using this technology to solve complex business problems. A lot of problems in business are not amenable to automation solely through conventional data processing techniques; but when we add these additional AI capabilities, we greatly expand our ability to automate what we are doing in business.

To summarize, AI is part of an explosion of new information processing tools and techniques that have greatly expanded our ability to computerize. It is a whole new world out there. Before, primarily all we could automate were fairly simple paper pushing and number crunching types of applications. But now we can go into a whole new realm of automation. Previously we had been working with straightforward, static applications that were kind of production-line oriented. Now we are able to go into more complex, dynamic, custom, solution-oriented applications.

Hardware and Software Trends

In the hardware area, we have new workstation tools—microcomputers that can basically put the power of a mainframe on your desk. We have languages, such as shell languages, that provide the user with 60 percent of the system right out of the box before he even gets started programming. Previously, with traditional data processing capabilities, we were only able to address maybe 5 percent of the problems that potentially could be addressed. With these new techniques available to us we now have a way to go after the other 95 percent that we have not been able, nor even begun, to touch.

There is a movement toward traditional programming languages. We have knowledge representation tools and inferencing tools available in COBOL and C. Originally if a person wanted to do serious work with AI technology, he had to be a LISP or a PROLOG programmer. Those languages, LISP and PROLOG, will continue to be very important, but in a lot of instances they are not good alternatives. Sometimes there is a need to do something in C or COBOL. Even in instances where one may resort to LISP and PROLOG, the recent implementations coming on the market have provided capabilities to interface and pass data between LISP programs and C programs and COBOL programs very easily.

Examples

Let me give you some examples of the types of things that we are able to do. We have used the integration approach to save a company half a million dollars in system development costs. It is hard to call the system an expert system because it generates journal entries, and I do not think too many people would call a journal entry generation system an expert system. However, it takes input about some very complex business transactions through a microcomputer work station. On the microcomputer work station is an artificial intelligence–based program which generates the journal entries to account for a complex business transaction. The business transactions were complicated in that they dealt with material transfers between production sites for an oil and gas company involved in moving materials from domestic to foreign sites. There were many variables. The transaction could involve moving materials from a wholly owned site to a partially owned site. It could involve fully depreciated materials or brand new materials; there are all kinds of permutations, and we were having difficulty getting it implemented using conventional data processing design and programming techniques. In fact, the accountant who had been doing this process manually had almost convinced us that it could not be automated cost effectively. We had spent three months working on the design and were not making any headway with it. As a last ditch effort we decided to approach it using expert systems techniques.

Within six weeks we had a system built that could handle 95 percent of these complex business transactions. The system could generate journal entries that might be 20 or 30 lines long. We showed the prototype to the client. We had a handle on the design; we were ready to program it in COBOL. By the way, it was going to take us six months to write the COBOL program. The client said, "You've already got 95 percent of the processing; why don't you just add the additional 5 percent and let's implement." So we did, and the system is up and running today, and the client provides testimonials that say they saved half a million dollars just in development costs by using an expert systems approach to a traditional data processing problem.

Another example is a production scheduling system that we did for a metal products manufacturer. We were able very quickly to get the system in place and thereby avoid delays in bringing online a new $10 million manufacturing facility. This system downloads forecast information from a traditional distribution system and uses that information in conjunction with information about both machine and trucking capacity to generate a production schedule. There is a lot of intelligence involved in doing the production scheduling, but the thing that saved the company money was the fact that we were able to get the system in place in four months.

The war story on this was that the company had made a strategic decision to consolidate their manufacturing operations into one central location to cut down on the raw materials inventory. They had scheduled this plant to go into production on January 1, and the engineer who was going to be in charge of the scheduling sat down in August to figure out how the scheduling would be done. He found out that it was going to take him five days to schedule one day of production through the facility! If that were the case, they would not be able to bring the facility online until they got some automated support for production scheduling.

We knew that writing a COBOL program or FORTRAN program was going to take a lot longer than four months, so we went in with an expert systems approach. We had a little bit of a complication because the expert, the engineer, had told us how he wanted the production scheduling to be done, and we had some doubts about whether his approach would solve the business problem. So we proposed the development of a prototype within six weeks. We showed him the prototype of exactly what he had asked for; he looked at it and said, "You know, guys, you gave me exactly what I wanted, but now that I see it, I can see it's not going to solve the business problem." In the two and one-half months we had left, we were able to implement a system that did solve the business problem. Because these systems are so flexible and maintainable, we were able to build on what we already had, modify it, get the system in place by January 1, and get the production facility online.

As a third example, internally at Arthur Andersen we had a need to provide a flexible, maintainable pricing module for some distribution control systems software that we had developed. Pricing cannot be considered, in any sense of the word, an expert function, but it is something that required thought. Every time we went to a new client to install the software, it had to be modified. So we used an expert systems approach to provide a version of the pricing module within an overall conventional distribution control system that made it very easy to modify pricing from client to client.

Guidelines

Through having done all this, I have developed a few guidelines I think are critical to accomplishing successful integration. The first thing that has to be done is to make the AI systems compatible with traditional computing. In the past that has been very difficult because the tools did not lend themselves to integration. Several developments, over the last 18 months to two years, however, have given us the capability to be compatible with traditional data processing, as discussed above in the section on hardware and software.

The second guideline is embeddability. In the past AI programs had to run independently of conventional programs. We now have the capability to embed AI code both inside of a conventional program—IBM's Knowledge Tool product is a very good example of a tool that allows us to do this—and we are able to put conventional code inside of an AI program. We have system software compatibility now. For a long time we were forced to run under operating environments that were written in LISP on LISP machines. At this point we have tools that run under all the major operating systems.

An important part of embeddedness is the ability to access corporate data. In the past, in the 1985 time frame, if you wanted to get information into an expert system, you had to enter it through the keyboard because we lacked good access to databases on mainframes and minicomputers. Now, most of the major vendors have provided some sort of capability, built-in capability, to access conventional databases. Examples of vendors who have provided this are AION Corporation with their ADS product, which has good integration with IMS and DB2. KBMS also has this capability, and even the very high-end tools like KEE from Intel-licorp are in the process of providing for access to mainframe databases.

Embedding is also impacted by hardware. Today we have a movement to-wards conventional processors—you no longer have to go out and buy an $80,000 LISP machine. One of the most exciting things is the advent of very powerful microcomputer workstations that provide LISP machine capability for $5,000 to $30,000. One interesting example of this is the Explorer Board from Texas Instruments which provides in a MacII package all the capabilities of a LISP machine at very reasonable cost. So, we are able to do everything that we are able to do on a LISP machine in this more acceptable vehicle.

The third guideline is the need to address a business problem. In a lot of instances companies have taken a technology or an expertise orientation in em-ploying AI technology. They have said, "Here's this technology solution, and we're going to go out and find a problem for it." Those systems tend to end up sitting on the shelf, because they fail to address a business problem. Or, they go after expertise and only expertise. They automate the expertise and not the business processing that goes around the expertise. I am coming more and more to the opinion that expertise is highly overrated. I think that the value of an expert is not so much in his ability to make a decision but in his ability to make that decision work after he has made it, to follow through and do all the things that are necessary to carry out the decision. So we have to be able not only to assist him in making the decision, but also in doing all the things necessary to make the decision work.

For example, in the past, the way that we went about implementing these systems is depicted on the top part of Figure 4.3. We would do things like drop an insurance application on an insurance underwriter's desk and give him an underwriting expert system to work with interactively, looking at the insurance application and answering a lot of questions. Then the system would make an underwriting recommendation that he put in his out box. Somebody would have to pick that up, go to the policy issue system, and enter it through a data entry terminal. Systems like that get very good reviews up front, but they end up not being used. A much better way, and the only way for systems to provide real value, is an integrated approach: Take the insurance application through a data entry system and then make the information that was entered through the data entry system available to an insurance underwriting expert system. Moreover, the underwriting expert system would probably have two components. I would have a black box component which would be able to underwrite a lot of the insurance policies without a human ever having touched them and send them directly on to the policy issue system. For the cases that it could not handle, it would provide its analysis to the insurance underwriter; he would interactively come up with a recommendation, submit it back to the expert system, and again it would go directly to the policy issue system. The entire problem needs to be addressed, not just a part of the problem.

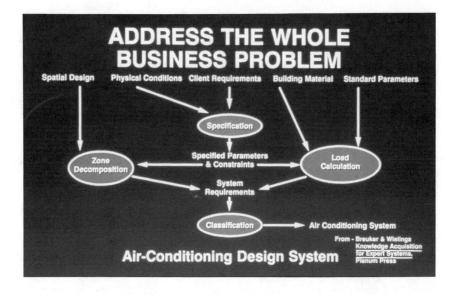

Figure 4.3. The Whole Business Problem and Nothing but the Business Problem

Another example of addressing the entire business problem is illustrated by the following air conditioning design system problem. This particular business problem has four major components. It has a specification component involved in specifying the requirements for the air conditioning system. It has a zone decomposition problem involved in breaking down the building that has to be air conditioned into the components that are going to have to be air conditioned. It has a load calculation problem to figure out what size of air conditioning unit is required. And it has a classification component, which, once the requirements have been defined, classifies the particular system so it can be matched to available air conditioning system configurations. This problem has multiple facets. The specification problem can be handled easily by an expert system. However, the zone decomposition problem requires a lot of special reasoning that we have difficulty doing in an expert system mode right now. So that turns out to be a computer-assisted manual process, with the human in the loop. The load calculation problem is a conventional program. The classification program is another expert system. Now, if we had gone in targeting just the expertise, we would have maybe just implemented these two "expert" components and forgotten about the other two. Had we done that, we would not have had a solution to a business problem. Again, the guideline is that the entire business problem has to be looked at and a total solution to the entire situation has to be implemented in order to provide enough value to get somebody to use the system.

The fourth guideline is not to default to traditional computing. It is true that anything that can be done using expert system techniques can be done using conventional data processing techniques. The converse is also true. Just because you can do something using conventional techniques, however, does not mean you need to default to that. In general, the guideline I go by is if a system or business problem involves a high transaction volume and if the problem complexity is low, then that is a traditional computing problem. If, however, a business problem has a fairly high complexity and it has a low to medium transaction volume, then I need to attack it using an intelligent computing technique. We have been able to expand the scope of what we can automate. In the past we have only been able to do fairly high-volume low-complexity applications cost effectively. Now, however, we can do a much larger group of problems with intelligent computing capability which allows us to expand the level of complexity we can address.

My final guideline is that the system has to perform adequately for an industrial-strength business problem. This is a challenge in high-transaction volume environments. The jury is still out on this one. There are some very good developments in the area of performance. For example, we are working with AION Corporation to develop a high-performance option for their software package ADS that AION thinks is going to increase the performance of their software anywhere from six to ten times. We now have the capability to do low to medium transaction volumes. The good news is that most of the complex problems tend to be low to medium transaction volume problems. They are not airline reservation types of systems that are getting hundreds of thousands of transactions going through in a short period of time.

part V
Technology Forecast

5

The Sixth Generation Computers: Optical Connectionist Machines

Kristina M. Johnson
Mike Kranzdorf
University of Colorado at Boulder

The dominance of symbolic processing in artificial intelligence (AI) research is being challenged by a new wave of parallel distributed processing (PDP) systems, which promises better fault tolerance, and the flexibility of learning without extensive preprogramming. These systems require massively parallel computation and are therefore very slow when simulated on conventional serial computers. Optical computing systems offer a natural parallelism to imbed these new highly parallel architectures. In this chapter we compare symbolic processing and parallel distributing processing and review several optical implementations of parallel distributed processing systems—the sixth generation of computing.

INTRODUCTION

Neural networks (also known as connectionist architectures and parallel distributed processing (PDP) systems) are groups of simple, highly interconnected processing units, which act collectively to perform computable functions. A unit in a neural network, like a real biological neuron (see Figure 5.1), contains a numerical activation value that is communicated to other units in the network through synaptic-like interconnections. The strength of individual connections determines the influence of one unit on another unit. The output of a particular processing unit is attained by combining activation values from input units, weighted by the synaptic connections (see Figure 5.2). These neural-like networks exhibit properties of associative memory, recognition, database search, learning, and computation.

Neural networks are open to many interpretations. They operate as biological models, cognitive models, engineering problem-solving tools, and artificial intelligence (AI) tools. Each paradigm provides a different, though not necessarily distinct, framework within which to discuss a specific connectionist system. For example, neuroscience involves, in part, the study of networks made of

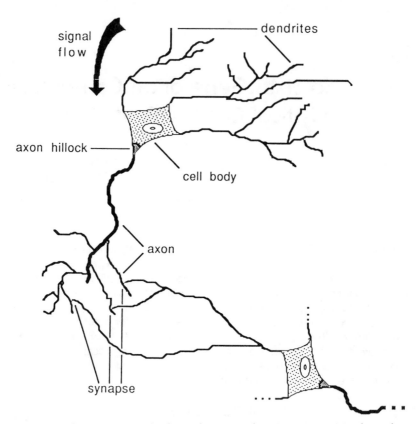

Figure 5.1.   Representative biological neurons showing connectivity through synapses

real biological neurons. Biologically inspired models are usually focused on a single aspect of behavior in a simple nervous system, such as the physical response to an environmental stimulus. A primary concern of these models is their biological and evolutionary plausibility.

Cognitive models usually seek to provide explanations of higher level human behavior, such as natural language understanding, learning and memory, and scene recognition. In general, the goal of such a model is a coherent explanation of a specific behavior within a larger conceptual paradigm. The representation of knowledge is integral to these studies, and ability of a system to learn a given behavior is often an important constraint in cognitive modelling. It is often very difficult to distinguish cognitive models from AI models, which more generally mimic human behavior rather than explain it. Thus, AI models may be concerned less with human information processing and more with implementation considerations, such as appropriate data structures and algorithms.

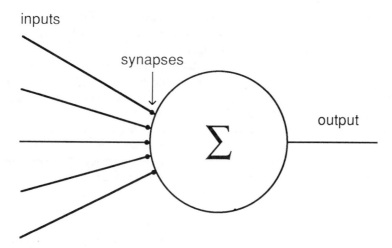

Figure 5.2. A simulated neuron which sums its gated inputs to yield an output value

Related engineering and problem-solving models are generally concerned with convenient implementations of appropriate algorithms. Optimization methods and signal recognition techniques are representative problems. Although biological plausibility is not an issue, inspiration for engineering problem solving is often gleaned from biological systems. Airplanes and birds both use wings and thrust to attain flight; however, early flying machines that mimicked their biological counterpart were not very successful.

All of the above disciplines have been influenced by the recent renaissance of neural network research. The remainder of this chapter focuses primarily on the comparison of traditional AI and neural network approaches to problem solving. Optical implementations of neural networks, the sixth generation computers, are also presented.

Symbolic Artificial Intelligence

The principle underlying most mainstream AI research is known as the *symbolic paradigm* (Smolensky, 1988). The basic components of "intelligence" are seen as those that are immediately available through introspection. Simple cognitive entities, such as physical objects, actions, and opinions, are the building blocks. Complex thoughts and activities are achieved through the combination and evaluation of these symbols. This is known as symbol manipulation, which is the computational strategy underlying such environments as LISP. Complex combinations of objects and procedures (both symbols), known as schemata and frames are often used in AI models (Minsky, 1975).

Expert systems. Most expert systems are made from *production systems,* which are environments for the evaluation of numerous IF-THEN–like statements. These rules are usually a representation of the knowledge of an expert in some field. Since in the symbolic paradigm this is the appropriate representation of human knowledge, these systems should be able to correctly mimic the expert, which has supplied the knowledge. In practice, however, many difficulties are encountered. Human experts rarely follow such strict rules in their own cognitive processes and thus have difficulty retrieving knowledge in rule-based form. When this information is consolidated it is often riddled with exceptions to be processed along with the rules. Experts operate more through heuristics and analogy than rules. Knowledge in these forms is very hard to quantify, especially when translating into an external symbol system. The resulting expert systems are usually not tolerant of inputs, which do not match the IF part of the rules exactly. Difficulty also arises when the domain is not sufficiently covered by the rules. Some examples of expert system domains include medical diagnosis, production floor management, process control, and customer account evaluation.

Knowledge bases. Systems which contain information in addition to rules are generally called knowledge-based systems. Such information could be background knowledge relevant to the domain, better rule handling and organization, or prototyping and generalization abilities. Large databases are often available to those systems. Knowledge bases hold great promise for creating more adaptable systems that can learn their domain through instruction or example.

Connectionist Artificial Intelligence

Many kinds of connectionist systems are being investigated and used for AI applications. There are two common ways of characterizing such networks. The first concerns the knowledge representation within the network. Information is local to units or is distributed among many units. The second is in the system's ability to acquire new knowledge. A given system may or may not have the ability to learn. Systems that learn do so either with or without a teacher and are known as supervised or self-organized, respectively. The latter applies to symbolic AI systems as well, but is primarily discussed in regards to neural networks.

Representation. Neural networks that assign the meaning of their units to the kinds of entities found in symbolic AI are known as *localist* systems. The connections between these units represent their relationships in the problem domain. Extracting meaning from a localist network is relatively simple. The activity level of each unit represents the amount to which the indicated concept is involved in the current state of the network. A list of all the units' meanings and their current activity levels can yield a complete description of a network's current "thought." Different *patterns of activity* across the units represent different "thoughts." These systems are very much like the semantic networks found in traditional AI.

At the other end of a continuum of representation encodings are *distributed* or *coarse coded* representations, in which such localization of concepts to units is not possible. Rather, units correspond to so-called *microfeatures* of the environment. A localist unit is replaced by a group of units whose activity levels represent the feature in question. No single unit can be said to represent any single entity. This makes the interpretation of activity patterns more difficult, but makes their interactions more subtle (and interesting). Many concepts can be represented and thus interact in a single group of units. Such complex interactions are very difficult to achieve with symbolic representations. The ability to manipulate symbol-like entities in such a manner is one of the most promising and exciting aspects of connectionist research. In this sense, connectionist systems are often said to obey soft constraints rather than hard ones (rules). Similarly, while localist representations define and limit the concepts available to a system, more distributed representations allow flexible interpretations of what concepts are in existence or are available. Distributed representations also have the advantage of better fault tolerance and noise immunity. For example, the failure of any single unit does not in general greatly disrupt the system as a whole. In contrast, failure of a localist unit, which represents a word, means that the word can no longer be expressed.

Learning. Along with the information contained in the units, there is information in the connections between them. A unit (or group of units) can be defined as a concept, which is then available to the system. Similarly, a connection between two units (or groups of units) implies that the two concepts are related. The units can then influence each other as the concepts would interact in the real world. In the case of a more distributed representation, the connectivity pattern within a population can restrict and shape the activity patterns, which are likely to occur. While this is also applicable to localist systems, in the case of distributed representations it deeply affects the way concepts evolve and are realized.

A network's connectivity pattern generally defines potential connections among units, not the specific strengths. It is these strengths that embody a given system's knowledge within its framework. Connection strengths may either be part of a system's definition, or may be learned by the system through experience. The former scheme is usually restricted to localist networks, where the correlations among predefined conceptual units are taken from the real-world problem domain. Connectionist implementations of databases are good examples of such systems (Bein & Smolensky, 1988).

Supervised learning. Many problems require learning the input/output relationships in domain knowledge. For instance, recognition and categorization problems are often well specified with respect to the distinctions between the groupings. Connectionist systems may be a good solution to this task. There are several techniques for modifying connection strengths in order to reproduce input/output pairs of activity patterns (Rumelhart, McClelland, & the PDP Research Group, 1986). This is in contrast with most symbolic techniques, where the rules that generate the mapping must be specified a priori. Connectionist systems offer a good solution to such learning-by-example problems, which are difficult for rule-based systems. Most successful connectionist models are of this type. Character recognition and loan analysis are prominent examples of supervised learning (Fukushima, 1987).

Unsupervised learning. Another type of categorization problem requires the system to classify inputs. This is an example of unsupervised learning. An unsupervised system forms an internal representation of the environment and uses that to respond to further inputs. The architecture of such systems usually contains information about the expected domain. Control and other feedback systems are often found in such situations and may benefit from connectionist implementation (Barto, Sutton, & Anderson, 1983).

APPLICATIONS OF PDP

In this section we compare PDP and expert systems approaches to solving problems in translating written text to speech, solar flare prediction, and optical inspection. We use these three examples to illustrate the power and potential of PDP networks to solve problems when the inputs and outputs of a system are well known, but the mapping between them is difficult or impossible to determine.

NETtalk vs. DECtalk: Text Translation

Language and text translation is of extreme interest, as ultimately facsimile machines and telephones may provide translation capabilities from one language to another. We believe future telecommunications systems may achieve this advanced state through realizing the potential of parallel distributed processing.

PDP networks are not preprogrammed; they learn relationships between patterns by trial and error. For example, to learn the association between the written word "apple" and its phonetic pronunciation, the word is appropriately encoded and presented to the network. The first few responses of the network to this input usually result in an incorrect pronunciation. An error signal is generated by comparing the network pronunciation to the desired pronunciation. This error signal is used to adjust the strength of the connection weights according to a learning rule. The weights stop changing when the error tends toward zero.

A simple PDP network that translates written text to speech has been developed by Terry Sejnowski at John Hopkins University (Sejnowski & Rosenberg,

1987). NETtalk is a computer simulation of the connections between 200 neural-like processing units. A real power of PDP networks is their ability to learn new patterns without excessive preprogramming. To translate a new language like French, examples of written and spoken French are sufficient to train NETtalk. Traditional expert systems approaches, like DECtalk (Digital Equipment Corporation, 1985) developed by Digital Equipment Corporation, would require pre-programming phonological rules of French, along with a table or dictionary of French words. Creating such a dictionary alone takes months of extensive programming. NETtalk, on the other hand, can be trained by example in a few days.

TheoNet vs. Theo: Solar Flare Prediction

Solar flares are a brightening in the coronosphere of the sun due to a shift in the sun's intense magnetic fields. A strong flare has the energy equivalent of 10 million hydrogen bombs. Flares have shorted out power stations in Canada, where the long transmission lines are not well shielded by the Earth's magnetic field. Flares also disrupt radio communications and influence the Earth's climate. In space, solar flares have pushed satellites 100 km out of their orbital position and have shorted circuits on the space shuttle. A major flare causes x-ray radiation that is lethal for astronauts in space. The thin skin of shuttles and the space station is no protection from this deadly radiation. Fortunately, most manned activity to date has taken place during periods where the sun has been relatively quiescent. However, just as the space shuttle is being readied for its return to space, the sun is climbing toward solar maximum. During the next few years, manned space activity will have to be carefully coordinated with solar activity.

For these reasons, predicting solar flares is a vital task. The U.S. maintains a permanent office to measure solar activity and issue flare forecasts. The Space Environment Laboratory (SEL) is located in Boulder, CO, at the National Bureau of Standards building. Because of the difficulty in predicting solar flares, the THEOPHRASTES project was created. THEO, an expert system, has been developed to assist forecasters in their predictions. Tests have shown THEO to be more effective than the SEL forecasters at predicting solar flares, and rivals the best experts in the field. The THEO expert system uses 500 rules gleaned from drawings made by experts to predict solar flare activity. Gary Bradshaw and Paul Smolensky, assistant professors of psychology and computer science, respectively, at the University of Colorado, Boulder, and their students have been experimenting with a connectionist version of THEO, called TheoNet (Fossard et al., 1988), that learns to predict solar flares. Because of the learning component, TheoNet can readily add new sources of observation to its predictions as new instruments are created to make measurements from the sun.

TheoNet can also be quickly adapted to make longer-term predictions of flare activity, beyond the 24-hour predictions made by THEO. In comparison to Theo, TheoNet requires only 17 processing units, interconnected to 5 hidden units and three output classifying units for low, medium, and high flare activity.

It is possible to extend THEO in these same directions; however, this involves extensive knowledge engineering using experts in solar physics. These experts are generally Air Force personnel with two-year tours of duty. Solar flare activity has an 11-year cycle. Therefore it is difficult to develop an expert system with an 11-year perspective. TheoNet can learn from experience, much the way human experts learn. The relatively small size of the network needed makes TheoNet an ideal system to implement in optoelectronic hardware. We are currently implementing TheoNet in an optical system described in the next section.

OPTICAL CONNECTIONIST MACHINES

Parallel distributed processing is extremely time-consuming to perform on traditional digital computers for two reasons: computers operate serially using a Von Neuman architecture and process digital information. Learning the relationship between input and output patterns in PDP networks requires many adaptations of analog connections. For example, NETtalk (Sejnowski & Rosenberg, 1987), a PDP network that learns to translate written text to speech, requires adapting 10,000 connections between 200 processing units. Running on a VAX 780, NETtalk learns to translate at a rate of 2 letters/second. After a day of training, NETtalk translates written text from a first grade primer to spoken English.

Sophisticated speech translation, pattern recognition, and robotic control will require making connections between an even larger number of processing units. These networks will be difficult to implement in digital or analog VLSI, where processing units are generally confined to a two-dimensional wafer and the interconnections between units occupy over 70 percent of the chip real estate. Connections between these processors is further limited by crosstalk due to the finite mass and charge of an electron. Photons have no mass or charge; hence, this kind of crosstalk is minimal in optical systems by comparison. Because photons can cross paths, optics offers a third dimension to exploit for making the high-density interconnections required by large neural-like networks. Optical systems are inherently parallel, which allows a quadratic increase in processing speed over serial machines. The optical power required to interconnect processors is independent of the interconnection distance, as compared to electronic systems where the communication cost increases linearly with separation between processing elements (Smith, 1987). Other advantages of optics in computing include scaleability through high fan-in and quantum power conversion and impedance matching (Miller, 1989). Currently there are two classes of optical architectures for implementing neural networks: those based on holography (Gabor, 1948; Leith & Upatnieks, 1962) and those employing optical matrix-vector multipliers (Goodman, Dias, & Woody, 1978; Goodman & Johnson, 1981).

Holographic-Based Machines

Holography is derived from the Greek root *holos,* meaning whole, and *graph,* meaning written or to write. By retaining both the amount of light or amplitude, and its propagation distance, or phase, the hologram records a three-dimensional image of an illuminated object. To record both object amplitude and phase, a hologram requires the interference of two beams of light. One beam is reflected from the object and the other beam serves as a clock, recording the time of arrival of the object light. These are referred to as the object and reference beams, respectively, as shown in Figure 5.3.

The hologram is an associative mapping between the object and reference beams. Illumination by the object beam produces the reference beam, and vice versa, as shown in Figure 5.4. The application of holography to associative memory was recognized independently by van Heerden, Gabor, and Sakaguchi (van Heerden, 1963; Gabor, 1969; Sakaguchi, Nishida, & Nemoto, 1970). Humans perform the same task when they play association games like "Password" and "Name that Tune." The contestant is required to associate the appropriate word or song with a partial reference word or tune. These researchers tried to illuminate the hologram with a partial reference beam to retrieve the entire object. Simple holograms, however, do not perform this task well.

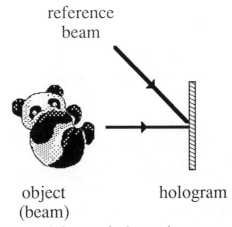

Figure 5.3.   Interference of object and reference beams, recording a hologram

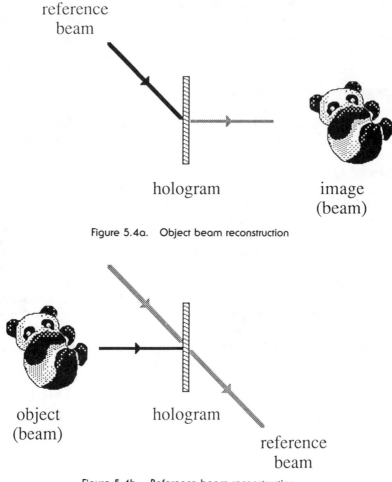

reference
beam

hologram

image
(beam)

Figure 5.4a.   Object beam reconstruction

object
(beam)

hologram

reference
beam

Figure 5.4b.   Reference beam reconstruction.

Figure 5.4.   Associative memory through hologram reconstruction

Recently, investigators have succeeded in performing holographic associative recall of data from partial or noisy inputs (Anderson, 1986; Soffer, Dunning, Owechko, & Maron, 1986; Psaltis, Brady, & Wagner, 1988). They employ holographic resonators to iteratively reconstruct complete, noise-free images from incomplete or noisy input data.

Figure 5.5 is an illustration of an optical holographic associative memory

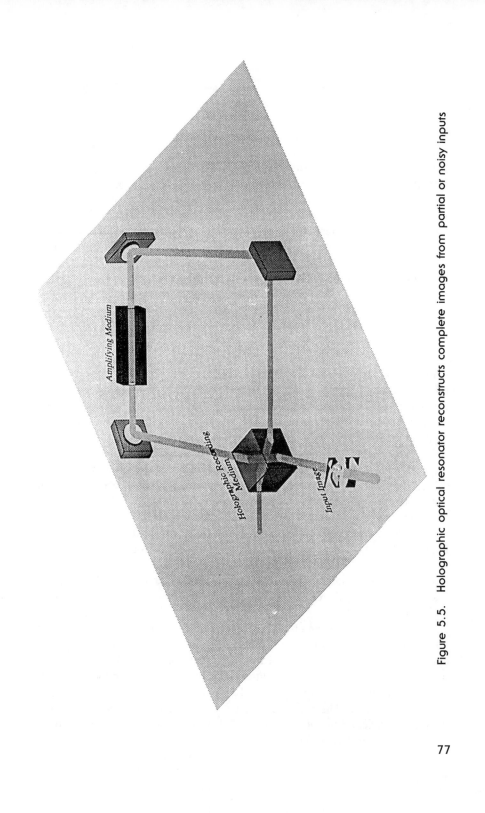

Figure 5.5. Holographic optical resonator reconstructs complete images from partial or noisy inputs

77

system (Anderson, 1986). Information to be associatively recalled is stored in the holographic recording medium. Here the interference patterns are analogous to connections between processing units in a PDP network. The input image, which is part of an object stored in the medium, illuminates the hologram. A reference beam that has a close association to the input image is diffracted by the holographic medium. Since the input is a partial or noisy image, the reference beam is also noisy or incomplete. The reference beam is reflected by mirrors through an amplifying medium and back to the hologram. The amplifying medium serves to "reward" the input images best matched to the objects stored in the hologram by increasing their brightness. Since there is only finite energy, this also serves to decrease the brightness of ill-matched patterns. As the images move around the resonator, they generate a new reference beam which, upon illumination of the hologram, reconstructs a closer approximation to the desired image. This process continues until a complete image is retrieved from the holographic memory.

Matrix-Vector–Multiplier-Based Machines

Another approach to optical associative memory employs matrix-vector multipliers (Psaltis & Farhat, 1985; Farhat, Psaltis, Prata, & Paek, 1985; Fisher, Lippincott, & Lee, 1987; Kranzdorf, Bigner, Zhang, & Johnson, 1989) as shown in Figure 5.6. An input vector consists of an incoherent source array of light emitting diodes (LEDs) that are turned either on or off. Light from LEDs turned on is imaged into a column that illuminates a corresponding column of pixels in the matrix mask. Anamorphic optics positioned behind the mask sums the transmitted light and images the light onto a one-dimensional detector array. The output detects the result of a vector-matrix multiplication.

The pixels in the matrix mask represent the synaptic weights in a PDP network, and the LEDs and detectors, the activation value of the processing units. Photographic film can be used as the matrix masks for performing Hopfield-type associative memory (Hopfield, 1982; Psaltis & Farhat, 1985). Supervised and unsupervised learning algorithms require adjusting the connections between processing units, and, therefore, an adaptable matrix mask must be used in this architecture.

Figure 5.7 illustrates an optical architecture for performing supervised learning. Again a linear array is imaged onto a two-dimensional matrix of weights. A cylindrical lens sums the transmitted values from the matrix. The output vector is incident onto a polarizing beam splitter (PBS), which breaks up the output into negative and positive weights encoded as horizontal and vertical polarization states, respectively. The two polarization states are separately detected and subtracted in parallel electronics. The result, when compared to the desired network response ("the teacher"), generates an error. This error is used to dynamically

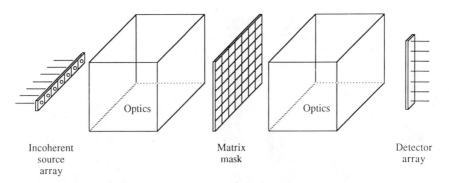

Incoherent source array

Matrix mask

Detector array

Figure 5.6. Optical matrix vector multiplier with photographic mask

change the weights of the spatial light modulator according to a learning rule designed to minimize the error between system output and desired responses (Widrow & Hoff, 1960).

The system described here is capable of learning the hetero-associative input-output relationships between 16-bit long vectors (Kranzdorf, Bigner, Zhang, & Johnson, 1989), as shown in Figure 5.8. This system development is Phase I of a

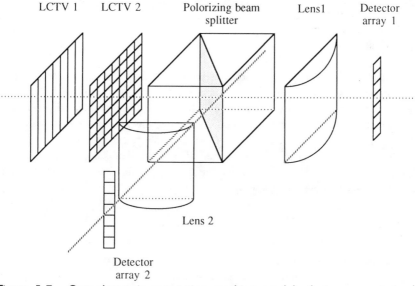

LCTV 1   LCTV 2   Polorizing beam splitter   Lens1   Detector array 1

Lens 2

Detector array 2

Figure 5.7. Optoelectronic connection machine module that uses supervised learning

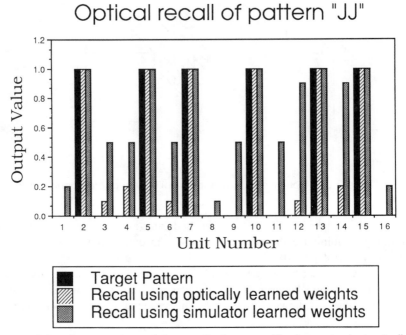

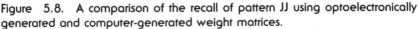

Figure 5.8. A comparison of the recall of pattern JJ using optoelectronically generated and computer-generated weight matrices.

five-year effort by the National Science Foundation Engineering Research Center for Optoelectronic Computing Systems at the University of Colorado, Boulder, to build optical PDP networks with several thousand interconnected processing elements. Work in progress includes increasing the network size from 16 to 1,000 processing units, developing PDP learning rules optimized for optical implementation, studying biological neural networks, and applying these systems and methods to applications in pattern recognition, language acquisition, robotics, and associative memory.

Optical Inspection

Inspection systems are essential to realizing fully automated manufacturing. The main goal of inspection in the industrial environment is to differentiate between defective and nondefective objects, signaling their removal from the assembly line. The inspection of manufactured glass is generally performed by a human operator. It is a tedious and costly task. Electronic machines can find large defects, but have difficulty achieving high resolution at assembly line speeds. This is due to the serial nature of these machines. Optoelectronic parallel processing methods (Cormack, Johnson, Zhang, & Cathey, 1988) can rapidly differentiate between defects in glass jars using the apparatus shown schematically in Figure 5.9.

In this system, glass jars are illuminated with laser light, which is filtered by a two-dimensional matrix mask that acts like a real-time low-frequency filter. Light scattered by defects will weakly illuminate the mask. Light transmitted by the rest of the jar will strongly illuminate the mask. A camera senses these differences in object illumination and turns off pixels associated with the strong illumination. Only defects, if present, are imaged by lens L2 at the output. A two-dimensional detector array (camera) can be used to detect the presence or absence of light, corresponding to the presence or absence of object defects. The advantage of optical parallel processing is the capability of quickly answering the question: Is the jar defective? This system is based on the vector-matrix multiplier architecture previously discussed. This task can also be performed using holographic techniques as follows.

Novelty Filtering

A novelty filter is capable of recognizing and displaying what is new or different in a particular scene of interest (Kohonen, 1984). The eye performs like a tracking novelty filter when it responds to a sudden motion in its field of view. Hawks soaring above a field find it easier to locate moving prey using a similar mechanism. Other applications include sorting and comparing patterns, such as fingerprints, photographs, and defects on an assembly line. An expert system would use a table look-up method to perform the same task. The larger the database, the more time-consuming the tasks. Figure 5.10 shows an optical tracking novelty filter which performs this same function quickly using highly interrconnected optical systems.

The optical tracking novelty filter (Anderson, Lininger, & Feinberg, 1986) consists of a Sagnac interferometer with one mirror replaced by a phase conjugate mirror (Pepper, 1986). The phase conjugate mirror is somewhat similar to a bicycle retroreflector; light incident on the mirror retraces its path exactly upon reflection. The output of phase conjugate interferometer is usually dark (Ewbank, Yeh, Khoshnevisan, & Feinberg, 1985). If a TV monitor connected to a video camera is placed in one arm of the interferometer, interesting things happen. The phase conjugate mirror takes time to reflect light, unlike an ordinary mirror. If the scene viewed by the camera detects motion occurring faster than the phase conjugate mirror reaction time, it will be displayed at the output of the

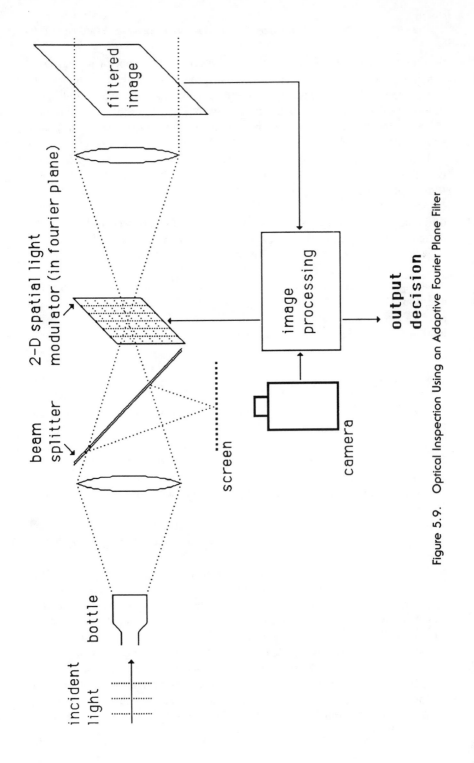

Figure 5.9. Optical Inspection Using an Adaptive Fourier Plane Filter

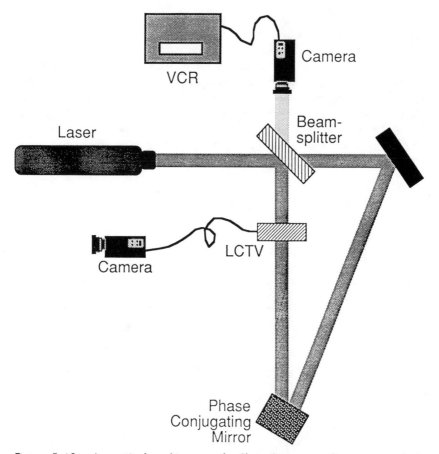

Figure 5.10. An optical tracking novelty filter. A two-port linear network that detects changes in a scene. It continually adapts, or becomes habituated, to the current scene.

interferometer. Although early in its development, the tracking novelty filter is an optical parallel distributed processor with the potential for sorting and matching objects and tracing new or novel events in a particular scene of interest.

CONCLUSIONS

In this chapter, we have compared parallel distributed processing networks and expert system approaches to problem solving. Expert systems have applications for solving well-defined problems that can be programmed with a traditional computer algorithm approach. PDP networks show potential for solving problems when the inputs and outputs are known, but the mapping between them is unknown. This is often the case in problems ranging from process control to process management.

Optics have potential advantages over electronics in implementing PDP networks, including large fan-in, parallelism, and high connectivity. To realize this potential, new algorithms and architectures need to be developed that are not constrained by implementation in electronics. There is a real need for better optical devices and components for such systems. Although optical parallel distributed processing is in its infancy, it will have a major impact on solving problems that are not well-defined and therefore cannot be approached using traditional computational methods.

REFERENCES

Anderson, D. Z. (1986). Coherent optical eigenstate memory. *Optics Letters, 11*(1), 56.

Anderson, D. Z., Lininger, D., & Feinberg, J. (1986). Optical tracking novelty filter. *Optics Letters, 11*(2), 45.

Barto, A. G., Sutton, R. S., & Anderson, C. W. (1983). Neuronlike adaptive elements that can solve difficult learning control problems. *IEEE Transactions on Systems, Man, and Cybernetics, 13*, 5.

Bein, J., & Smolensky, P. (1988). *Application of the interactive activation model to document retrieval.* (Tech. Rep. CU-CS-405-88). Boulder, CO: University of Colorado.

Cormack, R., Johnson, K. M., Zhang, L., & Cathy, W. T. (1988). *Optical Engineering, 27*, 358.

Digital Equipment Corporation. (1985). *DECtalk DTC01 Owner's Manual*, No. EK-DTC01-0M-002. Maynard, MA: Digital Equipment Corporation. [See also Pisoni, D. B., Nusbaum, H. B., & Greene, B. (1985). *Proceedings of IEEE, 73*, 1665.]

Ewbank, M. D., Yeh, P., Khoshnevisan, M., & Feinberg, J. (1985). Time reversed by an interferometer with coupled phase-conjugate reflectors. *Optics Letters, 10*, 282.

Farhat, N. H., Psaltis, D., Prata, A., & Paek, E. (1985). Optical implementation of the Hopfield model. *Applied Optics, 24* (10), 1469–1475.

Fisher, A. D., Lippincott, W. L., & Lee, J. N. (1987). Optical implementation of associative networks with versatile adaptive learning capabilities. *Applied Optics, 26*(23), 5039–5054.

Fossard, R., Ceci, L., & Bradshaw, G. (1988). *TheoNET: A connectionist network implementation of a solar flare forecasting system (THEO).* To appear in the Proceedings of the 1988 Neural Information Processing Systems Meeting. Denver, CO.

Fukushima, K. (1987). A neural network model for selective attention. In M. Caudill & C. Butler (Eds.), *Proceedings of the IEEE First International Conference on Neural Networks* (Vol II). Piscataway, NJ: IEEE Service Center.

Gabor, D. (1948). *Nature, 161*, 777.

Gabor, D. (1969). Associative holographic memories. *IBM Journal of Research and Development, 13*, 156.

Goodman, J. W., Dias, A. R., & Woody, L. M. (1978). Fully parallel, high-speed incoherent optical method for performing discrete Fourier transforms. *Optics Letters 2*(1), 1–3.

Goodman, J. W., & Johnson, K. M. (1981). *Incoherent matrix vector multiplier: Final report.* (Tech. Rep. #L701-1). Stanford, CA: Stanford University.

Hopfield, J. J. (1982). Neural networks and physical systems with emergent collective computational abilities. *Proceedings of the National Academy of Sciences in USA, 79,* 2554–2558.

Kohonen, T. (1984). *Self-organization and associative memory* (Chap. 4). New York: Springer-Verlag.

Kranzdorf, M. (1986–1988). *Mactivation.* Boulder, CO: Kranzdorf.

Kranzdorf, M., Bigner, B. J., Zhang, L., & Johnson, K. M. (1989). Optical connectionist machine with polarization-based bipolar weight values. *Optical Engineering, 28*(8), 844–848.

Leith, E., & Upatnieks, J. (1962). Reconstructed wavefronts and communication theory. *Journal of the Optical Society of America, 52,* 1123.

Miller, D. A. B. (1989). Optics for low energy communication inside digital processors: Quantum detectors, sources, and modulators as efficient impedance converters. *Optics Letters, 14,* 146.

Minsky, M. (1975). In P. H. Winston (Ed.), *The psychology of computer vision.* New York: McGraw.

Pepper, D. (1986). *Scientific American, 254,* 74.

Psaltis, D., Brady, D., & Wagner, K. (1988). Adaptive optical networks using photorefractive crystals. *Applied Optics, 27*(9), 1752–1759.

Psaltis, D., & Farhat, N. (1985). Optical information processing based on an associative memory model of neural networks with thresholding and feedback. *Optics Letters, 10,* 98.

Rumelhart, D. E., McClelland. J. L., & the PDP Research Group. (1986). *Parallel distributed processing. Volume I: Foundations, and Volume II: Psychological and Biological Models.* Cambridge, MA: MIT Press/Bradford Books.

Sakaguchi, M., Nishida, N., & Nemoto, T. (1970). *IEEE Transactions on Comp. C-19,* 12.

Sejnowski, T. J., & Rosenberg, C. R. (1987). Parallel networks that learn to pronounce English text. *Complex Systems, 1,* 145–168.

Smith, P. W. (1987). *IEEE Circuits and Devices Magazine, 5,* 9.

Smolensky, P. (1988). On the proper treatment of connectionism. *Behavioral and Brain Sciences, 11,* 1.

Soffer, B. H., Dunning, G. J., Owechko, Y., & Maron, E. (1986). Associative holographic memory with feedback using phase-conjugate mirrors. *Optics Letters, 11*(2), 118.

van Heerden, P. J. (1963). Theory of optical information storage in solids. *Applied Optics, 2,* 393.

Widrow, B., & Hoff, M. E. (1960). Adaptive switching elements. *IRE WESCON Convention Record, Part 4, Sessions on Computers Man-Machine System* (p. 96). Proceedings of the Western Electronic Show and Convention held in Los Angeles, CA, August 23–26, 1960, and sponsored by the Institute of Radio Engineers.

part VI
Corporate Applications

6

Intelligent Systems: Paying Dividends in Internal Controls

Craig S. Atkinson*

Chemical Bank

Two expert systems applications have recently been developed at Chemical Bank: one to assist in foreign exchange audits and another to assist in telecommunications audits. This chapter begins with a brief history of AI from the corporate view, emphasizing the need to go beyond prototypes to integrate applications into the work environment. The development of the foreign exchange auditing expert system is explained, and the technology transfer philosophy at Chemical Bank is illustrated. Benefits and return on investment from the system are presented, including the observation that one of the strongest benefits could not have been forecast—changes in work patterns. After a brief mention of a second auditing application, keys to successful implementation of AI technology are presented, including the importance of iterative development, hardware selection, technology transfer philosophy, and the importance of a champion. The chapter includes a discussion of two potential applications—one for line managers and one for investment traders.

A BRIEF HISTORY OF AI FROM THE CORPORATE VIEW

In 1986 it seemed that LISP machines were the answer. In discussions with young people coming out of universities—a potential source for building an AI staff—their first question was, "Where is my LISP machine?" That was part of the mentality. Also, part of the mentality was, and still is, the separation of "business types" and "technology types." Back in 1986, AI was viewed as a cult or a religion. However, the industry has changed.

By 1987 there was a noticeable shift. The vendors started to wake up. "This is not all R&D!" "This is not a religious experience but an economic experience"—hopefully with tangible results. On October 19, 1987, however, *Forbes* was asking, "What happened to those "Expert Systems" that were supposed to transform the world of business forever?" After all the publicity and PR, what had actually happened? While a lot of systems were being developed, where were they deployed?

---

*Craig Atkinson is currently vice president of Research and Development within the Strategic Technology and Research Group of Manufacturers Hanover Trust Company.

The answer may be that the efforts were geared around prototypes. While prototyping is an important process, a year or so ago too many people viewed it as the end product.

For example, when Chemical's efforts were getting underway, the vendors and the people in universities said, "We'll build you a prototype!" The next step was . . . refining the prototype! When asked, "But what do you do next?," the answer was, "We'll build another prototype!" At this point Chemical's response was, "Wait a minute! Time out! There's something wrong here!" Building prototypes could be a measure of success in the university environment but not in the business world. A lot of people scurried around and built prototypes that they claimed were end products without knowing what the next steps were or even how to get to the next steps.

In February 1988, the *Spang-Robinson Report* noted, "From our survey, it appears that AI is emerging as a strong force in the current economic uncertainty." On March 3, on the front page of the business section, the *New York Times* reported, "Trouble for many of the Artificial Intelligence companies"— very negative reporting on the industry. By late 1988, what was a cloudy situation was becoming less so due to integration and embedded applications.

GETTING STARTED

When we started we had a management sponsor, which made our job a lot easier. The management sponsor was the Chief Technology Officer (CTO) in the corporation, who reports directly to the President of the Bank. He believed that there was value in this technology for Chemical Bank. In the third quarter of 1986, we spent a couple of months looking at the industry, talking with a whole series of people, and trying to get an idea of what other people were doing.

From this we developed a strategy: Form a core group that could support the entire bank. We wanted to increase awareness, we wanted a focal point, and we wanted to get AI systems out and successfully in use. Getting some systems out would result in the establishment of joint partnerships with users, absolutely key to our strategy, and would provide us with additional experience, which would enhance our development capability.

Seeds, Water, and Fertilizer

Part of the strategy was to provide three types or levels of AI services, which termed *seeds, water,* and *fertilizer*. *Seeds* were basically education, communication, and a lot of demonstrations—trying to make people more aware of the technology.

The *water* was consulting support—application selection, implementation issues, and project management. In some cases we spent more time choosing the right applications than we did in actual development.

Fertilizer was the provision of some level of development capability. It also included vendor/industry liaison. For example, together with other New York–based financial services companies, we founded SMART/F$, the Society for the Management of Artificial Resources and Technology/Financial Services. This users' group was very popular, and 250 to 300 people attended meetings. It has been beneficial in providing visibility and credibility to the industry, certainly in New York, and has also been a way to put pressure on vendors.

Recruiting AI Personnel

How does a company get AI people such as we have? What types of AI people do we have? Within the company at the time of this presentation, we have six people working on knowledge-based systems. Five of the six people have advanced degrees but do not perhaps conform to traditional patterns. The blending of their skills and educational background is what is important. We hired three people from the outside, and three of our best people came from within and blended their skills into an effective team.

THE FOREIGN EXCHANGE AUDITING ASSISTANT

We chose foreign exchange auditing as an application because of its contribution to Chemical Bank's bottom line and because of the increasing volatility of the foreign exchange trading market. Foreign exchange trading grew in Chemical Bank by 60 percent over a three-year period. Foreign exchange trading volume at Chemical Bank was $750 billion a year worldwide. Successful trading at this volume can have a very significant impact on the profitability of the bank. Because of the number of trades, the range of irregularities are beyond the grasp of human auditors. There was no conventional software for performing automated audits at "human levels of expertise." Anything that could help manage this highly volatile situation would be beneficial.

Only two auditors in the company knew how to accomplish foreign exchange auditing. This was very scarce expertise. In developing this application we had high visibility without much risk. We believed it had strategic growth potential both as a control tool and as an auditing tool.

At the beginning, the Knowledge-Based Systems Department sponsored management seminars on AI to create awareness and acceptance of the technology. We formed a partnership with EDP Auditing who obtained funding from corporate R&D for the project. They contributed conventional programming, knowledge engineering, and project management.

For this application we consciously avoided integration issues—remember, we were doing this development in late 1986 and early 1987. We were able, therefore, to develop something very, very quickly. We built an operational prototype, running with live data, as early as February 1987. It was determined by a consulting company that by not worrying about integration—that is, by not embedding the application in the IBM System 38 environment—we would save a half million dollars.

The AI application was developed on a Symbolics AI workstation, using the ART expert system shell. Foreign exchange trading was done on a series of IBM System 38s. We would take log tapes off these IBM System 38s and load them onto the Symbolics. We affectionately called our exchange of data between the IBM mainframes and the Symbolics machine the "Chevy Method of Transmission"—the tape was taken, put in the Chevy, and delivered to another location. A more affectionate name for it was "Sneakernet." Because we want to expand the application internationally, we have spent some time in the last few months moving the software to more traditional hardware platforms.

Initially, the prototype trade auditing system was not online every day, so we could afford to run tapes around. Going that next step and hooking the Symbolics to an IBM System 38 was just too intimidating to consider.

The Trade Auditing System's Process

The application produces an exception report that is the heart of the system. It mimics what auditors do in looking at mounds and mounds of paper, randomly going through a day's trades and trying to identify some pattern of trading activity. The system examines all the trading data based on the rules in the expert system shell and produces a summary report. The system operates in either an automatic mode or an interactive mode.

In the interactive mode, the auditor looks for different types of patterns. The system plots each day's transactions against average and closing prices. The human auditor, via mouse, identifies off-market trades. This triggers the presentation of similar transaction data from the bottom of the screen display. The auditor looks for patterns of off-market activity and analyzes and interprets trade information, recommending items for further research.

Initially, the system handled trades in dollars and pounds at the New York City branch. It has been expanded to handle deutsche marks and yen and is planned for roll-out to additional branches.

Benefits

Benefits of the system were increased monitoring of trader activity, the ability to leverage extremely scarce expertise, and increased audit frequency and scope.

Finally, the success of this system established Chemical Bank as a leader of technology in the banking industry.

We also made some quantum leaps in reducing auditors' fear of technology. The expert on this system was the type of person who would not even look at a PC. However, when we had a very sophisticated workstation for him, we could not get him away from it. He understood the value of what it added to his job. This caused a change in his job and was a significant, positive by-product of AI technology.

Return on Investment Analysis

The scope of the audits increased by a factor of 30. The difference between being able randomly to look at 1,200 trades and being able automatically to look at 36,000 trades is very significant: It changed the way the auditor could attack the problem.

Beyond scope, the expert system was able to investigate and report on patterns a human would have been unable to detect in the normal, allocated time. The system effectively captured and extended auditing expertise. When the primary auditor was called overseas, junior auditors were able to use the system.

We plan to expand this approach into other high risk instruments. The system has made it easier for us to promote this new technology; it is a lot easier to show people the technology than to talk about it. We have demonstrated this system to over 200 people in the bank and, in doing so, have discovered similar types of problems we can address. People ask, "Can you do the same thing for us?"

Having the system has given us a lot of flexibility. When comments appear in the newspaper on the trading activities of different institutions, we can query the system and have rules modeling these trading practices within a matter of hours.

TELECOMMUNICATIONS AUDITING SYSTEM

Because of the success we had with our flagship currency exchange auditing application, we helped auditing develop a second application that now is part of our technology transfer program. This second application is PC-based. It is not as sophisticated as the first but is a good example of the technology. In telecommunications auditing, auditors are able to perform two audits a year, each taking 300 hours. What a boring, laborious process this is!

One of the telecommunications systems audited was SWIFT, the Society for Worldwide Interbank Financial Telecommunications. All the major banks participate in SWIFT. People have to look very stringently at the access codes associated with SWIFT, and there are various levels of access, depending on the types of funds transfers.

From an auditing perspective, the reduction in the auditing hours was projected to be from 150 to 4 hours, a savings accrued twice a year. Further, as was the case for the exchange auditing system, senior auditors can now let the junior auditors do the analysis while they spend time on more important things.

Some of the benefits we project from the telecommunications auditing system will have nothing to do with auditing, a phenomenon we observed with the foreign exchange system. While this started out as an auditing application, some of the periodic reports were sent to the head trader of the bank. What started out as auditing tools remained auditing tools but also became operational tools. We believe this is a significant finding.

Because the telecommunications auditing system is PC-based, we are going to expand it to do other types of related applications. Again, building one system is the catalyst for building others.

POTENTIAL APPLICATIONS

AI for Line Managers

There is a lot of potential benefit from AI technology for senior management. The banking industry's transaction systems generate more information than people can possibly assimilate. Highly paid professionals who need that data cannot get it because it comes in a form they cannot analyze. We see some potentially strong benefits in this area for high-level people who have to make critical decisions based on lots of information.

Intelligent Trading Systems

Many people are talking about intelligent trading systems. So are we. We are talking to people in the capital markets area about extensions of the foreign exchange auditing system. We believe that the information coming out of the various trading information systems can be beneficial to the trader. We do not, however, believe that we will see AI technology used to make trading decisions and replace traders. Traders act on a wide variety of decision factors—information-based, management-directed, and instinctive—for each type of trade and financial instrument. What we can do, however, is to provide the traders with additional information that help them make decisions.

KEYS TO SUCCESSFUL IMPLEMENTATION OF TECHNOLOGY

Iterative Development

Iterative development is crucial to success. It enables us to understand the "vision" of the project by starting small and growing. The acceptance of early prototypes determines the development path. Flexibility is the key—planning for change, initiating change, and accommodating change.

Hardware Selection

Hardware selection is difficult. It depends on the type of application, the industry, and a view of the vendor's future. Our evolved strategy is to get some experience both at the low end and the high end of the hardware spectrum. We did the telecommunications audit system on PCs and the foreign exchange system using Symbolics. Because of its power, we would not be where we are today had we not purchased Symbolics. We are also doing some things with Digital, a key vendor in our organization from the standpoint of delivery.

All of Chemical's data centers are IBM based. For us, moving into the mainframe environment will happen in 1989. We have one or two specific applications in mind, and the data are all resident on the mainframe. For now, however, we have consciously decided to let other people break trail with mainframes.

Technology Transfer

Our approach to the dynamics of technology transfer is shown in Figure 6.1. For new technology we try to provide a greenhouse environment. Talking with vendors, consultants, and universities is the beginning—getting in touch with research products and processes. The next step is assimilation—looking at new technology to see what has to change before we consider bringing the technology into Chemical Bank. At the moment, for example, there is a lot of talk about neural networks. For that technology, we will do a scan, but we will not start putting in neural networks just because that is what everybody is reading about. The technology has to be a fit.

We do not adopt technology for technology's sake. What we are trying to do and what we have done are to provide value-added applications with the added value applied to the targeted business unit. This is key to our strategy.

The Role of Centralized AI Development Group

We do not want a centralized AI development group at Chemical Bank. First of all, a central AI group will continually be in the maintenance business. The central group should not be doing maintenance; that should be done in the business units. More important, our organization is set up with decentralized business units that have support groups, and AI applications expertise belongs in those support groups. Our whole approach, therefore, is to get the technology into the respective businesses, not to keep it contained. If that means, as we have

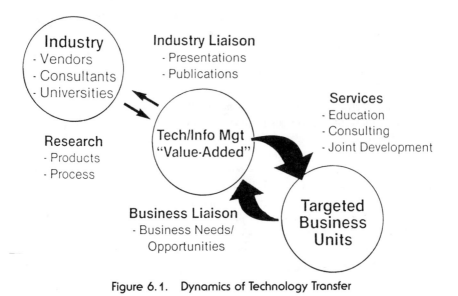

Figure 6.1.   Dynamics of Technology Transfer

recently done, transferring one of our people to the business unit, then we will do that. That presents problems to a manager because it forces the rotation of personnel, but the key is to get the technology out there. It is not going to do any good staying in our shop.

The Importance of a Champion

Part of success stories like our joint partnership with EDP auditing stems from the fact that the vice president in charge of EDP auditing sits on the Technology Advisory Board of Chemical Bank, composed of the senior technology officers of each business unit. With a champion, success becomes a catalyst; other people want to know why the champion's unit is suddenly using AI technology. This causes peer pressure to develop other things.

In the future we have to get more of a commitment from key people to relate a specific problem and solution. We find that people are very receptive to identifying applications for us. The problem is that potential users have a laundry list of more immediate priorities. The key is trying to blend this new AI technology with existing priorities.

Beyond the management sponsor and Chief Technology Officer championship of AI, there is interest at the highest levels in our organization. Recently the president of the bank spent time in our office and made some very interesting comments and observations. He was impressed not only with the technology but also with how this technology is a catalyst for change—how people have changed the way they are doing their jobs now that they have access to this technology.

Success Is an Individualized Affair

Finally, the specific solution to technology transfer depends on the organization. There really is no right or wrong solution. You hear a lot of people doing some very interesting things with entirely different sets of approaches. Ultimately, however, each organization must choose its own approach.

7

Underwriters' Workbench: The Fireman's Fund Experience in Applying an Expert System

Donald K. Stratton

Fireman's Fund Insurance Company

This chapter describes the conception, development, and fielding of Fireman's Fund Automobile Workbench I. The motivation for the development of this system was poor performance in the automobile insurance business due to inconsistent application of policy by underwriters and a large increase in the number of new underwriters. The project was begun based on the initiative of a senior user management champion of AI. The solution was a system of five components run on the IBM mainframe operational environment at Fireman's Fund: data entry, consultation, review, and reporting interfaced to a common DB2 database. Expert system technology was used only in the consultation subsystem. Automobile Workbench I was introduced, accepted, and routinely used by 130 underwriters. Details of project timeline, user acceptance, computing environment, performance, results, problems, and future plans are provided.

INTRODUCTION

Fireman's Fund is the eleventh largest property and casualty insurance company in the country. It has been in existence for 125 years, having its beginning on the west coast. The San Francisco earthquake of 1906 resulted in a fire that wiped out all the company's records, but it survived to meet all its claims. It has the reputation of being innovative and responsive to its customers.

Although Fireman's Fund has a 125-year history, it is actually a young company. For many years it was a wholly owned subsidiary of American Express. Then, in 1985, it became a publicly held corporation through the largest public stock offering in the United States at that time. Today, American Express, our former parent company, owns approximately 20 percent of the stock.

Fireman's Fund is a nationwide company and has three divisions: Commercial, Specialty, and Personal Insurance. Workbench was designed for the Personal Insurance Division, which handles the type of insurance we all buy to insure our homes and cars. In 1986, our Personal Insurance Division had a problem, the same one that all of our peers in the insurance industry were facing at that time: We were losing money in our automobile business. Costs of repairs, legal fees, and legal settlements were all contributing to cause the problem. We had an earned premium that year of about $350 million. However, it was costing us $1.10 for every dollar of premium. We had a loss ratio of 69.6. No company can stay in business and absorb that kind of loss. Thus, the business managers of Fireman's Fund decided to address this problem using expert systems.

There were various reasons Fireman's Fund was losing money on automobile insurance. First was the underwriting philosophy. There are two ways of looking at whether a risk should be accepted. One is desirability, whether it will be profitable to write. The other is eligibility, whether it meets certain criteria laid out by the company. In 1986, we used eligibility as the criteria for writing a risk. This was not necessarily profitable. Also, in the early 1980s, because of an insurance cycle downturn, we had a reduction in staffing. Then, in the mid-1980s the underwriting staff was increased with a number of inexperienced, unseasoned underwriters. Over half of them had less than three years of experience. As a result, we took on business that was eligible but not necessarily desirable or profitable.

Second, we had inconsistent underwriting. We had 130 underwriters spread over three different geographic locations. The underwriting was largely manual with very little automated assistance. While we had written underwriting guidelines, written communication is subject to interpretation by the reader and inherently permits inconsistency. Furthermore, attempting to change direction was a very difficult process, because it had to be accomplished with written communication, and we could not be sure that every individual would get the message.

Underwriters are under a lot of pressure; they are in the "hot seat" and must make some decisions that can have a big impact on the business. Sometimes, however, the decisions were being made just to move something off the desk. There was a lack of discipline in the way in which a risk was evaluated. Each underwriter would consider different elements of an application and would view an application differently. It was also difficult to get an underwriter to document the rationale for his or her decisions. All of these factors were contributors to the loss we were experiencing.

Fireman's Fund wanted to use expert systems to solve the problem: to have consistent underwriting, use a disciplined approach, and to switch its underwriting philosophy from eligibility to desirability. In other words, look at risk differently.

The process began with prototyping in 1986. There were two separate prototypes intended to evaluate two things: the technology and our new underwriting philosophy. One approach was on the PC to develop the new underwriting philosophy, while the other was on the mainframe trying to build a large expert system that reflected our current approach. Those two efforts were conducted independently, beginning in spring of 1986 and finishing in November of that same year. The result of the two prototypes was the decision to build a system combining the knowledge base (PC version) with the mainframe approach.

Fireman's Fund has three locations where it does underwriting: eastern region with offices in Allentown, a midwestern region with offices in Omaha, and a western region with offices in San Diego. Each office has approximately 40 underwriters. The system was to handle only automobile new business in all three regions and was to support all 130 underwriters. We wanted to have the ability to understand what was happening in the system, to capture the results of a decision, and to be able to track it and monitor it. In short, we wanted to be able to assess whether the philosophy was working in the field.

We didn't want the underwriters to do data entry. The system had to have a separate data entry facility so clerical staff could enter the application data and the underwriter would only be involved with the consultation. We wanted user acceptance and involvement. We were very cognizant that we were changing the underwriting philosophy and the corporate culture in the field. We wanted the acceptance of both the underwriting field management and the underwriters themselves. Finally, we also knew that building the system was an evolutionary process, and as a consequence we wanted one that was easy to expand as we learned of its impact on the business as well as the data processing side.

AUTOMOBILE WORKBENCH I

The system that was developed was called Automobile Workbench I. This system performs four major functions:

- It reformats application and motor vehicle reports (MVRs) into a logical order for decision making.
- It requires the underwriter to evaluate each underwriting characteristic individually. Thus, the system forces all underwriters to view the application and consider relevant characteristics of the risk in a disciplined, consistent manner.
- The system requires the underwriter to exercise judgment and to document the rationale for his or her decision.
- The system provides management reports to monitor the business decision.

The system does not make the decision to accept or decline the risk. The company has four programs: Vantage, Economy Plus, Regular Auto, and Superior. The system evaluates risks against the profile of an ideal risk for our best class of business, Vantage, but requires the underwriter to make the final decision. The system will merely flag any elements of concern within the risk.

There were four major functions in the design of the initial Workbench as seen in Figure 7.1: data entry, consultation, underwriter review, and reporting. The data entry subsystem used ISPF screens and COBOL programs to update a DB2 database. The consultation function is the expert system portion using the IBM interactive ESE package on TSO on an MVS system. It reads and writes to the same DB2 database used by the entry system and is the only part of the system that involves ESE.

The underwriter review is an inquiry/update facility used by underwriters subsequent to the consultation for reviewing the application, consultation results, and their decision. It uses ISPF panels, COBOL, and the same DB2 database used by the consultation and data entry subsystems. The underwriter review is important because initially the underwriter may not make a decision without further information, or the agent may call and ask why a decision was made, and they need to get into the system to find out what they have done. The reporting subsystem produces reports by COBOL programs and by QMF.

Figure 7.2 provides an overall picture of the Automobile Workbench. You will note that the DB2 database is central to all four components. This was one of our key design features. We wanted an integrated system on a DB2 database to allow us to capture the data and look at the results of the system. Below is a description of how the system works.

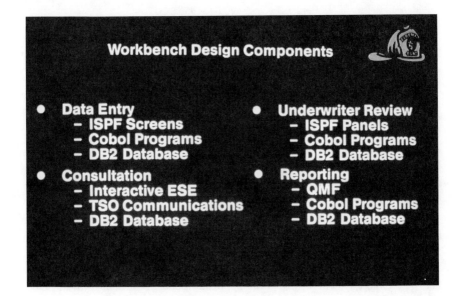

Figure 7.1. Workbench Design Components

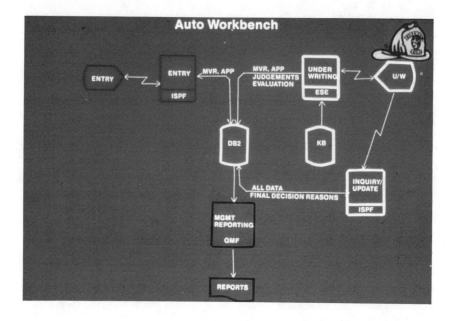

Figure 7.2.   Auto Workbench

Data Entry

When a new automobile business application is received by the personal insurance regional office, it is first screened to see that it is complete, the agent being consulted for any missing data. A motor vehicle report is ordered for all drivers on the policy. The MVR and application data are entered into the ISPF-based entry subsystem and written to the DB2 database. The subsystem has the ability to add, delete, or change data on the database. When data entry for an application is complete, the application is filed temporarily and a rating worksheet with the application number written on it is sent to the underwriting department.

Consultation

Underwriters then initiate an ESE consultation, specifying the application number. The expert system will read the application and MVR data from the DB2 database. The system will display selected relevant data to the underwriters through a series of screens and ask the underwriters questions that require judgment and to which they must respond. For example, after displaying information on a vehicle, it will ask the underwriters to classify the vehicle as standard or nonstandard. The underwriters are asked seven different sets of questions about the operators or about the car, each requiring their judgment. Following their responses, the system will evaluate the risk and then allow the underwriters to view all the application data but not the system recommendation. After the application data are viewed, the underwriters are asked to accept or decline the business and to place it in an appropriate program. Only after the underwriters have placed the risk in a program can they see the system recommendation. At that time the system shows them the underwriting "flags," elements of the risk to which they should pay particular attention. In addition, it shows how the risk compared to the ideal profile for our best class of business. Then, finally, the underwriters are required to document the rationale for their decision. All of this is then stored back into the database.

Underwriter Review or Inquiry/Update

The underwriter review subsystem, also called the underwriter inquiry/update facility, is used by the underwriter after the consultation has been completed. Many times the underwriter will need to talk to the agent before releasing a policy for issue. The underwriter may, for example, place the risk in a different program than requested by the agent. Or, the underwriter might receive a call from the agent several days or weeks later asking for the rationale for the underwriter's decision. Since all the data are saved on the DB2 database, the underwriter can use the TSO-based inquiry/update facility to review the information. The TSO subsystem is much faster and less expensive operationally than a repeat of the consultation. This subsystem could have been written using IMS or CICS. TSO was chosen because it was faster for development. Thus, the inquiry/update just reads the database and bypasses the expert system, and if the underwriter changes a decision, that is saved back into the database.

Running an expert system online takes time. It is not fast; it is not like being on a PC and using spreadsheet or word processing software and getting an instantaneous response. There are some areas that have a long response time and the underwriters must patiently wait for a minute or two. In the interest of conservation of time, we decided to bypass repeating the consultation, since we already had the system evaluation, and allow the inquiry/update function with TSO. As a result, using this system, if the underwriters decide to change a decision or perhaps defer making a final decision until they call an agent, they can get on the system very quickly, make a final decision, and get out. It gives the underwriters all of this information online at the terminal.

Management Reporting

The reporting subsystem initially consisted of a series of QMF monthly management reports and ad hoc reports to help us monitor the use of the system and the completeness and accuracy of the knowledge base. The reports were created by batch processing. The reports were developed by a user working with the team. Subsequently, some of the more difficult reports were converted to COBOL, which provides considerably less expensive processing.

Initial Concerns

When we started building the system, we had a lot of concerns. I designed the system and was manager of the project, and I was very concerned whether it would work. We were using new technology; this was the first time we had used expert systems in a production environment, and it was only the second DB2 application to go into production. We were trying to tie all this together and just did not know if it would work or not technically—nor whether it would be accepted. We asked ourselves whether it would so disrupt the culture out in the offices that we would get foot-dragging and resistance that would cause the system, even though it might work, not to be used.

Additionally, we were not certain that the system could support 120 underwriters and were not sure how much it would cost to run.

Another concern was whether it would consume too many resources. We used ESE, and there was not too much information available on what kind of CPU utilization it had and what kind of resources it would use. So, our equipment planners were especially worried that it might take our online system that supports 4,000 users to its knees.

We had a very optimistic date: We wanted to have the system up and running within three months. And, given the above, we wondered whether we could get it completed in three months.

It was very successful in every respect. As may be seen in Figure 7.3, the project began in mid-December, taking the PC prototype completed in October and converting it into ESE. The ESE-based underwriting system was installed into the production system in March in the eastern region, and we trained our first underwriters in the system. After resolving a few problems, implementation in the first personal insurance region began in April and roll-out to all three regions was completed in July. It did work and it worked very well.

Project Team

The project team consisted of four people: one business person who did the QMF reports and coordinated the effort in the field, one automobile underwriting expert, one programmer to do the DB2, and one knowledge engineer who developed the knowledge base. While IBM claims that a user can "build a system with ESE," our experience indicates that it really requires someone who at least thinks like a programmer and has some programming or system design background. This background is necessary to design the knowledge base for optimal perfor-

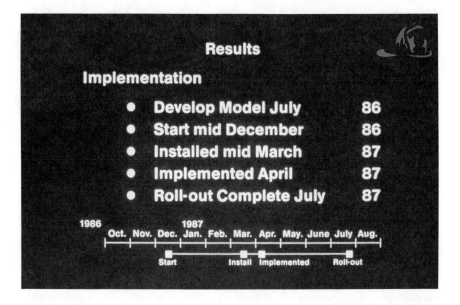

Figure 7.3. Results

mance. System design skills are also required on the team to insure that a system's design uses the best features of ESE while at the same time minimizing its use of computer resources.

Acceptance by the Users

The system was well accepted by the users, and there were a couple of reasons for this. It was sponsored by the senior vice president of underwriting, and he wanted this tool to be the way to change the underwriting philosophy and actually to change the culture of the underwriters in the field. He said "You will use it." So we had a very heavy top-down approach. However, this does not necessarily by itself ensure success.

We tried to get the underwriters involved very early in the prototypes and the very early reviews of the system. We reviewed things with them, going through the knowledge base on paper, and did a lot of education. When we arrived at our final user testing, we brought underwriters in on-site. When we went out into the field to train teams of from six or eight people at a time, we first trained the trainer. That person then became the champion, and he went through and trained one team in each region. Each region also had a coordinator, who eventually became responsible for training. When the trainer went back and trained the next team, he trained with the coordinator assisting. By the third time, the coordinator trained on his own. In this way, we kept the users involved.

Initially we had lots of feedback in terms of how the system was going to interact with the user, and we made massive changes in the first three months of the system's life. We added the inquiry function because the response time was just too long. To go back into the consultation just to change a decision was time consuming. We changed how we presented the data to the underwriters several times. In other words, we responded to the problems that came back to us from the field, and with the expert system shell, it was very easy to do. We were able to change the knowledge base and how the information was displayed very quickly.

Computing Environment for Automobile Workbench I

Figure 7.4 is a diagram of Firemans Fund's computing environment. We have a 3090-600. This is our development side during the day and our batch operational production system each evening. Then we have a 3090-400 split between VM, which is our office automation and information center development, and our

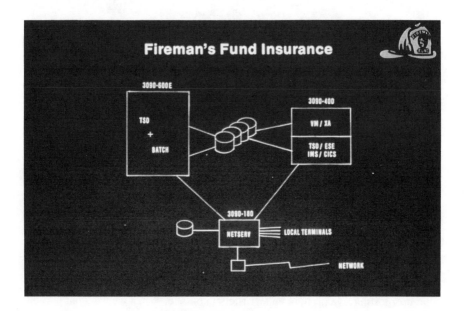

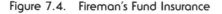

Figure 7.4.   Fireman's Fund Insurance

production system, which is IMS and CICS. We had a special version of TSO in production where we ran our Workbench.

We have about 4,000 IMS users, and we were very concerned that adding ESE to this environment would impact them. This was a considerable concern. We have another 3090 front end that handles only communications.

Figure 7.5 represents the offering after we had it installed for about three or four months. This is IBM ESE Release 1.0. We started out with 398 rules, 396 parameters, and 22 FCBs when originally introduced. We put it in for about a week, and unfortunately we had a very long response time. So we had an IBM expert come out for one day to work with our knowledge engineer to review the knowledge base and come up with ways to improve performance. Our knowledge engineer totally restructured the knowledge base and had it out in the field in two weeks.

Performance

ESE Release 1.0 provided some facilities that allowed us to improve performance. The Knowledge Engineer reduced the number of rules to 346—down by one-third—with fewer FCBs and parameters. The CPU usage went down a third,

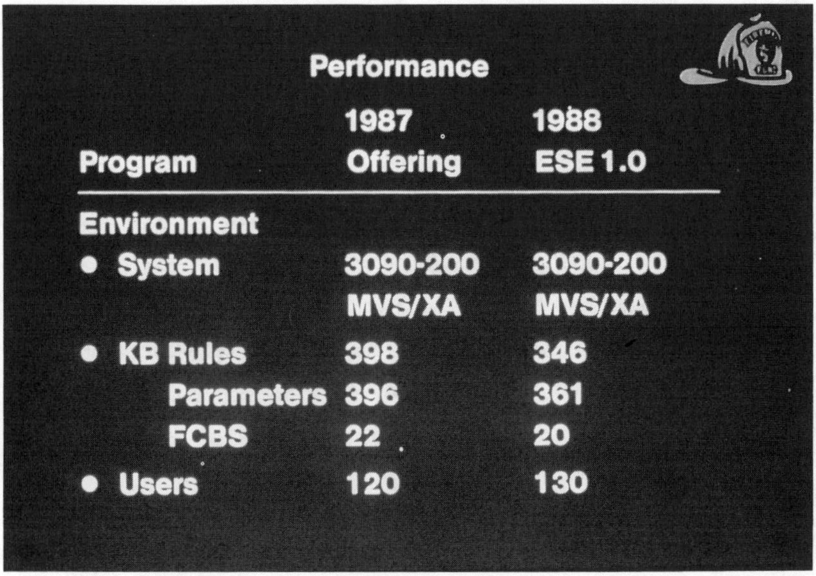

Performance		
Program	**1987 Offering**	**1988 ESE 1.0**
Environment		
• **System**	3090-200 MVS/XA	3090-200 MVS/XA
• **KB Rules**	398	346
Parameters	396	361
FCBS	22	20
• **Users**	120	130

Figure 7.5.   Performance

and response was reduced by a third. With the ESE Release 1.0 shell (it is like a 5th generation language) you get tremendous productivity.

We began the project supporting 120 underwriters and now it supports 130 who use the system daily. In addition, there are approximately 30 underwriting staff and management people who use the system occasionally.

The resource utilization of the system, while expensive, was a pleasant surprise (Figure 7.6). Under both the program product and offering we use approximately 3 percent of the CPU, a much lower percentage than predicted to support 130 underwriters. Under the ESE program, offering a consultation used 17 CPU seconds. With the program product ESE 1.0, the same consultation required 9 CPU seconds. While this is still expensive, it is acceptable, and the underwriting department believes the benefits outweigh the costs.

The knowledge base requires an average working set of 2.2 meg under ESE release 1.0; it required 2.5 meg under the program offering (see Figure 7.7). Response time varies depending on the amount of IMS and CICS activity in the system. Generally we have an average response time of 3 seconds between screens. However, the consultation does have a couple activities that take much longer. Loading the knowledge base now takes approximately 40 to 50 seconds and refreshing it for a second consultation takes approximately 25 to 30 seconds.

The target elapsed time for a consultation with underwriter interaction is from

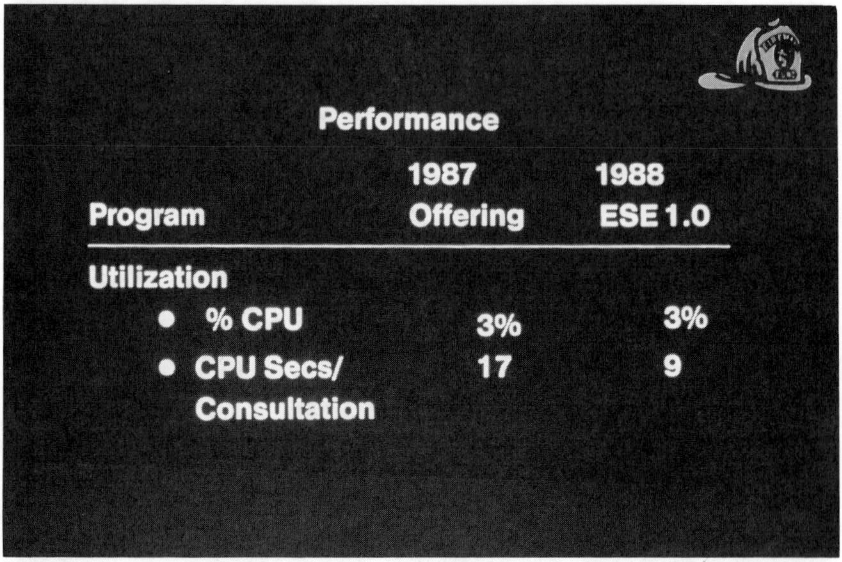

Program	1987 Offering	1988 ESE 1.0
Utilization		
● % CPU	3%	3%
● CPU Secs/ Consultation	17	9

Figure 7.6.   Performance

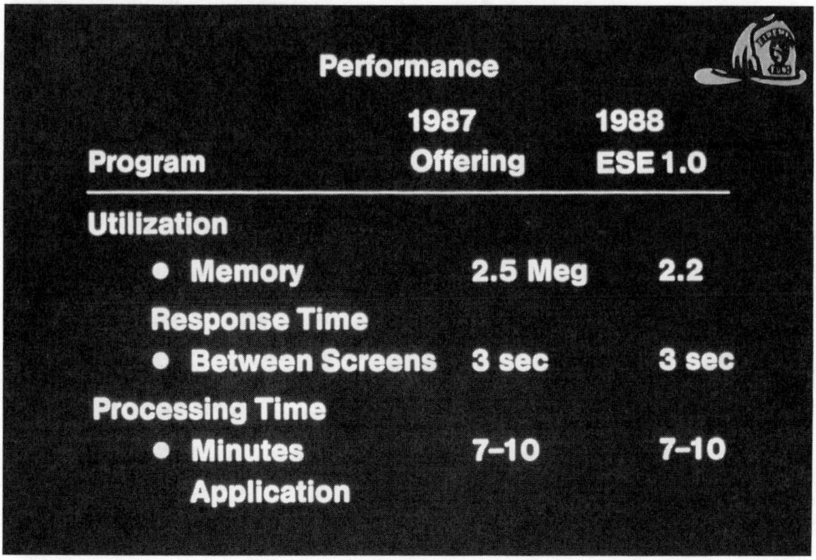

Performance		
Program	1987 Offering	1988 ESE 1.0
Utilization		
• Memory	2.5 Meg	2.2
Response Time		
• Between Screens	3 sec	3 sec
Processing Time		
• Minutes Application	7-10	7-10

Figure 7.7. Performance

7 to 10 minutes per application. System response will support this goal. However, we often find underwriters spending 20 to 30 minutes per application because they will "study" the screens.

Today we have approximately 15 concurrent users of the system. All automobile new business is processed through Automobile Workbench.

Results

From both the system development perspective and the performance perspective, we were successful. From the business perspective the system was very successful. The system helped achieve the business objectives and provided some unanticipated benefits. The benefits are outlined in Figure 7.8.

The system helped achieve a disciplined approach to underwriting. The underwriters now view the application in a predetermined sequence, make a series of component decisions based on relevant data; then, considering all the components, the underwriter makes a final decision on the risk.

This systems approach has led to consistent underwriting and consistent documentation. Every application for a new automobile policy is treated in the same

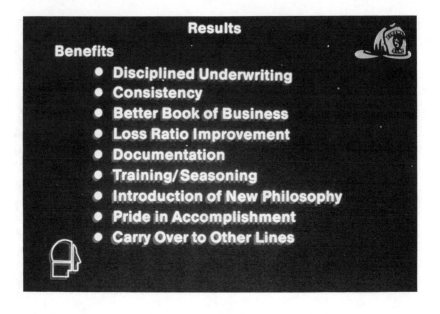

Results

Benefits

- Disciplined Underwriting
- Consistency
- Better Book of Business
- Loss Ratio Improvement
- Documentation
- Training/Seasoning
- Introduction of New Philosophy
- Pride in Accomplishment
- Carry Over to Other Lines

Figure 7.8. Results

way. Every underwriter, regardless of location, considers the same factors in making his or her decision.

A side benefit we are realizing is training. Since all underwriters are stepping through the system, we are getting a lot of training for the new underwriters. They now know what they should be looking at, why they should be looking at it, and in what order. Now, they are led through the process, and the system gives them help. It reconfirms what they have already done and gives them feedback for getting it right.

We now have a much better book of business. The book characteristics are closer to the type of business that we target from a marketing standpoint. In addition, we have reduced the loss ratio by 5 points and are now better than our competition. We have a better loss ratio for automobile now than our competitors. It should be noted, however, that the expert system is only one of several factors that led to this improvement. However, it was a major factor.

Underwriters are now documenting their decision rationale on every automobile risk. The system requires them to do so.

The system has trained both inexperienced and experienced underwriters in the desired approach to evaluating a risk while they are processing business. The system has also been used as a nonproduction training tool for a group of underwriter trainees.

The system certainly facilitated the implementation of a new underwriting philosophy—desirability instead of eligibility. It would have been very difficult to change directions without the system to consistently force consideration of appropriate factors. The system was developed with a small team of business and data processors and was completely driven by the executive sponsor in the underwriting department. The partnership of systems and users worked extremely well. The executive sponsor had a clear vision of what he wanted to accomplish. The team took tremendous pride in the ability to deliver the system in a short period of time. We have taken a new technology and successfully transferred it into the business world and received good results.

Finally, the system provided an unexpected benefit. The discipline practiced for automobile underwriting was carried over to other personal lines of business, such as homeowner's insurance, even though there was no expert systems support.

Problems

However, there were some problems. It still takes too much underwriter time per application. The cost is still too high. Even at 7 CPU seconds per consultation, processing a piece of business is expensive. Also, it takes too much time for an underwriter to underwrite with the system. And, we still have duplicate entry. We built an integrated system but we did not integrate it into our other processing systems. The underwriting expert system and the policy rating and issue system are not connected. Consequently, once the underwriter decides to accept a risk, it must be entered into our policy processing system. We needed to address all of these problems, and Auto Workbench II, introduced in 1989, does address them.

AUTOMOBILE WORKBENCH II

Figure 7.9 shows the architecture of Automobile Workbench II. It is several orders of magnitude more complicated than Automobile Workbench I. Auto Workbench I was totally rewritten to produce the new system: It has a different knowledge base, a different database. It is four times bigger than the first system we built. It still uses a DB2 database and we still do management reporting using QMF. We have added automatic MVR ordering and table classifications that are fed into DB2. The expert system with the knowledge base is now run in the batch without underwriter interaction. The underwriter interfaces with the inquiry/update, which is the major piece of the system. Now the underwriter only has to get onto the screen; the response is very fast with no long delays. The underwriters can look at their work, make their decisions, document them, and the system manages the work flow. There is a decline process that is also fed

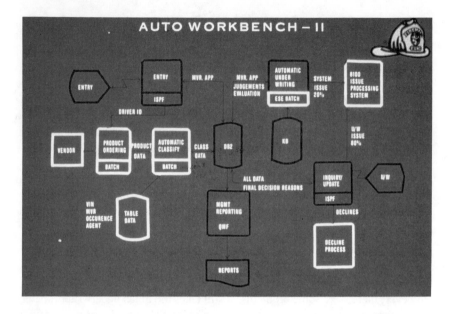

Figure 7.9.   Auto Workbench II

because certain things have to be done if you decline business that is different than if you accept.

The data entry function is very similar to the Workbench I entry subsystem. The major difference is that MVR data are not keyed into the system. Upon entry of the application data, a MVR is automatically ordered from Equifax, our source for those reports. When the MVRs are received, which may be several days later, they trigger the running of a series of batch programs. One set of programs classifies the MVR occurrences.

One of the problems in the insurance field is customer service—getting an application out in enough time to get it into the customer's hand. It takes from one to two weeks. The Work in Process subsystem, a key part of the new system, automatically routes information electronically—in short, it is quick and eliminates most paper.

This subsystem is used to put work items (applications that have been through the batch expert system) on the underwriters electronic work queue or in-basket. The underwriter then views his queue, sees which applications must be processed and sees the system recommendation (auto issue, review, decline). The underwriter then selects an item from his queue and reviews the information via the underwriter review function (inquiry/update). The underwriter is required to make a decision and document his rationale and then release the policy for processing. If the expert system recommends issue, the underwriter does not have to review the application. It is simply released for processing. Only risks qualifying for the best program available in a state can be automatically sent to the issue queue.

Because the underwriter does not interact with the expert system, but uses the inquiry/update subsystem to review an application, the process of evaluating a risk requires a great deal less underwriting time. We consistently get good response time from this TSO/COBOL subsystem. In addition since the processing intensive part of the system, the consultation, will run in batch in nonprime hours, the CPU utilization and cost for that utilization will be less than it is today. Also, at some future date, when we gain additional confidence that the system is making appropriate recommendations, more of the business can be automatically issued without underwriter review.

The Work in Process subsystem allows the tracking of time, tasks, and actions during the underwriting of a new business automobile risk. It provides valuable management information that allows us to improve service to our customers.

We believe that this system will provide a very positive service to our underwriting staff and help the underwriting department achieve their objectives.

The batch expert system has table-driven functions, has reduced costs because the long consultations are done at night and, consequently, uses overnight CPU time, which is more economical. The expert system reads the classification data, MVRs, and application data, evaluates the risk, and writes the result and system rationale to the DB2 database. The classification information formerly supplied by the underwriter during a consultation is supplied or entered with application information during the entry process. The vehicle is classified as standard or nonstandard, and so on. The expert system also writes a record to the Work in Process system. That system puts an entry on the appropriate underwriter's queue.

The system recommends action on an application. It is state specific. That is, it considers the unique rules of each state in the United States. The system also considers each company underwriting program and recommends the appropriate program for the application. Workbench I only measured the risk against the ideal profile for Vantage, our best class of business.

For an applicant qualifying for the best program available in a state, the system recommends automatic issue. The system also recommends which applications should be declined and for all others recommends the appropriate program and requires that an underwriter review the application and system recommendations.

The system has both a novice and expert mode. In expert mode, which is used by all Fireman's Fund experienced underwriters, the underwriter uses the underwriter review (inquiry/update) subsystem to review the application, MVRs, system notes and recommendation, and makes and documents his decision. In novice (training) mode, the inexperienced underwriter is forced to respond to classification questions through the underwriter review subsystem, to make a decision, and then to view the comparison of the system results with his responses. The application is routed to the supervisor for review and approval prior to release. Novice mode is intended to provide an "on the job" training facility in the production environment.

We currently have an interactive expert system for property business—homeowner's and dwelling fire new business. The current system, called Property Workbench I, is in production in one regional office and supports only one state. This system was intended as a prototype for Property Workbench II, a system that is similar to Automobile Workbench II in concept. It will also be a batch expert system and will be introduced in early 1989.

8

The Use of Expert Systems to do Risk Analysis

David W. Erbach

Great-West Life Assurance Co.

This chapter begins by introducing an important class of problems—risk analysis. The risk analysis task is sized by risk level and risk frequency. Special problems of risk analysis from an expert systems point of view are presented. The beginning steps of knowledge engineering for risk analysis are presented through descriptions of several approaches to risk analysis by expert systems. Challenges to expert systems technology endemic in the risk analysis problem are stated—and these serve as generic issues for the field as a whole. The chapter closes with the consideration of some longer-term management issues, including the belief that progress in this field will be slow after the "low-hanging fruit" is picked.

INTRODUCTION

This chapter offers a survey of the problems of using "expert systems" to do risk analysis. The concentration is on financial risk analysis, particularly insurance underwriting. This is a subject that is not very well developed yet, so there is no broadly accepted model of how to do the job. In any case, the varied kinds of risk analysis undertaken in various circumstances may require different treatment. These depend on such factors as the amount at risk, the nature and quality of information available, and even the legal context in which the decision is made.

The opinions in this chapter are entirely the author's. They do not necessarily represent the views of the Great-West Life Assurance Company, its professional underwriting staff, or the practices that Great-West currently uses in support of its own product lines.

RISK ANALYSIS AND INSURANCE UNDERWRITING

There are many kinds of risk analysis undertaken by various organizations. A surprising variety of these, from where to drill oil wells to evaluating the structures of prospective corporate leveraged buyouts, are susceptible to expert system evaluation.

Many of the ideas of this chapter are applicable in several of these areas. But I'm going to concentrate primarily on the problem of risk analysis in insurance and finance, where it is commonly known as underwriting. Even with this restriction in scope, the problems vary greatly in size, character, and complexity.

At the smallest scale of risk, but highest volume, there is the example of credit card transaction approval. Here, when credit is extended, it is rare that the amount will exceed a few hundred dollars. The sum at risk is precisely known, and after a few months, the customer's payment habits are usually well established.

One of the most publicized examples of an expert system in this business is the one that American Express has developed. This was a very nice piece of work. Several descriptive sketches of the system's organization have been published. One can infer from them the majority of the complexity came from the difficulty of linking all the hardware and software cleverly enough that the relevant information could be assembled in one place rapidly enough to complete the transaction in a few seconds. In this case, the actual risk analysis is one of the least of the problems.

Risk analysis problems on a larger, but still systematic scale, occur in areas such as property or automobile insurance. Here the size of the typical risk is larger. But the contract can generally be reviewed and repriced each year.

Life and health insurance exhibit risk on a still larger scale. The size of the

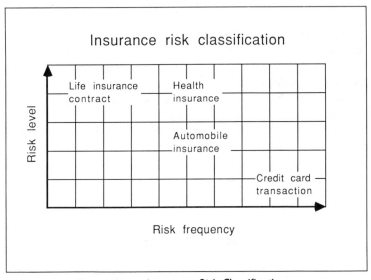

Figure 8.1.   Insurance Risk Classification

contract can easily be $100,000 and more. The effective risk is also larger because such contracts are generally unmodifiable (at least, to the disadvantage of the client) for the life of the contract. It is precisely this distinction that makes term life insurance generally much cheaper than "whole life" policies.

In this general area of insurance risk analysis, the most sophisticated example I know is the system which Nippon Life developed, in association with a Japanese software house, to deal with the medical parts of underwriting. Nippon Life is the world's largest life insurance company, thanks to the strength of the yen. As of some time ago, I understand their system can deal with some 400 diseases and clinical conditions. Similar systems are under development by Lincoln National Insurance Company and Capsco, a Canadian affiliate of SwissRe Corporation.

At the most extreme are the kinds of contracts that the Syndics of Lloyds may be willing to write if you have an oil tanker you'd like to slip through the Persian Gulf in one piece. Here there are millions of dollars at risk in each event, and even though the event may happen lots of times, the context changes on a daily basis. So, it's hard to imagine anyone dreaming of confiding this job to an expert system.

THE SPECIAL PROBLEMS OF RISK ANALYSIS FROM AN EXPERT SYSTEM POINT OF VIEW

It's well known what contexts tend to be promising ones for expert system use. The things that help include characteristics like:

- A large number of relatively similar problems.
- Logic that is not too vague or baroque.
- Data that are not too extensive and in a form that is easy to manipulate by computer.

Of course, I am leaving out all the political and technical issues that come into play in any particular circumstance. In the case of risk analysis, we can add the following characteristics:

- An expected risk per event that you are comfortable trusting to a machine.
- A predictable risk context. (Life insurance is very price-competitive with lots of thin margins. But it has lots of actuarial data experience behind it.)
- Risk indicators that are not too hard to deal with.

A quick look at even this short list shows why credit card transactions, automobile insurance, and life insurance are noticeably easier problems than health insurance or ocean-going marine.

APPROACHES TO RISK ANALYSIS BY EXPERT SYSTEM

The American Express cases and the Nippon Life systems represent extremes of risk-based products to which expert systems have been applied. Between them lie many examples in various stages of completeness from my own and other insurance firms.

Here are two more cases which I think are instructive to compare, because they come from very similar contexts. They are the cases of Fireman's Fund, and of my own firm.

Fireman's Fund, the large San Francisco-based insurer, recently produced a system to help underwrite certain kinds of casualty insurance. They have been relatively public about it, and even made a television commercial with IBM.

My understanding is that the Fireman's Fund people were faced with a number of problems. These included inconsistent underwriting and a shortage of skilled underwriting staff. They had decentralized underwriting, and even let marketing people modify underwriting decisions in certain cases. So perhaps some inconsistency was inevitable. Also, perhaps it's no surprise that an insurance company competing in the San Francisco job market would not have it so easy. To help solve the consistency problems, they decided to centralize some of their underwriting. But some of the underwriters didn't want to be centralized. So they ended up with more problems of staff shortage and inexperience. The result was their casualty expert system underwriter, which has received some publicity.

They've obviously been very happy with the expert system underwriter they developed, and feel they've been able to deal with their problems.

In contrast, a project in my own firm involved underwriting for certain life insurance lines. Now Manitoba is not the kind of place you would mistake for San Francisco Bay. With only a few thousand employees, Great-West is the largest private company in a radius of 500 miles and one of the few local firms that competes across the continent. The result is that we tend to have access to the best people from a population of about a million and that our employee base is fairly stable. So our problems are not usually a *lack* of expertise but *bored* expertise. One of our major goals is to do the easy (read: boring) parts of the business with expert systems so that our expert underwriters can move on to more interesting problems.

So we and Fireman's Fund, even though we are both working in an area as narrow as insurance underwriting, are after quite different things. I think this contains a managerial law: Don't believe anyone else's benefit analysis about expert systems. You can do a lot of different things with them. So it pays to think carefully about the particular opportunities of your own situation.

For the rest of this paper, I'd like to discuss some of the things that should be thought about, if you propose to do risk analysis by expert system.

Partitioned and Overlapping Reasoning

If you want to devise an algorithm for an automated underwriter, one of the first issues is the question of what indicators of risk you are going to use. For instance, with automobile insurance, there are many factors that indicate an increased frequency or cost of accidents. Here are a few, and no doubt, you can think of others:

- the age of the car and the price when new
- the size of the engine
- the number of miles the car is driven annually
- the age of the owner
- the amount of alcohol the owner drinks
- the city or town in which the car is driven most frequently.

The simplest approach to risk evaluation is just to allot some points for each of the criteria you select. Then you can let the sum correspond to an evaluation of the total risk. That is equivalent to the assumption that the indicators of risk do not overlap or interact.

In the interests of simplicity, that is the process that has often been adopted. But it's done because being more accurate was too hard to administer. The problem with this simple approach is that not everything that counts is countable. With a computer to help in the collection and analysis of information, there is no reason one can't do this job better. More accurate assessment has many prospective advantages. It should lead to lower prices for better risks with attendant prospects for increased market share. It can lead to the acceptance of fewer bad risks with implications of improved profitability.

However, if you set out to be more accurate, your actuaries will probably remind you that risk indicators often overlap in their indication of risk. There are two possibilities. The overlap may indicate double-counting, so that the real risk is less than the sum of the risks would suggest. Alternatively, the risks may interact to create a joint risk that is greater than a mere sum would suggest. For instance, big engines and alcohol behind the wheel are an extra dangerous combination.

So at the very beginning, you must choose whether and how to deal with overlapping risk indicators. If you allow your indicators to overlap, you can use the redundancy to make them check each other. You can get more accuracy and a higher assurance that you haven't overlooked anything. But, as we'll see later, the design, maintenance, and testing will all get noticeably trickier.

If you keep your risk indicators independent, then the maintenance and testing get easier. But you will have less assurance that you have covered all the risk issues.

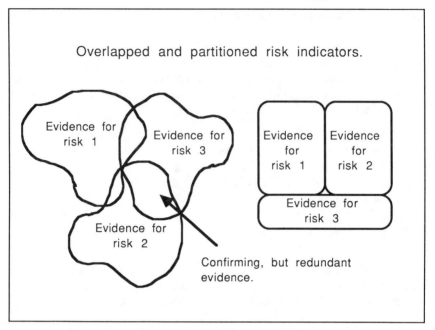

Figure 8.2.   Overlapped and Partitioned Risk Indicators

This is the beginning of the knowledge engineering process. There are both actuarial and design implications of the choice you make.

Removable Data and Rules

In some problem areas, old knowledge never becomes wrong. It may become irrelevant, or it may be superceded, but your main risk in keeping it around is unnecessary carrying costs. In chemical analysis, for example, presumably techniques that used to work still will, even if better techniques have displaced them.

But in some contexts, old information can become wrong and potentially damaging. Expert systems that work with such contexts have a very special set of design problems, ones about which I've seen all too little in the literature. For instance, some people buy life insurance as part of an overall financial plan. If an expert system to analyze a client's financial circumstances uses information left from pretax reform days, the assessments it produces may be baloney. So, how are you going to insure that you can purge your system of obsolete information and rules if you must?

For that matter, if the external rules are changed, how will you insure that you can remove certain parts of the system and replace them with others? That happens, for example, if you decide that you are not going to allow gender as an indicator of probable lifespan in the calculation of pension annuity benefits.

There isn't an easy answer to this. I know of no textbook specification of how to do this. The ease of doing the job properly depends on quality of the software architecture. But it is also heavily influenced by such things as the partitioned or overlapping logic adopted in various components of the system's reasoning.

It does help if you understand carefully how your system makes its inferences. That sounds like just a self-evident piece of common sense, but there is a little more to it than that. Part of the common wisdom about expert systems is that they are nonprocedural, so that you don't have to specify, or even understand, their internal sequencing very precisely. Some of that is true. But my experience suggests that, for large expert systems, you can't be cavalier.

Distribution and Control Problems

You only need one copy of some expert systems. I read recently about one that a California utility designed to help in maintenance of a particularly troublesome earthfill dam, whose caretaker was about to retire. Presumably troublesome earthfill dams are really one of a kind.

But underwriting is something that an insurance company wants to do a lot of. Of course, in the first place, underwriting is central to the whole industry. But even more, because of brokers and independent insurance agents, there is not even reason to expect that all the users will be regular employees, with the company's best interests at heart. So how will you control the expert system?

One approach is the one Mutual of New York has taken. Their electronic underwriter runs in their head office. They do data collection in the field, ship a file to head office, underwrite it there, and transmit the results back to their offices. They are able to complete this process rapidly, sometimes in less than an hour. The whole approach is a sober one, with which I have sympathy.

But it's hard to avoid the feeling that it's dodging the issue a little. The trend in business these days is to get the process over rapidly. Suppose you want to get an electronic underwriter into the hands of your marketing people, so that you can underwrite business properly, and still issue it on the spot? How can you assure that people who aren't permanently hooked to your network don't use old versions of the expert system? How can you assure that it isn't treated as a sort of computer game, with overenthusiastic marketeers trying to find ways to get marginal business past it?

This one is not a trivial exercise, which is probably why the MONY people chose the approach they did. In substance, the problems here are probably not dramatically different than those of distributing any other application that actually matters. But since underwriting lies at the very core of an insurance company's affairs, one needs to be very comfortable that everything is unfolding as it ought.

SOME SPECIAL PROBLEMS OF RISK ANALYSIS

Testing Expert Systems

Testing expert systems is a tricky affair. With normal software, one would like to do an exhaustive test of all combinations of input possibilities. But with expert systems for risk analyses, that's usually both a practical and conceptual impossibility. It's a practical impossibility because the variety of acceptable input data is very large. This contrasts, say, with an expert system for monitoring a machine, where the number and range of inputs is precisely foreseen. But more than this, it's a conceptual problem. If your problem is simple enough that you can foresee all the input possibilities and sequences, then you probably don't need expert system techniques to solve it. You might want to use them anyway, because they are fast to write. But, however big the return on investment one might calculate from such projects, it's not really exploiting the technology to its limits.

So for many important classes of expert systems, you're forced to adopt some sort of statistical testing process. We find that this process, like many aspects of expert system design, lies between art and science.

Naturally, one would like to work from proper statistical results about the client base and risks you're dealing with. But many combinations are infrequent. So from the point of view of business prudence, there are all the pitfalls of small sample statistics lying in wait. Here it's worth having someone who knows statistics properly available.

Another idea is to create statistically suitable test data. But it's also hard, and error-prone, to pretend that one has thought of everything in advance, and hence is creating complete test data. We dealt with this one by creating a random client generator, which uses some real data picked more or less at random from our customer files, complemented with statistically suitable artificial data. For instance, it will choose real occupations and medical conditions but artificial demographic data. The combinations you get out of this can be quite entertaining. But we also discovered that they are a very good test of an expert system's resilience and completeness.

The process of confirming one's confidence in a system probably comes down to the issue of confidence in the people who are commissioned to do the work.

Then there is the problem of testing new releases. How do you know that a new release still treats the old cases properly? The obvious thing is to keep old cases around and run through them on a batch basis. But unfortunately, the software doesn't give much help here. I don't know any commercial shell that will let you keep a file of cases, and then run through them all again with, say, the ages of all the individuals increased by 15 years. The lack of good test facilities is one of my biggest gripes with most of the commercial software available in this area.

Creating a Database of Decisions

With some problems, once you have a possible answer, it's easy to check if the answer is actually right. If it is, often you don't need to care anymore how you got it. But underwriting is not like that. With the natural time lag between policy issue and claims experience, if you make a mistake in underwriting, the distance between crime and punishment can be long, even years.

People doing many kinds of risk analysis really do have to care about this. After all, if you lose money through adverse claim experience, you want to know if are suffering from poor underwriting, or from a statistical fluke.

So to understand your risk analysis procedures over the long term, you have to develop a way of storing decision mechanisms. Unfortunately, there isn't an obvious way to do that. Most expert systems will answer a basic "how" question. But they don't automatically store anything like the chain of reasoning (or messages) that resulted in the decision.

The problem isn't even easy from a theoretical point of view. I invite any data-structure enthusiasts to try to debate the relative merits of, say, relational and hierarchical structures, for dealing with this problem. We are actively investigating this one; if anyone comes up with a bright idea, I'd be pleased to hear about it.

Maintenance for the Long Term

The problem of long-term maintenance of expert systems is another one that, in my view, has been underrated. The problem is particularly acute for risk-oriented expert systems. Everyone I've discussed this with just grimaces.

Not many of these systems have been around for long, so there isn't much experience to investigate. Probably the best example is Digital's famous XCON, which has several dozen people doing the maintenance.

Most of us would want our expert systems to last as well as any other software, say 10 years, or so. And in most organizations, several dozen people is not a reasonable number to have looking after one piece of software.

For orthodox software maintenance problems, most companies have developed a sort of rough architectural discipline that tries to divide and conquer. One's first idea with large expert systems is to try something similar. But now we run into conflict with earlier issues. If you partition your problem in the interests of easy maintenance, you lose the ability to have some redundant analysis for risk confirmation purposes. If you don't, you turn maintenance into an even more confusing matter than it inherently is.

The essential of the problem here is the same as often recurs in the design of expert system software: The extreme positions are all demonstrably bad. So it comes to making compromises based on the particular circumstances at hand.

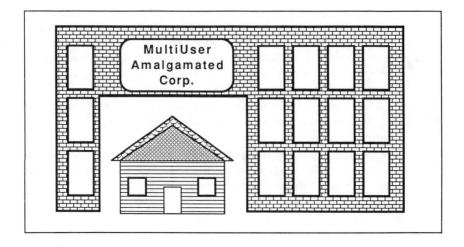

Figure 8.3.   Problems of Pioneering: How to Handle Expert System Maintenance for the Long-Term?

And people with some experience tend to be able to find better compromises than others.

The Data Acquisition Problem

Another problem that is particularly bothersome for some kinds of risk analysis is the need to consider various types of data. If you are doing your risk estimate by just giving points for a few indicators, you're home free. But, for complicated cases, our own professional underwriting staff use a combination of numerical, text, and binary data from the application, voice data from a telephone interview, graphical data from an electrocardiogram, and even handwritten notes from doctors. The combination of varied species and varied sources of data presents a problem that, for the foreseeable future, just can't be handled in its full variety. So you have to compromise and often restructure and simplify the data that are to be considered.

That has its good and bad side. On one hand, it enforces a discipline in the way the risks are evaluated, which is often a good thing. On the other, it does infringe on the professional turf of the underwriters. They may argue, with considerable force, that an expert system underwriter is just a sort of parody of

the real thing and quite unable to mimic the feel for a case that a professional underwriter develops.

The Historical Release Problem

Underwriting is a process that gradually evolves. New occupations, like video store manager, appear. Others, like elevator operator, disappear. New tax laws in Canada give tax credits for individuals. Old tax laws give income deductions. But the liabilities involved in an insurance contract remain. So how are we to be sure that our new contracts are underwritten taking full account and discount of our past experience?

The problem doesn't go away even if you keep yourself to one copy of your underwriter in your head office. If you want to run old files through your new release, for test purposes, say, what do you do with reasoning that has been removed from the system? If you don't remove it, what becomes of your maintenance burden? Could it possibly be sensible just to keep all the old releases around?

If you don't restrict yourself to copies of the system in a head office, how does one update the field versions? How does one get rid of the old field versions so that even Mr. Murphy cannot find one to run at an inconvenient moment?

These problems, too, have their analogies with ordinary software. How does one assure that standard spreadsheets are doing what they are supposed to? I gather that some corporations have gone so far as to pass around rigid copies of personal computer software and forbid people to do any customization. I myself wouldn't want employees whose understanding of what they are doing is so weak that they couldn't be trusted in such circumstances. But, no matter how much control you try to exert, there isn't much you can do about independent agents who are self-employed and not forced to use your services.

We happen to have already puzzled out a solution to a problem similar to this. It arose from the need to give the latest interest rates for annuity quotations. We transmit information daily using encryption techniques. This allows us to keep rates for several days around, without people being able to get access to yesterday's rates for today's transactions, even though yesterday's transactions may not have been completed yet.

In principle, you could do the same thing with your underwriter. But there are two differences: underwriting policies don't change all that fast, and an entire underwriter represents a file of considerable size. If telecommunications facilities were free, you'd just redo it all each day anyway. But they aren't, yet. The process that's best depends, of course, on the nature of the network you have available and nature of the computers to which your system is to be delivered. Our own thinking has to be based on a sort of worst case: the desire to make an underwriting expert system accessible to thousands of people, not all our employees.

SOME LONGER-TERM MANAGEMENT ISSUES

There's Time to Think

I think the subject of expert systems is going to evolve much more slowly than much of the popular technical press would lead us to believe. The reason is that I think the subject is fundamentally pretty hard.

Of course, pioneers often find low-hanging fruit amidst the territory they are the first to explore. There are reputations to be made in picking some of it. But I think the situation has some ominous reflections of the earliest days of software. When no one in a firm had automated anything before, it was easy to do something and get a lot out of it. It was only when the somethings started to get large, middle-aged, and crowded that hell started to feel like other people's computer programs.

It's much the same in expert systems. The biggest gains will ultimately be gotten out of some very large systems, which are tightly fitted into existing software and broadly distributed in terms of both users and geography. And we are far, far away from understanding how to build such things effectively. Even the question of how to represent knowledge most effectively is, in many contexts, quite unsolved. I would say that, at least once a month, we run into a problem that just does not appear to me to be conveniently expressible by any of the standard techniques of knowledge representation, much less by most commercial software.

All this says nothing about the need for computer systems that can deal in at least the most basic kinds of mixed data species.

People are beginning to sense this. There is some soul-searching in the press. The most famous startups haven't made too many fortunes yet. Several of them, both in hardware and in software, are losing venture capital hand over fist. There are lots of people at conferences, and lots of trees that have been sacrificed to commentary about the subject. But even now, some of the most frequently cited examples of success are 10 years old. So I think we've got lots of time yet and a great shortage of experience.

A Question of Pace

All of this means that corporate managers are faced with a difficult question of pace. On one hand, it's tempting to rush in and pick some of the low-hanging fruit. On the other, it's pretty clear that the hardware, the software, and even the underlying theory, are all in rapid evolution. A cynical approach to all this would be to try do something spectacular, and then get promoted before the cracks start to appear in the foundations.

For people who are more sanguine, and inclined to contemplate the longer-term view, here is my perspective on the state of the art.

Expert systems are misleadingly named. In the right context, and with sufficient development effort, programs developed with expert system techniques are undoubtedly capable of doing the work of experts. Some are performing at that level now. But the name carries a misleading connotation that there is some sort of gap between the problems you can apply expert systems techniques to and whatever it is that software tends to do now. In truth, there is not much distinction. Such distinction as there is comes mostly from the fact that expert system techniques, particularly the use of "shells," greatly improve the speed at which you can write software. The actual software coding becomes a smaller job. That, in turn, makes it possible to devote a larger proportion of the development to a careful exacting treatment of the actual problem at hand. It is this that makes it possible to get performance up to "expert" standard with a manageable amount of development effort.

As a result, I think expert systems, and especially expert system shells, ought to be thought of as the correct inheritors of the term "fourth generation" software. They are sharply aimed at the rapid production of software to deal with high volume problems. The goal is the same as that of third generation languages, while the means are more advanced. In contrast, what is more standardly called "fourth generation" software is aimed at making it possible to deal with one-of-a-kind questions. However worthwhile that job, it is certainly not the natural successor of the third generation.

In many organizations, the easiest promising prospects for the use of expert systems are involved with the work of people who are nearer amateurs than highly trained experts. That's certainly the case in the simple categories of underwriting. I gather from acquaintances that it's also frequently the case in other industries. Viewed in this sense, expert systems are simply a natural and necessary step as we strive to create software more rapidly, more cheaply, and with a closer fit to the task at hand.

The variety of tasks to which we could apply ourselves is unlimited. On one hand, there is some impressive low-hanging fruit. But at the high end, there is a very considerable discipline involved in doing expert system development well.

This variety is what makes it interesting, rewarding, and fun.

Using Knowledge-Based Systems in Financial Services: Methodology and Case Studies

Nelson Marquina

Coopers & Lybrand

The emphasis of this chapter is on the importance of having a development methodology for building an expert system that allows a company to move from a prototype into an actual implementation within any environment. Just such a methodology has been developed by Coopers and Lybrand and is fully discussed here. Included in this chapter are a survey of the involvement of the financial services field in artificial intelligence and a look into the short-term future where the concept of reuseable software (function-specific and industry-specific shells) is presented. Also included is a discussion of each of two case studies where this development methodology was applied in building an expert system: one called ExperTax, developed by Coopers and Lybrand for internal use, and the other called REIN-SURANCE, an underwriting expert system developed by this firm for a client company. The chapter concludes with a brief discussion of the benefits of using such a methodology.

INTRODUCTION

An important shift for the utilization of expert systems in business applications occurred between 1983 and 1985. Expert systems moved out of prototype development into the mainstream of industry. Of course, in many different places people are still in a prototype mode, but where expert systems have entered the mainstream, for example in the financial services and in manufacturing, the experience provides a model and a methodology for systematically developing expert systems for other industry applications. We now have people with understanding and experience who have built a large number of expert systems. In Coopers and Lybrand, the combined expertise of 52 people for the past four and one-half years has resulted in the development of a methodology for building expert systems and the tools to implement this methodology. In this chapter I emphasize the importance of having a methodology for building expert systems that allows you to move from prototyping to the actual implementation, be it embedded systems or integrated systems in some larger context, be it data processing, MIS, some financial service, or a manufacturing process.

First I will share with you the results of a survey of the status of AI in financial services; secondly, we'll examine the Coopers and Lybrand methodology; and thirdly, we'll review two case studies where the methodology was used in the building of two different expert systems.

SURVEY OF THE STATUS OF AI IN FINANCIAL SERVICES

Following are the results of a 1987 survey conducted for Coopers and Lybrand by Schubert, Inc. In the consulting business, we are market-driven, so we wanted to know—among other things—where the market was, where the market was going, and what the self-perception of the market was.

As illustrated in Figure 9.1, we know that 40 percent of the largest banks and brokers in the investment companies are currently using or developing expert systems; 10 percent are in the planning mode. About 47 percent are still not active in this area. Figure 9.2 shows how we broke the financial services into segments. Looking at the breakdown we see that of those people responding to the survey, 60 percent of the commercial banks are actually in one of those modes—planning, building, or using expert systems. Forty-seven percent of the security and commodity firms, 42 percent of the insurance companies, and about 10 percent of other specialty houses are in that mode. (These data are prior to Black Monday in October 1987.)

In the survey we queried success factors. Figure 9.3 indicates an interesting contrast in attitudes between the directors of MIS and the CEOs or top management of the organizations. Notice the difference between the two groups with

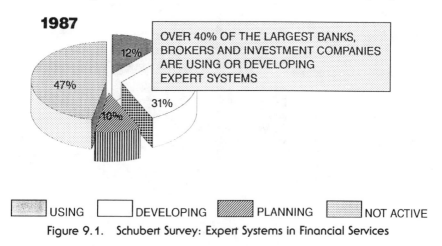

Figure 9.1. Schubert Survey: Expert Systems in Financial Services

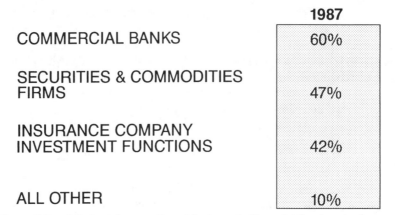

1987

COMMERCIAL BANKS	60%
SECURITIES & COMMODITIES FIRMS	47%
INSURANCE COMPANY INVESTMENT FUNCTIONS	42%
ALL OTHER	10%

Figure 9.2.   Schubert Survey: Expert Systems in Financial Services by Segment

respect to their attitude about the role of expert systems for survival or getting ahead of competition. Fifty-six percent of the directors of MIS felt that expert systems as a technology was crucial for them to survive. Within the top management queried, this view was held by only 34 percent; 53 percent of top management didn't have an opinion whether expert systems technology was crucial or not, in contrast to 26 percent of MIS directors. What this means is that top management in 1987 was in a wait-and-see mode. At this point in 1987, the burden of demonstrating the benefits of using expert systems technology was on the MIS or the data processing people. I mention those two groups because in the

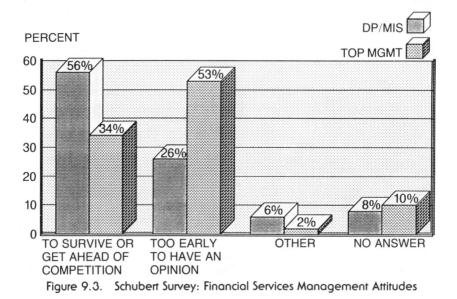

Figure 9.3.   Schubert Survey: Financial Services Management Attitudes

financial services industries, data processing and MIS are the owners of the expert systems technology.

As another part of this survey, we asked about the company's perception of where the expert systems market was today and where the market was going in the near future. People in the trading field felt that the areas where they needed expert systems technology or they felt expert systems technology had an impact were in foreign exchange trading, option trading strategies, trading risk assessment, pricing/analysis of data quality, and technical analysis/pattern recognition.

In investment banking, deal structuring was the activity that attracted people first to expert systems. The number of factors and the amount of data involved in putting a deal together was becoming unwieldy for human beings to do in a reasonable amount of time. Other application areas were in expert portfolio reviewing and business strategic planning.

Within the insurance field, interest was generated by underwriting, risk/product matching, and claims management.

In banking, interest in expert systems applications was equally spread among decision support systems for lending advisors, consumer and business loan reviews, credit scoring, and online customer assistance.

Let me summarize this section by presenting some statistics from our 1986 and 1987 surveys in the insurance industry. By comparing the 1986 and 1987 results, Figure 9.4 shows the progress in the utilization of expert systems in insurance applications. Overall the insurance industry moved towards either using or developing expert systems from 36 percent in 1986 to 63 percent in 1987. Similar changes are observed in other industries. Figure 9.5 shows the change in attitudes towards expert systems from 1986 to 1987. It is interesting to

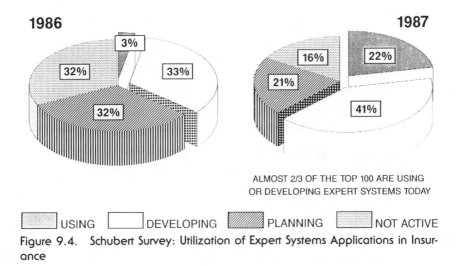

Figure 9.4. Schubert Survey: Utilization of Expert Systems Applications in Insurance

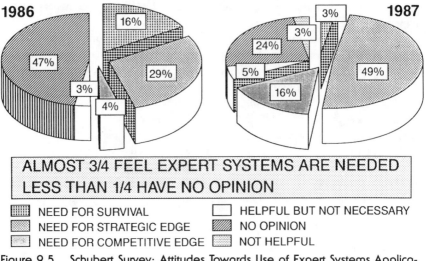

ALMOST 3/4 FEEL EXPERT SYSTEMS ARE NEEDED
LESS THAN 1/4 HAVE NO OPINION

▦ NEED FOR SURVIVAL   ☐ HELPFUL BUT NOT NECESSARY
▨ NEED FOR STRATEGIC EDGE   ▨ NO OPINION
▨ NEED FOR COMPETITIVE EDGE   ▨ NOT HELPFUL

Figure 9.5.   Schubert Survey: Attitudes Towards Use of Expert Systems Applications in Insurance

notice that the percentage of companies that felt expert systems were needed for survival actually went down to 3 percent from 16 percent. Figure 9.6 presents comparable results for the insurance industry; Figure 9.7 presents summary highlights for the financial services industry.

The Future of AI in Financial Services

In the short-term future, people in financial services definitely will want to use more expert systems. Once they experience the benefits of expert systems, it is not difficult to find more and more applications for their clients. Integration of

- ALMOST 2/3 USING, DEVELOPING, OR ACTIVELY RESEARCHING EXPERT SYSTEMS APPLICATIONS

- THIS 1987 FIGURE IS DOUBLE THAT OF 1986

- COMPANIES WITH EXPERT SYSTEMS IN USE WENT FROM 2% TO 22%

- ALMOST 3/4 BELIEVE THAT EXPERT SYSTEMS ARE CRUCIAL TO THEIR COMPANIES

- THIS 1987 FIGURE IS 1 1/2 TIMES THAT OF 1986

- UNDERWRITING AND CLAIMS ARE THE MOST FREQUENT EXPERT SYSTEMS APPLICATIONS

Figure 9.6.   Expert Systems in the Insurance Industry, Survey Highlights

- MOST ACTIVITY IN COMMERCIAL BANKING &
  SECURITIES INDUSTRY SEGMENTS

- POPULAR BANK APPLICATIONS:
  - LOAN REVIEWS & TRADING SUPPORT

- POPULAR SECURITIES FIRM APPLICATIONS:
  - OPTIONS TRADING & RISK ASSESSMENT

- 43% OF MAJOR FINANCIAL SERVICES INSTITUTIONS
  USING, DEVELOPING OR RESEARCHING APPLICATIONS

- 90% OF THESE BELIEVE EXPERT SYSTEMS ARE CRUCIAL

- 1/3 OF FIRMS NOT INVOLVED PLAN TO BE BY 1990

- MOST COMPANIES FAVOR EXPERT SYSTEM SHELLS
  FOR DEVELOPMENT

- PC / MAINFRAME FAVORED HARDWARE
  FOR FUTURE DEPLOYMENT

- LISP MACHINES LOSING FAVOR FOR
  DEVELOPMENT AS WELL AS DELIVERY ($)

- INTEGRATION INTO DP ENVIRONMENT IS
  A MAJOR CONCERN

- MIXTURE OF INTERNAL & OUTSIDE DEVELOPMENT

- KNOWLEDGE BASES ARE BEING MAINTAINED BY USER GROUPS

Figure 9.7.   Expert Systems in the Financial Services Industry: Survey Highlights and Additional Findings

expert systems with MIS and data processing departments will be a must in about one year. Clients will not buy services of consultant firms or the internal services of their own MIS/DP groups or expert systems groups to build expert systems that will exist in isolation. An evolution of domain-specific tools is imminent. Vendors are moving into the area of function-specific and industry-specific shells—shells, not tools. The best example of a function-specific shell today is Testbench developed jointly by TI and the Carnegie Group. Testbench is focused entirely on diagnostic problems and originally was intended to be used by the manufacturing industry. In a sense, we're moving toward the concept of reusable software where the shell itself doesn't change. It is the contents of the shell that changes.

There will be knowledge engineers specializing in specific-domain applications, which is already happening. The more we get to the mainstream of the applications of expert systems, the more the knowledge engineers need to know about the domain. Unfortunately, knowledge acquisition is not that automated yet, so the knowledge engineers must carry some of the burden of learning something from the domain experts and vice versa. Expert systems are becoming more commonly used in such a way that knowledge engineers now have to specialize on a few of the domains or areas of application.

Low-cost, standard hardware is becoming more available at all levels of organizations. At the hardware level, in particular, 386- and 486-based machines like the IBM PS/2 and Macintosh II, based on Motorola's 68030 chip, are powerful enough for the development of fairly large expert systems. In software tools, we have not just the domain-specific tools but the current generic tools. Think of software tools as a scale going from the language for building expert systems on one end, all the way to application-specific expert systems. If you start off with languages (LISP, C, and so on), then move to the tools (like ART, KEE, KnowledgeCraft, etc.), you get a partitioning in the middle of the scale between languages and tools, namely, the application-specific shells. In other words, an application-specific shell is an attempt to bring the power of AI tools to non-AI industry domain experts and end-users. Languages and powerful AI tools still require expertize in AI to use them.

Now, we have software vendors, such as Inference, that market ART and ART/IM who are moving toward end-user tools. They have software front-ends to allow people to use ART without having to learn the guts of LISP programming. MIS and data processing people are used to working with structured development methodologies when building software systems. When they looked at expert systems, they looked at it from that point of view. They asked, What is the structure? What is the technique? What supports the methodology for building it? How do you have cost control? Time control? How do you track people? Who's doing what, when? They have this mindset and that's why we had difficulty in introducing expert systems into that environment. The AI community have been asking for a number of years for a structured methodology approach to the entire knowledge engineering process.

Figure 9.8 summarizes how the financial services industry sees the future of expert systems utilization and their perception regarding the need for a disciplined approach to expert systems development.

DEVELOPMENT METHODOLOGY

Coopers and Lybrand's development methodology allows you to reduce the development cost for an expert system. It is a comprehensive, streamlined, structured, methodological approach. The development methodology should not

- INCREASINGLY WIDE-SPREAD *USE* OF EXPERT SYSTEMS

- INCREASE IN *SCOPE* OF EXPERT SYSTEM APPLICATIONS

- *INTEGRATION* OF EXPERT SYSTEMS INTO OVERALL DP ENVIRONMENT

- FURTHER EVOLUTION OF DOMAIN-SPECIFIC *TOOLS*

- KNOWLEDGE ENGINEERS *SPECIALIZING* IN DOMAIN APPLICATIONS

- LOWER-COST STANDARD *HARDWARE* USED AS
  TOOLS BECOME MORE CAPABLE

- *STRUCTURED METHODOLOGY* APPROACH APPLIED
  TO ENTIRE KNOWLEDGE ENGINEERING PROCESS

- REDUCED *DEVELOPMENT COSTS* DUE TO COMPREHENSIVE,
  STREAM-LINED STRUCTURED METHODOLOGY APPROACH

Figure 9.8.   Expert Systems in the Financial Services Sector: The Future

be new to data processing people, who follow these same stages. One starts with the definition of the system's requirements, which is nothing new, just part of the engineering process. The next steps are: solution definition, design and build, operational testing, transition to user, and maintenance as depicted in Figure 9.9. Each discipline has its own way of implementing this particular process. For instance, if one goes to a data processing department and you look at the procedure books, they will tell you exactly who is doing what and when, very precisely, under each of the development phases. Tools and techniques to support a high level of software project management already exists commercially for traditional software systems. In Coopers and Lybrand we have accomplished the same thing for expert systems.

I will now walk you through the requirements definition first and focus on that phase the most. At this point we are eliciting objectives that come directly from management. We want to know what they want, what the constraints are, the budget, people, time, and so on. We identify the sources of knowledge. Some of it is people. A lot of it is procedures, procedure manuals, books, drawings, and then at that point we determine whether an expert system is feasible, given this particular knowledge domain.

Users normally do not have a complete knowledge of what is needed. It is a sort of Catch 22—a chicken-and-egg type of situation. You have to start doing some of the expert system development before you know exactly what you need. The picture of the entire process at that point is not clear. Management needs to understand very early (in the first phase) what commitment is required, what the tradeoffs are, what the organizational implications are.

To address the needs stated above we developed a tool called FFAST that allows us to build knowledge models rapidly and efficiently. With FFAST we

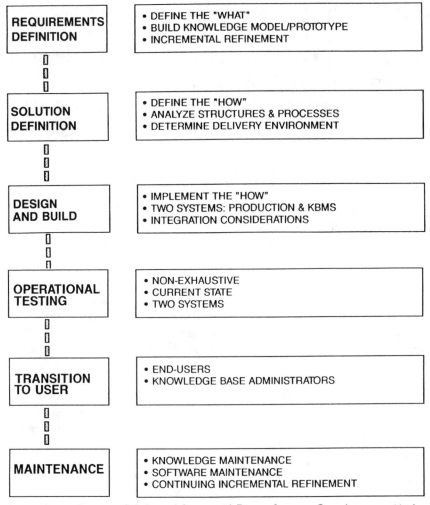

Figure 9.9.   Coopers & Lybrand Structured Expert Systems Development Methodology

can build a prototype of the eventual software system as part of the requirements definition phase. At this point in the process we have not chosen the deployment machine yet. We have not chosen the language to be used. We have not chosen a shell or tool for the actual system development. But there is a need for management and users to know what the system looks like before starting to build. That is why people talk about quick prototyping. That's what we faced three-and-one-half years ago. If you observe data processing people, you will see that they develop the requirements definition with pencil and paper and flowcharts. For expert systems it needs to be more than a flowchart, it also needs to be a prototype—a useable, testable, functional prototype. You can put test data through it and run it. It needs to be a tool for communication between the expert systems developers and management, end-users and experts. It actively involves the expert in the development process right from the beginning. The knowledge model is built based on the expertise or the understanding of the experts at that point, incrementally.

FFAST allows us to maintain a business event perspective. Computer Aided Software Engineering (CASE) tools suffer from the lack of this feature. It's the Achilles' heel in traditional data processing. The problem is that software people are trying to build a software system to manage a set of business events, say, loan applications. When they understand the system requirements, they translate the requirements into a language that is data processing specific, and the end-user does not understand that anymore. Management does not understand it anymore. They have data flow diagrams and entity relationships and tools to manage them. The point is that direct, effective communication is lost between the original requirements and the actual implementation. With a tool like FFAST we maintain that business-event perspective. It allows instant feedback between the knowledge engineers and the experts, that is in the knowledge acquisition and validation iteration, very early in Phase 1.

Let me explain how we do it, graphically. As depicted in Figure 9.10 we start with initial interviews between the knowledge engineers and the expert or experts. We have the initial interview to understand the domain language and build a data dictionary on paper. Very quickly we move to a room that we call the boiler room. It is a room with a partition in the middle, the experts on one end and the knowledge engineers on the other end. There is no communication either visually or by voice. All of this is videotaped. A business event is introduced to the experts: for example, a loan application. The expert is asked, What do you do now? Well, in one case I was working with a particular bank from a South American country. The expert looked at the application, and said "It's okay; approved." We said, "Wait a minute, what do you mean 'approved,' so quickly?" "Well," he said, "I know this client." So we blacked out the name and said "Now you don't know the specific name of the client. Now what?" Then he spent about a minute, and said, "Okay, I'll approve it." "Approve what?" we replied. "Well, I know the city where this client is located, and I know the local economy, and I know no matter what they're doing, they're doing well. I don't need to know who the client is." I said, "Wait a minute. Okay, you don't know the specific city now, what do you do now?" So we dissect it that way. At this point, at least we know that the entity "city name" contains informational value in making a risk assessment.

This process is being videotaped and with FFAST we build the electronic version of what is happening in this room. That is what happens in the initial knowledge modeling. At the end of each day, the experts see the electronic version of the knowledge model. We process case data through the model as it

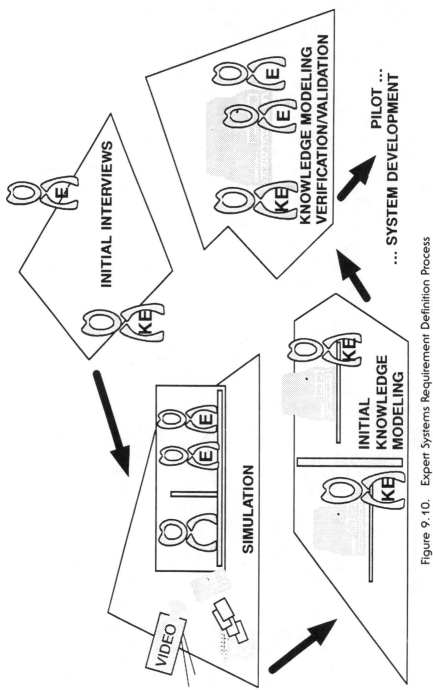

Figure 9.10. Expert Systems Requirement Definition Process

138

exists at that point. This gives opportunities for the experts to refine the knowledge model as it is being built. That iteration happens right on the spot.

Eventually we move to the knowledge modeling verifications and validation. That's when we bring in the test cases and some of the eventual end-users for validation. We ask: If you were using this system later on, how would you react? Do you like it? Does it have the right columns? Are the titles in the right place? Are these the right type of menu systems? So we build that into the design itself before we even decide what shell we're going to use or what platform we are going to deliver the eventual system on.

Let me just back up for a moment and give you an overview because the rest is fairly easy. Once you understand what you need to build and you can see it running, the building process is much easier. And that is what happened when at this point the data processing people came in. They got excited—they saw how we do requirements definitions. They recognized that they have exactly the same problem in software development, not necessarily expert systems, traditional software development. They wanted to know how they could use FFAST with their CASE tools. So, what we have done now is we have taken two paths. We have built a FFAST version for the traditional software development people. That allows them to build a knowledge model and from there go to COBOL, PL1, or 4GL or any other language. The knowledge model is used as part of the system requirements definition. If it is determined that what is needed is an expert system, we proceed with our knowledge-based approach. You end up with two systems at that point—a production system and a knowledge-based maintenance system. Two separate pieces of software. The testing again is the current state at that point and it has two systems, two different end-users—the actual application user and the knowledge-base administrator. The "transition to user" phase would focus on those two people as well as the software maintenance people. They know what needs to be changed, when it needs to be changed. That is why we now have knowledge maintenance as a piece of software and the user does the maintenance without our involvement.

CASE STUDIES

Case Study I: Expertax

The ExperTax application was developed for Coopers and Lybrand's internal use about four years ago for corporate tax accrual (see Figure 9.11). We build an intelligent questionnaire to assess the tax situation for a corporation. We used the top tax experts in Coopers and Lybrand in the U.S. to develop the knowledge base. ExperTax is deployed on PC compatibles in all 95 Coopers and Lybrand's U.S. offices. Eleven hundred tax advisors, tax experts that work with client corporations, use it on a PC laptop. The tax reform of 1986 required complete

- CORPORATE TAX ACCRUAL AND PLANNING

- INTELLIGENT QUESTIONNAIRE CREATED

- COMBINED KNOWLEDGE OF OVER 40 EXPERTS

- OVER 3,600 FRAMES AND RULES

- DEPLOYED ON PC COMPATIBLES AT ALL 95 C&L OFFICES

- FIELD USE AT OVER 1,000 U.S. CORPORATE CLIENTS

- COMPLETE REVISION FOLLOWING TAX REFORM ACT OF 1986 TOOK ONE MONTH

- MAINTENANCE DONE BY C&L NATIONAL TAX GROUP

Figure 9.11.   ExperTax Fact Sheet

revision of the ExperTax knowledge base; it took only one month to make that calibration. The knowledge-base updates were done by the National Tax Group requiring no further involvement of the AI group.

This effort began before we developed FFAST, so we used PC-based shells as a modeling tool. We modeled one section of the questionnaire to test the concept. We tested it with 10 cases to validate the requirements at that point. Based on the requirements defined in Phase 1, we determined that ExperTax would be a stand-alone PC-based production system. We used a proprietary LISP-based inference engine called Qshell, for Questionnaire Shell, and a separate knowledge-base maintenance system (KBMS) for full consistency checking of the knowledge base.

Coopers and Lybrand EDP Quality Assurance team tested the software, just like any other piece of software before it is sent to the field. Forty cases of four different branches were tested. Tax specialists conducted the training. The knowledge base is maintained by the National Tax Group. The AI group is completely out of the loop. To me that's an important measure of success. ExperTax is used all over the country and is maintained by the end-user community, the owners of the expert system.

Case Study II: Reinsurance Underwriting

The REINSURANCE underwriting application was developed for a client company. Figure 9.12 contains the fact sheet for this case study.

The REINSURANCE system uses 80 screens. By 80 "screens" I mean that the end-users are used to seeing 80 different data forms and screen layouts. These

- ASSISTS IN UNDERWRITING REINSURANCE TREATY SUBMISSIONS

- AUTOMATED USE OF UNDERWRITING MANUAL

- PROTOTYPE: OVER 80 SCREENS AND 1169 ACTIVE FIELDS

- KNOWLEDGE BASE: 700 RULES AND 1200 FRAMES

- 3 EXPERTS

Figure 9.12. Reinsurance Underwriting Expert System Fact Sheet

screens were designed at the beginning of the development process. We used three expert underwriters to develop the knowledge base. We used FFAST to develop the knowledge model. A Symbolics 3670 was linked to DBase III on the PC. We used parallel requirement definitions for each underwriting phase. Because of the modularity of the methodology, we can build the requirements definition in parallel, separately, and then integrate them later. The system was delivered on a PS/2 platform linked to an IBM mainframe. FFAST is now also used as a knowledge-based maintenancy system on the TI MicroExplorer, by the end-users themselves.

Having a strong internal expert systems group, the client was able to take over the expert system development of REINSURANCE at the testing and maintenance phase. In most applications, we conduct the testing ourselves. We also conduct the maintenance phase, by training the knowledge-base administrators in using FFAST and in how to update the knowledge base.

BENEFITS

Figures 9.13, 9.14, and 9.15 summarize the benefits of using a structured methodology for the development of expert systems. What we have observed and experienced is that our development methodology allows you to build the re-

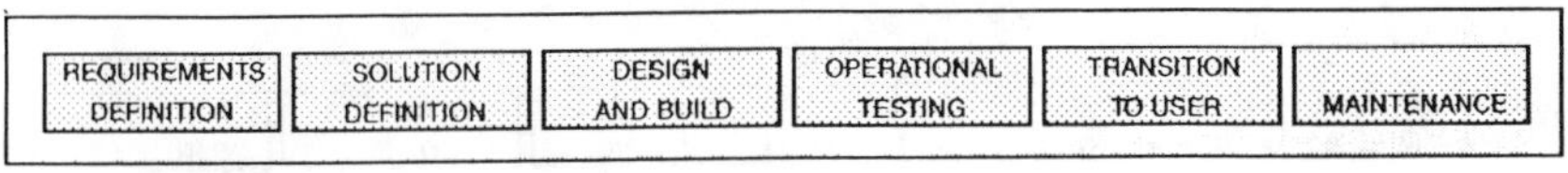

REQUIREMENTS DEFINITION	SOLUTION DEFINITION	DESIGN AND BUILD	OPERATIONAL TESTING	TRANSITION TO USER	MAINTENANCE

BENEFITS:
INCREMENTAL KNOWLEDGE MODELLING/PROTOTYPING

- DEVELOPMENT OF REQUIREMENTS DEFINITIONS FOR ILL-DEFINED PROBLEMS

- EXPERT INVOLVEMENT THROUGHOUT THE PROCESS

- MAINTAINS "BUSINESS-EVENT" PERSPECTIVE

- FULL VERIFICATION, VALIDATION, AND ACCEPTANCE BY THE USER

Figure 9.13. Coopers & Lybrand's Structured Methodology for Expert System Development

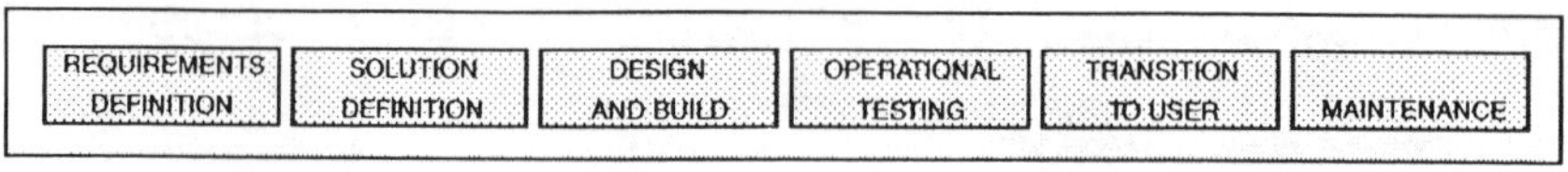

REQUIREMENTS DEFINITION	SOLUTION DEFINITION	DESIGN AND BUILD	OPERATIONAL TESTING	TRANSITION TO USER	MAINTENANCE

BENEFITS:

SEPARATION OF ORIGINAL KNOWLEDGE MODEL FROM DELIVERY SYSTEM

- POWERFUL DEVELOPMENT ENVIRONMENT

- OPTIMIZED, INTEGRATED DELIVERY ENVIRONMENT

Figure 9.14. Coopers & Lybrand's Structured Methodology for Expert System Development

quirement definitions for ill-defined problems, endemic in expert systems. The expert gets involved from the beginning, so there's ownership, early ownership, in the end results. The methodology enforces the maintenance of a business-event perspective, which impacts system maintenance throughout the life cycle of the software. You get full verification, validation, and acceptance by the end-user. The end-user sees how this system is going to look. They experience the eventual system's touch and feel in Phase 1, so they can impact how the system should be designed. From the development side, it allows you to eliminate a dependency from developers, very crucial in many industries. Knowledge-base management can and should be done by the users. Again it impacts the feeling of ownership and sustains continual evolution, as demonstrated in the ExperTax application.

Finally, we have observed that this methodology allows us to structure the development process itself, to have proper planning of the expert system development, and to maintain cost control. It also allows multiple member development teams, since you can split the system into pieces and modules. I believe we have a high degree of success for two main reasons: First, we know we are

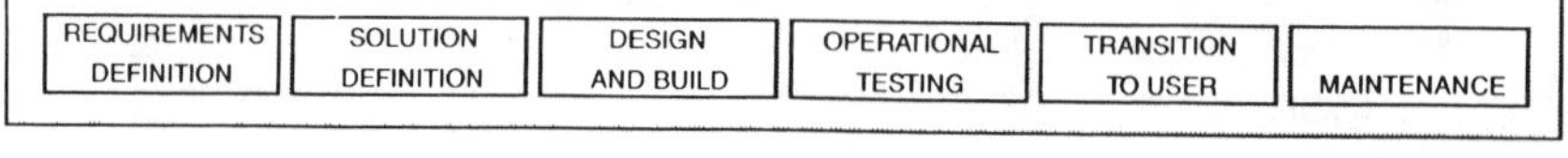

REQUIREMENTS DEFINITION	SOLUTION DEFINITION	DESIGN AND BUILD	OPERATIONAL TESTING	TRANSITION TO USER	MAINTENANCE

BENEFITS:

TWO-SYSTEMS: SEPARATING THE KNOWLEDGE BASE

- ELIMINATES DEPENDENCE ON ORIGINAL DEVELOPERS

- SYSTEM MANAGEMENT CAN BE DONE BY USERS

- SUSTAINS CONTINUAL EVOLUTION

Figure 9.15. Coopers & Lybrand's Structured Methodology for Expert System Development

meeting the requirements definition because we achieve a consensus at the beginning of what the requirements are; and secondly, management, experts, and end-users see a functional prototype of the eventual system before it is built. That, finally, ensures that the end-users will accept the final product.

10
Capital Expert System

Laurie Dowell
Jack Gary
William T. Illingworth
Tom Sargent

Texas Instruments, Inc.

Gathering information, necessary forms, and financial calculations needed to generate a "capital investment proposal" is an extremely complex and difficult process. The intent of the capital investment proposal is to assure management that the proposed investment has been thoroughly investigated and will have a positive impact on corporate goals. Meeting this requirement typically takes four or five experts a total of 12 hours to generate what is called a "capital package," or a request for investment. A Capital Expert System was therefore developed using Personal Consultant, a Texas Instruments AI software product. The completed system is hybrid and as such does not depend solely on rules but incorporates several different software packages that communicate through variables and functions passed from one to another. This chapter describes the use of expert system techniques, methodology in building the knowledge base, contexts, LISP functions, database, and special challenges that had to be overcome to create this system. The Capital Expert System is the successful result of a unique integration of artificial intelligence with business accounting, financial forms generation, and investment proposal expertise.

INTRODUCTION

Capital investment is required to sustain or improve business profitability. Industries that fail to invest capital may forfeit the ability to incorporate technological advances into their business plans and incur costs maintaining aging or obsolete equipment. If capital investments are not made for a protracted period of time, then higher product costs and loss of competitiveness in the marketplace can result.

A "Capital Authorization Request" (Figure 10.1), more popularly known as a capital package, is a financial proposal requesting management to make a capital investment. The intent of the capital package is to assure management that the

REQUIRED
DOCUMENTATION

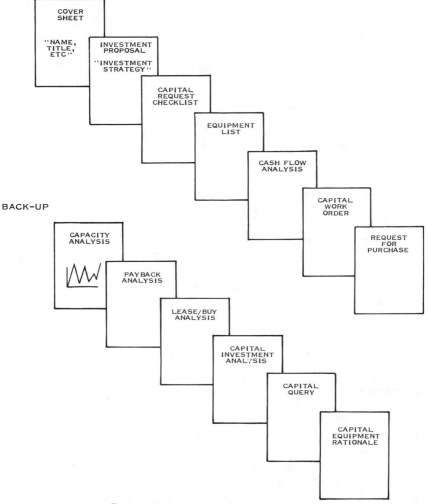

Figure 10.1.   The Capital Package

proposed investment has been thoroughly investigated and that it will be profitable and/or meet corporate goals. The package may be reviewed by as many as five levels of management; therefore, it must explicitly describe the total impact the capital investment will have on the organization's business strategies.

Gathering information, forms, and financial calculations needed to generate a capital package is an extremely complex and difficult process. Advice and help from many experts, especially in areas of engineering, manufacturing, product planning, facilities, financial planning, financial control, and capital administration are usually required to generate one capital package. Hours of consultation are required with many different experts to produce an economically justifiable and credible capital package. Inquiries indicate that 12 hours per package is not unusual, with the 12 hours usually spread over 5 to 10 days.

It became apparent that an expert system was needed for capital package generation. The Microwave Products Manufacturing Department within Texas Instruments decided to develop a system that would meet the following conditions. The system must:

1. Not be subjective.
2. Be extremely accurate and precise compared to manually generated packages.
3. Be highly productive.
4. Contain years of experience in multiple disciplines.
5. Ask pertinent questions.
6. Analyze requirements.
7. Recommend strategy and advise user.
8. Generate a "ready-to-present" capital package.
9. Perform on or above the level of human experts.
10. Possess the potential to become used company-wide (easy to use and run on a PC).

THE EXPERT SYSTEM

Description

The expert system was developed on a Texas Instruments PC using Personal Consultant, which is an Emycin-like program (Harmon & King, 1985) developed and marketed by Texas Instruments. The Capital Expert System is a backward chaining rules system that takes full advantage of Emycin's user-friendly interface and knowledge acquisition facilities. Use of Personal Consultant has accelerated development of the expert system (Figure 10.2). The completed Capital Expert System is a hybrid expert system. A hybrid does not depend solely on rules but incorporates several different software packages that communicate through variables and functions passed from one to another. In addition to Personal Consultant, the Capital Expert System was developed using IQ LISP and dBASE II.

The Domain

In 1985, the Defense Systems & Electronics Group (DSEG) of Texas Instruments management authorized over 1,500 capital packages. The packages origi-

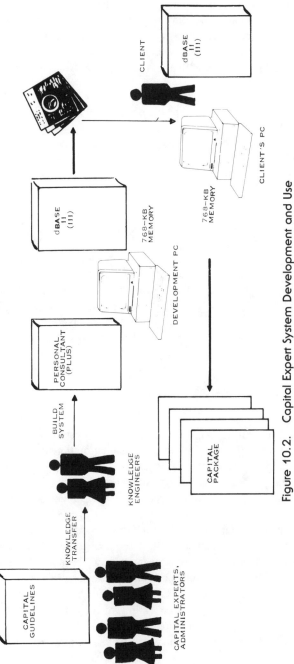

Figure 10.2. Capital Expert System Development and Use

nated from several hundred sources and used a variety of different engineering and accounting principles, making management's task of evaluating the packages difficult. Evaluation was further complicated by dissimilar forms of backup material used to support the packages. A technique to standardize the methodology used to generate packages was clearly needed.

Capital packages are classified into one or a combination of several categories including:

- Capacity.
- Cost reduction/productivity.
- Quality/reliability.
- Safety/legal/environmental.
- Development.
- New product.
- Sustaining/replacement.

The length of time required to manually generate a capital package depended on which category or categories the package qualified. A simple replacement package required half the documentation and a proportionate amount of time to prepare as did a capacity or productivity package. A cross-sampling of capital experts was polled to determine target times to complete ready-to-present capital packages. The times per category ranged between 4 and 15 hours distributed over 5 to 10 days.

The Consultation

A consultation with the Capital Expert System is a straightforward exercise that averages between 30 and 45 minutes. Consultation time depends on the number of items being requested, the user's familiarity with the items, and the category of the capital package. Previous consultations show that 70 percent of the consultation time is spent answering questions, 20 percent on computer computations, and 10 percent on printing forms.

During the consultation, the Capital Expert System will obtain pertinent information concerning the capital request by asking the client (user) a series of questions called prompts. These prompts have been designed to extract the information required to complete a capital package from a client unfamiliar with the capital guidelines. The client needs no prior knowledge of the capital process, but should have some understanding of the capital item being requested. The end result of the consultation is a ready-to-present capital package that contains all capital forms and backup documentation necessary to justify the capital request.

Use of Expert System Techniques

After the problem was selected, the next step was to analyze the knowledge to be included in the system and to select the proper tool. Harmon and King (1985) define knowledge acquisition as "the process the knowledge engineer goes through, studying the expert's behavior, uncovering the expert's underlying knowledge, and selecting and employing a tool to build a knowledge system." Basic information on how to complete a capital package can be found in the DSEG *Request for Capital Guidelines* (Texas Instruments Incorporated, 1986). These guidelines specify the required forms for a capital package, types of authorizations, rules for capitalization, and other pertinent information. The guidelines themselves represent many years of human expertise.

The heuristics, or "rules of thumb," were obtained from those familiar with presenting capital packages or the capital administrators and managers that reviewed the packages. A model expert system was built using the capital guidelines and the inputs from those in the Microwave Products organization that have prepared capital packages. Once the model was complete, demonstrations were held for a sample of the population of capital experts and administrators throughout the DSEG. The expert's recommendations and comments were recorded for later evaluation and incorporation. The demonstrations were a vehicle to acquire a vast assortment of expertise. However, the information was biased because of the inconsistency in the way capital packages were completed and reviewed. The knowledge engineers examined all of the inputs received and incorporated the most useful comments from the sample of capital experts into the expert system to create an efficient method for generating capital packages.

Choosing the proper tool to build the expert system was crucial to the development of the project. Personal Consultant was chosen to build the Capital Expert System for the following reasons:

1. The capital guidelines provide the rules for a rule-based system and are well suited to a backward-chaining and goal-oriented system like Personal Consultant. The rules are written in an if-then format and can be input easily in Abbreviated Rule Language (ARL).
2. Personal Consultant is user-friendly. The run-time version of the Capital Expert System uses menu selections to speed up consultation time and has help-functions for every question the user must answer.
3. The client copy may be distributed on a diskette for use on the Texas Instruments PC.
4. It is easy to update rules and parameters.
5. The improvements that will occur with conversion to Personal Consultant Plus include: conversion to PC Scheme, use of a full screen editor, speed of execution, doubled knowledge-base capacity, and integrated graphics capabilities.

Building the Knowledge Base

The knowledge-base development may be divided into five categories:

- Rules
- Parameters
- LISP functions
- Contexts
- Databases

A detailed explanation of each category follows below.

Rules. Rules represent the relationship between a parameter (variable) and its value. Rules also enable Personal Consultant to determine the solution to the problem. As previously stated, the basic rules for the Capital Expert System were obtained from the capital guidelines and the heuristic rules from consultations with a sample of capital administrators and package preparers.

The functions of the rule in the Capital Expert System are:

1. *Knowledge representation*. Rules are written in an "if-then" format. An example of a rule from the Capital Expert System is shown in Figure 10.3.
2. *Determination of flow of consultation*. Personal Consultant uses backward chaining or goal-oriented control to determine the flow of the consultation.
3. *Performance of simple calculations*. Elementary calculations are done within the rules using IQ LISP.
4. *Invocation of functions*. Since the Capital Expert System is a hybrid system that requires several calculations, database management, and printing of forms, several developer defined LISP functions are required. Functions are called or invoked inside rules to ensure their evaluation at the proper time.

Parameters. Parameters are used in Personal Consultant to save or store information in the knowledge base.

Parameters uses include:

1. *Variables*. Parameters may be compared to variables. In Figure 10.3, "item" is a variable that represents the name of the object requiring capital investment.

IF: The cost of the item is greater than or equal to 1,000 **AND** the useful life is greater or equal to 2 years **AND** the item is not software.

THEN: It is 100 percent definite the item is capitalized.

Figure 10.3.   Sample Rule

2. *User interface*. Parameters have properties that supply the question the user sees as well as the help function, if necessary.
3. *Goals*. Goals are stored in parameters. For example, the goal of the context FORM-GEN is forms (Figure 10.4).

LISP functions. The Capital Expert System contains a vast number of developer-defined LISP functions that serve the following purposes:

1. *Create dBASE II programs*. Developer-defined functions are invoked in the "action" of rules that write dBASE II command files that execute the dBASE II calculations and database management. This is done by writing LISP code that opens a command file as the output file, writes the dBASE II commands, and closes the output file.
2. *Graphics*. Graphics are invoked inside rules, contexts, and parameters. LISP is used to clear the screen, display the graphics, and return the Personal Consultant screen. The graphics are presently loaded onto the disk in compressed format.
3. *Open and close external files*. Developer-defined functions, invoked by rules, are used to open and close dBase II command files, print files, and input/output files. Once the files are opened, the data are manipulated or sent to output, then the files are closed.
4. *Print out forms*. Developer-defined functions are invoked by rules that open an output file as a print file, pass the parameter values from Personal Consultant to LISP as variables, and use "PRINT" commands to print out the forms. LISP functions print out the following forms: Cover Sheet, Investment Proposal, Capital Authorization Checklist, Capital Work Order (CWO), Facilities CWO, and capital package Analysis Sheet.
5. *Call dBASE II*. LISP functions allocate memory and load and execute dBASE II software using dBASE II command files.

```
FORM-GEN  [CONTEXTTYPES]
-----
TRANS: (this context will generate and print the proper forms)
INITIALDATA: NIL
GOALS: (FORMS)
RULETYPES: (FORM-GENRULES)
PARMGROUP: FORM-GEN-PARMS
PRINTID: FORM-GEN-
UNIQUE: T
PROMPT1ST: (Would you like to generate a capital package?)
ADDOCWITH: (PACK-TYPE CAP-JUST)
```

Figure 10.4. The Context FORM-GEN

Contexts. The purpose of the contexts is to separate the knowledge base into subtopics. The context organization is illustrated in Figure 10.4. The contexts are: Capital Justification, Capital Expenditure, Package Type, and Form Generation.

Databases. The need for data management capabilities in the Capital Expert System became apparent as the system was developed. Database capabilities are required in the knowledge base to store large amounts of data, to perform large calculations, and to generate forms. The dBASE II program was chosen over dBASE III as the software database manager because of the small amount of memory required (128 K) that allows sharing of memory on the run-time copy. Database capabilities are presented in the following lists.

1. *Store/save consultation information.* Data required to complete the Equipment List is prompted for in both the Capital Expenditure and Capital Justification contexts. This information must be stored in a database until the form is printed in the Form Generation context. The information will be retrieved and manipulated for other forms and calculations.
2. *Storage of constant information.* The Capital Expert System stores in a dBASE II file constants that are used in calculations and form generation. These constants are product build schedules, labor rates, and overhead rates. These database tables must be easily updated as changes occur and dBASE II allows this capability.
3. *Calculations.* dBASE II files are set up for payback analysis, capacity analysis, and depreciation.
4. *Form generation.* The following forms are printed as dBASE II reports: Equipment List, Payback Analysis, and Capacity Analysis.

The System

The Capital Expert System emulates the flow that a capital package originator goes through to complete a package. Personal Consultant organizes the knowledge base with the use of contexts. Each context represents a section or a subdivision of the problem. The developer specifies the number of instantiations of the context that may occur during any consultation. Personal Consultant provides the developer with the choice of instantiating a context "exactly once," "at most once," "at least once," or an unknown amount of times. The number of instantiations is determined by the values of the PROMPTEVER, PROMPT1ST, and PROMPT2ND context properties (Figure 10.5).

1. *Capital Justification.* The root context that is instantiated only once. Basic information about the user is prompted for in Capital Justification, along with unique items that are written to the Equipment List but are not standard equipment. The system prompts the user to determine if a facilities estimate is required

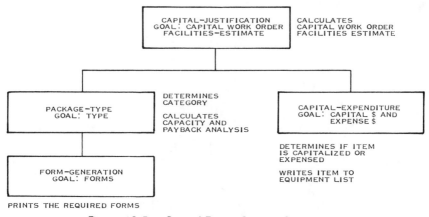

Figure 10.5. Capital Expert System Context Tree

and allows the user to enter the facilities amount. The Capital Expert System will, if required, prompt the user for CWO data and do the required calculations (Figure 10.6.)

2. *Capital Expense.* A child (subordinate) context to Capital Justification that is instantiated according to the number of items on the Equipment List. The Capital Expert System prompts the user for basic information about each item: description, cost, vendor, and quantity. The system determines whether the item is capitalized or expensed and writes the item to the Equipment List (Figure 10.7).

3. *Package Type.* Also a child context to Capital Justification that is instantiated exactly once per consultation. The Capital Expert System asks the user a series of questions to determine the category of the package. If the category is Capacity or Cost Reduction/Productivity, then further calculations are required. The system prompts the client for capacity data, informs the user of the required number of machines, and makes its recommendation. If a payback analysis is required, the system does the calculations, informs the client of the payback time in months, and makes a decision about the quality of the investment (see Figure 10.8).

4. *Form Generation.* A child context to Package Type and Capital Justification that is instantiated at most one time. In this context the Capital Expert System performs the depreciation calculations and retrieves and manipulates previous inputs. The user is prompted for the remaining information (mainly text) required to complete the capital forms. Personal Consultant invokes LISP functions that print the forms: Cover Sheet, Investment Proposal, Equipment List, Payback Analysis (as required), Capacity Analysis (as required), Capital Authorization Checklist, CWO (as required), Facilities CWO (as required), and the capital package Analysis (Figure 10.9).

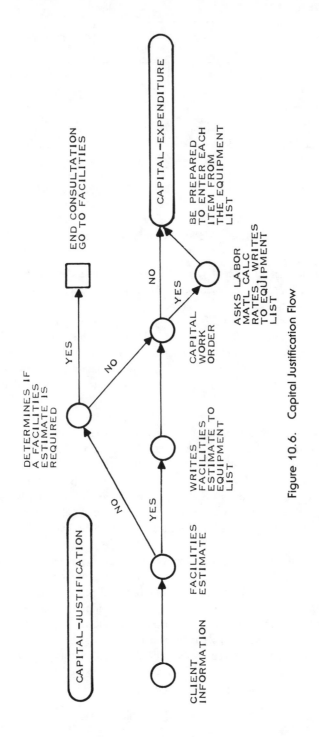

Figure 10.6. Capital Justification Flow

154

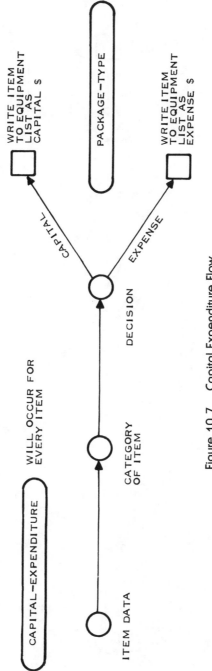

Figure 10.7. Capital Expenditure Flow

155

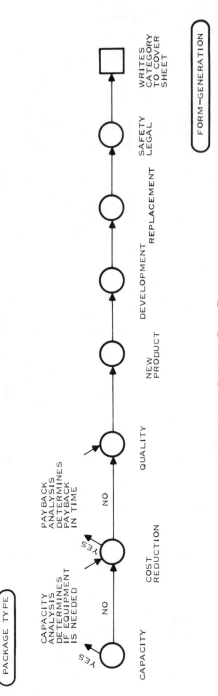

Figure 10.8. Package Type Flow

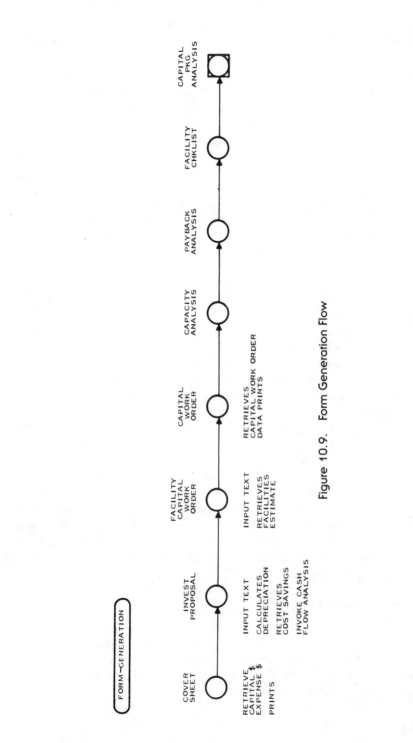

FORM-GENERATION

COVER
SHEET

RETRIEVE$
CAPITAL $
EXPENSE

PRINTS

INVEST
PROPOSAL

INPUT TEXT

CALCULATES
DEPRECIATION

RETRIEVES
COST SAVINGS

INVOKE CASH
FLOW ANALYSIS

FACILITY
CAPITAL
WORK
ORDER

INPUT TEXT

RETRIEVES
FACILITIES
ESTIMATE

CAPITAL
WORK
ORDER

RETRIEVES
CAPITAL WORK ORDER
DATA PRINTS

CAPACITY
ANALYSIS

PAYBACK
ANALYSIS

FACILITY
CHKLIST

CAPITAL
PKG
ANALYSIS

Figure 10.9. Form Generation Flow

Special Challenges

Data management problems arose during the attempt to build and manipulate an unknown number of files. The solution employed LISP functions invoked by Personal Consultant to write and execute a dBASE II program file and read the data back into Personal Consultant.

Memory problems became apparent when Personal Consultant, IQ LISP, and dBASE II were creating errors when approaching memory limitations of the system hardware (768 kilobytes). This resulted in an inability to initialize and assign variables. Other failures occurred to the hardware, especially to the keyboard, printer, and disk. The solution was to convert the system development version to swap out memory to a RAM disk when the system is required to perform data management routines using dBASE II. As the number and size of LISP functions grew, it became apparent that more memory problems would soon arise. To prevent additional problems, we made the large LISP functions disk interactive. This was accomplished by defining small memory-resident LISP functions that load, execute, and clear large LISP functions in memory as needed for execution.

The Capital Expert System requires extensive calculations and data management that far exceed the scope of Personal Consultant. The solution required the development of a hybrid expert system that performs most of the calculations and data storage/retrieval functions outside Personal Consultant. This is accomplished through the use of LISP functions alone or LISP functions invoking dBASE II.

When using Ashton Tate's dBASE II software for the data management of the Capital Expert System, two problems arose. The first problem was that dBASE II did not always read the entire contents of a program file written by LISP; the last 128-byte block of the program file were not always read. This problem was solved by adding four comment lines onto the end of the program file where it would not affect the program evaluation if the last four lines were not read and executed. The second problem occurred while performing nested Do-While and If-Then loops; dBASE II would lose its value of the variables. This problem was solved by frequently reassigning the correct values to the variables while nesting.

System Advantages

The Capital Expert System (see Figure 10.1 for a complete view of the system) has several advantages over creating a package manually including standard format, adherence to all guidelines, internal build schedule, financial planning approval, capital package analysis, and ease of updating.

- *Standard Format.* All capital packages will use the proper forms and accounting principles. This will provide management with a better means to evaluate capital proposals.
- *Capital Guidelines.* The Capital Expert System will ask for all pertinent information, not allowing the user to overlook any minute details.
- *Internal Build Schedule.* The internal build schedule, with its own update program, will allow end users to easily customize the build schedule to their application and to keep it current.
- *Financial Planning.* The system incorporates the recommendations of financial planning in its rules and calculations.
- *Capital Package Analysis.* A unique advantage of the Capital Expert System is the generation of a package analysis that informs the end user of the quality of the capital investment. The capital package analysis contains the Expert System's recommendations and the sign-off cycle with support data for capacity and cost reduction calculations.
- *Easy Updating and Maintenance.* The modular nature of the Capital Expert System allows easy updating and maintenance. Rules and databases can be removed, added, or changed without effecting the entire system (see Figure 10.10).

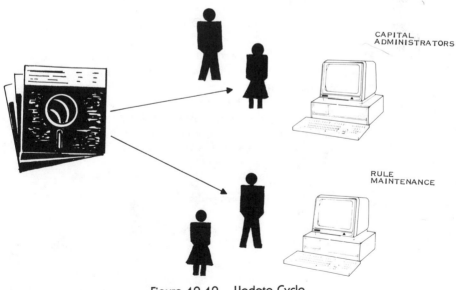

CAPITAL
ADMINISTRATORS

RULE
MAINTENANCE

Figure 10.10. Update Cycle

System Status and Plans

Knowledge engineers are currently evaluating and incorporating expert knowledge obtained from a sample population of capital experts, capital administrators, and financial planners. This knowledge will be used to make a complete general application that can be used throughout Texas Instruments. Financial Planning is also in the process of changing the capital request forms and capital guidelines. The Capital Expert System will be updated as changes are made. Plans include incorporating expert system defined graphics into the Capital Expert System to generate a capacity graph, when required.

The Capital Expert System will go through an extensive validation procedure by using Beta test users to surface possible problems. On completion of this testing cycle, the Capital Expert System will be available throughout Capital Accounting and the Information Centers. Currently, the Capital Expert System is undergoing conversion to Personal Consultant Plus and PC Scheme, which are AI software products of Texas Instruments. Once the knowledge base is converted, enhancements that are possible with the use of Personal Consultant Plus will be added. Since most consultations with the Capital Expert System will engage accounting and financial control people, it would be advantageous to have voice interaction with the computer. Future plans for the Capital Expert System include the addition of synthetic speech as the output and voice recognition as the system input.

CONCLUSION

The Capital Expert System is the end product of an unusual blending of artificial intelligence with capital accounting and investment expertise. Further integration of capital investment rules with an external database has resulted in a unique hybrid expert system. Employing this system in the preparation of a capital investment package not only provides the user with a ten-to-one productivity increase but ensures the user of an extremely accurate, very credible, and economically justifiable capital package ready for presentation.

REFERENCES

Harmon, P., & King, D. (1985). *Expert systems*. New York: John Wiley.
Texas Instruments Incorporated. (1986). *Request for capital guidelines*. Dallas, TX.

11

Expert Systems in Auditing and Aerospace Engineering

Bert L. Bivens

Lockheed Aeronautical Systems Company

A number of expert systems, either completed, under development, or being planned, are discussed. These include MEDCHEC, an expert medical insurance claims auditor; COMPOSER, an expert design aid for structural engineers working with composite materials; ATEX, an aircraft technician's diagnosis and repair assistant; and MSCST, a family of specialized aids to provide producibility expertise to engineering designers of thermoplastic composite parts. Two expert systems projects under study for future development are presented. Motivation and rationale for developing each system and development experiences are covered. The issue of "Why expert systems?" is examined, followed by a chapter summary that emphasizes that expert systems have arrived as useful tools in production settings.

INTRODUCTION

Lockheed is a large corporation with 100,000 employees. Throughout the corporation and our different companies a number of AI efforts are ongoing. These projects are so diffuse that the exact number of people really doing AI in the corporation is unknown; a good estimate would be at least 150 and probably more. This chapter focuses on work that is being done at the Information Services Branch of the Lockheed Aeronautical Systems Company (LASC).

LASC initiated efforts during 1986 to provide expert system development services for internal company applications. This startup work was premised on its being self-supporting, meaning that individual projects would be funded by their end-user organizations. This premise injected technical personnel into a marketing role, which included selecting good projects, justifying their selection using return on investment (ROI) criteria, and securing funding from skeptical, if not reluctant, user management.

One completed expert system, several currently under development, and some candidate systems for future development will be discussed in this chapter, providing a flavor of the range of potential areas where the technology can be applied. A descriptive summary of the systems is represented in Figure 11.1.

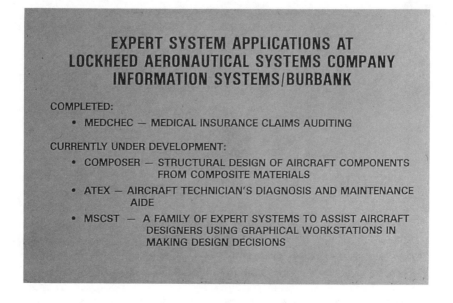

Figure 11.1.   Expert Systems Applications at Lockheed Aeronautical Systems Company Information Systems/Burbank

MEDICAL INSURANCE CLAIMS AUDITING

In looking for a suitable first application candidate expert system, the initial sifting process stimulated the interest of the manager of LASC's in-house group insurance operation. Due to rapidly rising medical costs, the company's commitment to provide medical insurance to employees and their dependents strongly impacted overhead expenditures.

As a cost-containment measure and as good business practice, group insurance was responsible for evaluating whether claims for compensation received from employees, physicians, hospitals, and laboratories were valid and payable under the rules set forth. Industry-wide experience suggested that 10 to 12 percent of the total dollar value of such claims were either fraudulent or over-billed.

An auditing team, consisting of a certified public accountant and two former claims processors, had been established to review claims after their receipt and processing. The volume of claims varied from 800 to 1,000 per working day. One auditor could manually audit a maximum of approximately 20 claims per day; therefore, the team of three auditors audited less than 10 percent of the daily claims. However, they had developed rules for selecting claims to audit and items to look for that improved their ability to locate illegitimate claims of high value more successfully than using random spot audits. The auditors were convinced that if an augmented set of the rules they used could be computerized, significant reductions in total claims expenditures could be achieved.

We were asked by our insurance risk manager to evaluate whether expert systems technology could be applied to help reduce claims expenditures. As a result of his request, we performed a cost benefit analysis of using an expert system. We estimated how much it would cost and he helped us estimate what the potential benefit of the system might be. A development plan was prepared, submitted to management, and approved.

The expert system, called MEDCHEC (MEDical CHarge Evaluation and Control), was developed over an eight-month period. Knowledge acquisition interviews with the auditors, a Lockheed physician, and the claims processors produced a knowledge base from which the logical underpinnings of MEDCHEC were created. Examples of rules in the knowledge base are:

- "The assistant surgeon's bill should not exceed 20% of the surgeon's bill."
- "If the lab tests that comprise a test panel are billed individually, they should be billed collectively as a panel and at a reduced rate."
- "There should not be bills for more than three consecutive physical therapy sessions without an intervening doctor's visit."

One thing to note about these rules is that some of them cannot be resolved solely by looking at a single claim. For example, if either a surgeon's bill or an assistant surgeon's bill is received, it cannot be resolved until the other bill is received. In this case, the first claim is put on hold pending receipt of the second claim so they can be compared and considered together. Likewise, a number of rules allow claims to be viewed in a historical context, utilizing information about both the patient's medical history and the claimant's billing history. Access to history files was often crucial for making good judgments about the validity of current claims.

Additional (nonmedical) rules were also needed because the expert system runs on a different computer than the claims transaction processing. These additional rules supported communication between the dissimilar computer types and controlled the overall auditing process. We had a very specialized minicomputer (sold by McDonnell Douglas and called Microdata). It used the Pick operating system and software written in Basic. This system was not easily integratable with existing AI software on our expert system computer, which was a Symbolics. A large part of our effort was involved in the interface between these two computers. On the Symbolics side, at least 50 percent of the rules we had to write had nothing to do with the medical insurance domain—they were simply related to communications.

MEDCHEC was developed to run at night after all claims data for the day had been computerized. Insurance claims were entered into the claims computer each working day by a group of claims processors, who make on-the-fly decisions about payments. At night, after the claims processing personnel have completed the day's transactions, the transaction data and associated employee and provider history data are brought over to the MEDCHEC computer. MEDCHEC analyzes the transactions one by one, comparing their individual circumstances (including historical facts) against predetermined auditing rules. MEDCHEC's analysis of the claims data preceded preparation of reports for further analysis by human auditors the following work day. The reports listed those transactions the auditors should analyze further and described what factors made those transactions good candidates for auditing.

In terms of results, MEDCHEC was able to audit 100 percent of the claims every night. In addition, detection of flagrant billing errors enabled MEDCHEC to instruct the check processing system to put automatic holds on payments. Starting from the first week of trials on the prototype version of MEDCHEC, hard savings averaging $1,500 per day were achieved. This dollar savings was sufficient to reimburse development costs in approximately five months. The prototype was quickly placed in production and used regularly thereafter.

For my organization, a very favorable result was that the climate for additional expert systems was greatly improved throughout the company.

STRUCTURAL ENGINEERING DESIGN AID

A second project for the Information Services AI group is currently under development to support the solution of a difficult engineering design problem. Performance requirements of new aircraft models dictate the use of materials that have higher strength-to-weight ratios than traditional metallic alloys. One such class of materials, called composites, combines dissimilar substances to produce new materials and unique properties. Composites aren't anything new. The Egyptians made bricks 2,000 years ago by mixing straw with clay, but such strategies have only begun quite recently in the aircraft business. The move to composites is accelerating rapidly.

A common type of composite in use today consists of high strength fibers (graphite, Kevlar, etc.), embedded in a resinous material. Vendors supply composite materials in rolls, ready for use by parts fabricators. A fiber generally has great strength along the fiber axis but not perpendicular to the axis. To satisfy the strength and stiffness requirements for a particular part, layers (plies) of these materials are combined together with each ply oriented to provide the structural characteristics required in a given direction.

Once detailed structural design requirements are known, it becomes necessary to determine the total number of plies needed and how many (and which ones) must be oriented in each of the required directions. If, for example, it is determined that 80 plies are required for a given part (such as a wing skin panel), the optimum orientation of each ply must then be determined. As the number of plies increases, the number of combinations of possible ply orientations becomes extremely large, and optimal (or near optimal) design choices are increasingly difficult and time consuming to find.

Designers select a design using rough rules of thumb and then submit the design to specialized analysis programs to determine whether it satisfies structural requirements. If the requirements are not satisfied, the designer analyzes how the design's actual performance varies from the required performance, refines the design, and repeats the process.

Expert designers can develop a near optimal design in as few as six iterations, but an inexperienced designer may require as many as 100 iterations to develop a comparable design. Existing software tools to help designers are fairly limited because this is such a new technology. Because of the scarcity of expert designers and support tools, and because of the rapidly increasing demand for composite designs, a project was initiated to capture the expert's knowledge and embed it into an expert system, thus making it available to all composite designers—the good and the not so good. This expert system will provide a valuable new resource.

Another interesting angle on scarce expertise is the artificial scarcity imposed by having to work on classified projects. In the military aircraft business we have a lot of classified projects and no one expert is cleared to work on all projects. So it would be very nice to be able to take a particular engineer's expertise and make it available where needed. We hoped to do this using AI technology.

An expert system, called COMPOSER (COMPosites Orientation and Stacking Expert Reasoner), was started in the spring of 1987. The approach used was to select an expert in the composites knowledge domain. Sometimes experts don't want to give up their knowledge, but in this case, our expert was nearing retirement age and was very anxious for the company to have his knowledge after he left. Knowledge acquisition sessions were conducted to determine the processes used by our expert. A knowledge representation strategy was developed, leading to an expert system prototype. Production designers were allowed to test the prototype and recommend improvements. The prototype was iteratively refined until it satisfied end-user requirements.

COMPOSER has now progressed to an operational prototype, which is in the process of being further refined. COMPOSER asks the designer to specify design requirements, material properties, and loading conditions; then, using rules specified by the human expert, it automatically generates a trial design. COMPOSER works interactively with a designer, allowing user intervention during the design process. Rules are also available to assist the user in refining the trial design, as desired.

Once a design is established, COMPOSER automatically generates the input

file required for the analysis program, submits the file to the program for execution, retrieves the output file, analyzes the answers, and recommends additional
design refinements. In a few hours, a design can be developed that would take an
inexperienced designer days or weeks using a manual process. Much of the
drudgery associated with setting up the input data file and submitting it to the
analysis program has been automated, contributing to the very rapid and error-
free nature of the process.

In addition to the expected direct labor-hour savings, a more financially
rewarding aspect of applying expert system methods to the engineering design
process results from the reduction of design time span. On a large project,
utilizing hundreds of engineering personnel, trimming one month from the total
aircraft design span will save millions of dollars. Shaving off even a few days
can save hundreds of thousands of dollars.

To date this expert systems development project has stayed on schedule and
within budget. Early tests of the initial operational prototype that is being tested
in a production environment indicate that considerable design acceleration will
be possible. Technical results to date have favorably impressed those who have
witnessed demonstrations of the current system. Planned refinements will produce additional cost reductions. An operational system target date of midyear
1989 appears to be very promising.

The success of the COMPOSER project stems from a variety of sources. The
foremost source is teaming with a willing, motivated expert. The use of state-of-
the-art inference engine technology—high quality development tools—was also
crucial. We wanted to use the best tools we could. For a shell we selected the
Automated Reasoning Tool (ART) marketed by Inference Corporation. We used
the high quality development environment on the Symbolics LISP machine. In
this effort, we also used an experienced expert system developer as a consultant
to reduce the project's risk.

The primary difficulty in the project was the restricted availability of the
domain expert. This individual was in great demand. Getting him away from the
projects that use him was difficult. Since we couldn't get very big slices of his
time, we planned very carefully so that when he was available we knew exactly
how we were going to use his time.

AIRCRAFT TECHNICIAN'S EXPERT SYSTEM (ATEX)

LASC's Product Support organization is concerned with assisting purchasers of
the company's products in keeping them in working order. Military aircraft are
increasingly sophisticated but must be maintained by military personnel who are
constantly being rotated to new assignments, shifted from one type of aircraft to
another, are often inexperienced, or who may not re-enlist after becoming skilled.

Maintenance manuals are becoming massive, post-flight data available for analysis is increasing with every new generation of aircraft, and higher aircraft performance levels demand improved maintenance at lower cost. Because of this, the trend in recent years has been to use artificial intelligence methods to meet the maintenance requirements of increasingly complex and sophisticated aircraft.

There are at least three main sources of data for this problem. One is the pilot debriefing. When pilots return from a flight, they use a debriefing station for communicating with a mainframe computer about problems encountered during their flight. A second information source is on-board computers. These constantly monitor test points, in some cases up to 10,000, during flight. The third source is maintenance manuals. The weight of maintenance manuals for the B1-B bomber exceeds the weight of the bomber. Clearly electronic methods are required to reduce this bulk and to facilitate information retrieval.

The general idea for ATEX is to download relevant subsets of these three sources of data into a portable computer that an aircraft technician can carry to the flight line. The computer-based expert maintenance aid will assist the technician in fault detection and isolation and provide advice in performing needed repairs. This work started in 1988 at LASC and will be an ongoing project for a number of years. It is expected that all future military aircraft will use this type of technology.

MANUFACTURING SCIENCE OF COMPLEX SHAPE THERMOPLASTICS (MSCST)

In 1987, LASC started work on the MSCST project, an Air Force contract to push the state of the art in building aircraft parts from a new kind of composite materials called thermoplastics. As part of this contract, LASC agreed to develop a product definition system architecture, and to create expert systems to assist aircraft modelers/designers. Three-dimensional modeling systems are being used to develop the geometric descriptions of aircraft parts, but developing the geometry requires designers to be knowledgeable about material properties, cost modeling, factory processes, and producibility constraints.

Since this information/knowledge is not yet available for advanced materials like thermoplastics, it was decided to encode the knowledge into computer-resident form as it is being developed through basic research. Thus, properties of these new materials are available through queries from designers during the modeling process.

Figure 11.2 presents a graphical representation of our product definition system architecture. The box on the left shows the process of collecting and developing knowledge that is needed about these materials. The knowledge bases in the center—quite a number of knowledge bases—hold different aspects of the information needed. This family of knowledge bases provides knowledge about

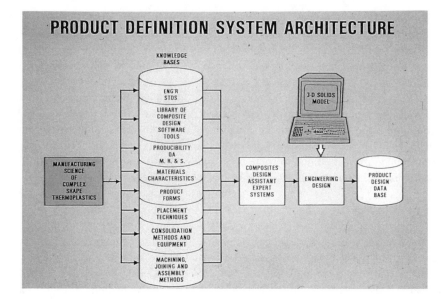

Figure 11.2.   Product Definition System Architecture

specialized niches of the design process, such as material selection, consolidation, heat transfer, joining and forming, tool design, and costing. The expert systems will be able to access these knowledge bases and communicate with designers working in a CAD environment to produce designs that then go into a design database. The design database is passed to the computer integrated manufacturing cycle where it is used by tool designers as well as manufacturing personnel.

As engineers design a new thermoplastic part at a CAD workstation, they need information. They need to know what kinds of material are being used, what are the properties of those materials, and how they interact with the geometry of the part. For instance, certain kinds of materials may be capable of only being bent a certain number of degrees without breaking. The problem is to bring the right information to the attention of the designer at the right time with a minimum of effort being required on his part.

In current CAD environments it is very difficult to design a part that is producible the first time it is sent to the factory floor. As a result, many designs are sent back from manufacturing to the designer for rework. This process is very expensive and inefficient. We would like to be able to develop producible designs the first time.

Because this design knowledge involves many different areas of specialization, a number of individuals are required to supply all the knowledge needed for particular designs. We hope to centralize that knowledge into expert systems and to integrate these expert systems with a 3-D CAD system on common hardware so that getting the right information at the right time is easy.

Work has begun on the material selection expert system, and several of these systems will be operable in late 1989.

CONCEPTS FOR FUTURE PROJECTS

The following are a few concepts being analyzed and debated for possible future implementation.

Proposal Development

A principal activity of businesses, especially major defense contractors, is writing proposals. Proposal development is a highly specialized domain of expertise, which in turn relies on other domains of expertise for much of its content. Most proposals are written in response to a "Request for Proposal" (RFP) issued by the contracting agency. With minor variations between various agencies, most RFPs follow a general pattern while imposing specific requirements that each responding company needs to address to improve its chance of winning the competition.

Generally, proposals must be written in a few weeks or months, depending upon their size. The time is invariably too short, making respondents feel they could have performed better if they had more time. Analysis of the proposal development process has uncovered a number of areas ripe for automation.

Development of the Requirements Interface Matrix (RIM), for example, is a time-consuming process undertaken early in proposal development to assure that requested items in the RFP are addressed. By optically scanning the RFP document, and putting its text into a computer, the RFP can be searched for key words, such as locating "shalls" and "wills" which require a response.

An expert system could be written to control and monitor this process. Likewise, once the proposal development process is underway, the inverse of the RIM, known as the compliance matrix, could be monitored by an online system that continuously reviews material supplied by the various proposal authors. Information fed to the proposal manager by an expert proposal monitoring system on a daily basis would assure that there are no missing items. A number of other ideas for assisting individual authors and tracking the proposal development process have been suggested. These artificial intelligence components would be combined with conventional software, procedural innovations, and specialized hardware to provide an integrated systems solution. An overview of the proposal authoring and management system is provided in Figure 11.3.

Management Control and Information System (MCIS)

To assist in the management of defense contracts, LASC is developing an online system (MCIS), capable of presenting current status information on all aspects of a project's technical, manufacturing, budgetary, and schedule histories. Specific requests for information cause MCIS to extract it from appropriate databases, formulate it into user-friendly formats, and display it back to the requester through color graphics. Access to the system will be provided to customers, team partners, vendors, and in-house users, with appropriate security controls.

A bottleneck is presented by the need for the manager-user of the system to explain to the computer just what needs to be displayed. High level managers, many of them at least, tend not to be comfortable with using computer systems. Further, they often progressively converge on which information they want or need but have difficulty in explaining what information they want at the outset. Often the information they want is of an ad hoc nature. Even carefully planned menus designed to show standardized types of information may not cover what a manager is interested in. While the answer to such an ad hoc query would be in

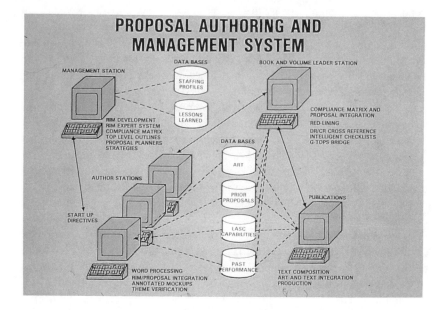

Figure 11.3. Proposal Authoring and Management System

the system, the lack of a menu to index it may require specialized database query knowledge that a manager ordinarily would not have or be expected to have.

Under consideration is how best to build expert system interfaces that can conduct dialogues with users unskilled in database query, determine exactly what information they desire, and automatically structure the queries needed to retrieve and present that information.

Keyboard entry is generally not effective for high level management personnel. Many managers are not comfortable with typing. Thus, our planning includes the eventual addition of voice recognition equipment to the system to allow the user to talk to the computer instead of using a keyboard.

The planned approach is to equip terminals with additional hardware that can convert spoken commands into strings of phonemes. Software would convert phoneme strings into readable text using knowledge of what types of queries to expect. Once the translation into natural language is complete, an expert system —using some of the same knowledge about query intent—would generate the appropriate database query formats. This type of interface has great potential for widening the use of information tools to those who can use most advantageously the information they have to offer—high-level executives. Such systems today are very experimental and border the edge of feasibility.

WHY EXPERT SYSTEMS?

All of these projects could be accomplished with "conventional" software techniques. However, using an expert system shell avoids the problem of recreating the inferencing logic for each program. Further, using a sophisticated development environment greatly accelerates the rate of development and lowers the cost. Having the program written in the form of rules that can be easily read, deciphered, and modified greatly simplifies maintenance and lowers life cycle cost. Fast prototyping methods allow concepts to be tested quickly and discarded if nonoptimal.

The difference between an expert system and conventional software is the separation of the inference engine from the domain knowledge. Inference engines can be written in virtually any computer language. An expert system shell is a program that includes an inference engine and allows for insertion of specific knowledge bases. But in order to satisfy the types of applications presented, it is not necessary—only desirable—to separate the inference technology from the knowledge base. For years we mixed them all together. It's not a very neat and clean way to do it, but that's the way software was always developed before expert system technology.

There is a downside to using expert systems. If you use the most sophisticated hardware tools to get into the game, the ante is high. Experienced and knowledgeable AI practitioners are scarce, and they command higher salaries. The technology has a different feel to it. Attitudes about it are sometimes negative, and it normally requires an adjustment period before it takes root in an organization. Porting software to conventional hardware environments may be difficult.

SUMMARY

Expert systems technology has arrived, and although it has caused some birth pangs, it seems to be here to stay. Expert systems provide terrific competitive advantages to those who have them against those who don't. Introduction of new technology into an organization often triggers waves of new thinking about how to improve the ways for conducting business.

A variety of applications of expert systems technologies has been discussed. New ways to apply the technology are being uncovered daily. Awareness of the potential of expert systems will lead to increasingly broad use of the technology in many areas of business. These applications will have dramatic, positive effects on productivity, product quality, and profits.

12
Achieving Competitive Advantage in Manufacturing with Knowledge Systems

Perry W. Thorndyke

FMC Corporation

Manufacturing, a dominant sector in the United States economy, provides a fertile area for intelligent automation. Knowledge systems are finding broad application to manufacturing operations in FMC Corporation, a diversified machinery and chemicals company. Four manufacturing applications of knowledge systems at FMC are presented as examples of the use of the technology to enhance competitiveness. The applications span manufacturing from design to production planning and production control. They include the automated specification of wellhead components and materials, the development of product blends in a carrageenan plant, control of raw material inflow in a phosphorous plant, and an automated part gaging and inspection system. Benefits obtained from these applications are presented along with a vision of the potential AI technology has for the future of manufacturing.

MANUFACTURING PRODUCTIVITY AND KNOWLEDGE BOTTLENECKS

This chapter focuses on manufacturing and indicates some of the approaches FMC has taken to achieve competitive advantage in manufacturing through the use of knowledge systems. Within FMC, knowledge systems technology is being applied to all business functions. However, as a manufacturing company FMC can particularly benefit from high quality and cost-effective manufacturing processes. Manufacturing holds the key to competitive advantage in many of FMC's businesses.

Knowledge systems can contribute to manufacturing competitiveness in many ways. I illustrate these with four applications of knowledge systems to a variety of manufacturing activities within FMC. Two of the applications address discrete parts manufacturing for mechanical parts, and two of the applications address chemical processing applications. One of the chemicals applications is a continuous processing operation, and the other is a batch processing application. These applications illustrate both the diversity of FMC's manufacturing businesses and the range of manufacturing applications for knowledge systems.

The needs of United States manufacturing companies in their drive to remain competitive in the world market may provide the principal driver for AI research and development in the 1990s. One only need look at the lineup of the largest U.S. companies to see how predominant manufacturing operations are in the gross national product of the U.S. economy. Of the Fortune 10, five of the companies are directly involved in manufacturing and four others—oil companies—also have heavy manufacturing components. FMC, with annual sales of over $3 billion, derives its revenues from manufactured products and processed minerals.

However, recent trends in the competitive position of U.S. manufacturing companies in the world marketplace are unsettling. Over the last 25 years there has been a steady decline in the percentage of manufactured goods sold in this country that are produced by U.S. manufacturers. Similarly, the percentage of manufactured goods sold abroad that were produced by U.S. manufacturing companies is declining. Measures of the productivity of manufacturing operations in the U.S. indicate that the rate of productivity improvement of U.S. manufacturing companies is much slower than for other highly industrialized countries, such as Germany, France, and Japan. This rate is measured as output per employee hour in manufacturing. Clearly, an improvement in the effectiveness and productivity of manufacturing processes and personnel will be a key factor in maintaining a strong position in the world manufacturing economy.

Now, let me turn to FMC as a case study and use FMC as a microcosm of American manufacturing companies to illustrate some ways in which I think we can regain our competitive edge through the use of intelligent manufacturing systems. FMC is nearly as diverse as the U.S. manufacturing economy. Approximately one-third of the $3 billion in sales comes from defense systems; one-half comes from sales of agricultural and industrial chemicals, including bulk commodity chemicals, specialty chemicals, and precious metals; and the remainder comes from more than a dozen different commercial machinery and equipment operations. The commercial machinery businesses serve diverse industries ranging from petroleum to food processing to material handling.

Historically, the role of manufacturing within FMC has been similar to that of most other manufacturing companies. Information and requirements created within the marketing and engineering functions is passed down to the factory floor where the product is produced. In fact, if the process is unpacked a bit, one sees that information passes through many hands: engineering, drafting, manufacturing engineering, quality engineering, production planning, and so on down to the shop floor where production schedules are put in place and goods are directly manufactured.

The problem with this traditional process is the sequential flow of information from engineering to manufacturing. Typically there are many cycles, or iterations, through the design and manufacturing process. If, for example, a design released to the shop floor for a part cannot be produced cost-effectively, feedback goes to the design engineers who may have to redesign the product. Each time an operation goes through the design and production cycle, it creates expense, takes time, and contributes to the overhead cost associated with the manufacturing process.

Another problem arises from the fact that the various specialists in the chain from design to manufacturing have highly specialized and compartmentalized knowledge. Taken together, they constitute a large staff of people, which, in some instances, can create knowledge bottlenecks at various stages in that process. These specialists often have computer tools available to them to help streamline their functions. For example, there are many commercial tools available for computer-aided design and computer-aided analysis, several of which are used at FMC. But typically only a few people know how to use effectively any given tool, and the tools are often not integrated with one another. So there is considerable technology available but little integration or broadly distributed expertise about how to use these tools. At the same time, many functions could be aided by computer automation, but the tools are not yet available— specifically, knowledge tools (as opposed to information processing or data processing tools) that add value by contributing expertise as well as performing data manipulation functions. So while on the one hand there are too many tools available, on the other hand there are also too few tools available, which slows production of results.

Two approaches to unblocking some of the knowledge bottlenecks and to reducing costly iteration between design and manufacturing are (a) to bring manufacturing considerations forward into the design process—so-called design for producibility—and (b) to expand those pockets of knowledge that constitute both knowledge bottlenecks and labor-intensive knowledge processing. Our approach is to find valuable know-how of key individuals that cannot be used often enough, or quickly enough, in the manufacturing process. We then attempt to automate what these most skilled experts do in order to make that expertise available across the entire spectrum of times, locations, and tasks requiring that skill.

FOUR EXAMPLES

This strategy can be illustrated with some concrete examples from within FMC. I'll describe four specific applications: one application that focuses on each of three major steps in the manufacturing process (i.e., design, process development, and production) and a fourth application that integrates the entire process in order to reduce the iterations from production back to design.

Typically, the manufacturing process starts with a product requirement or order. The requirement then goes through a *design engineering* process resulting in a product specification, blueprint, or configuration description. The second major activity—*process development*—aims to produce a plan for manufacturing that product according to the part and process specification. The process specification goes to the plant for *production* of the finished goods. From a knowledge processing viewpoint, the design process is essentially a spatial reasoning process—reasoning about parts, their geometries, how they fit together, and what tolerances are necessary to insure the fit-up of various parts constituting the product. Production is primarily a temporal reasoning process—estimating production times, production schedules, when machines will be available, how long a part will use a certain machine, and so on. Process development requires reasoning both about space (the characteristics of the part) and time (production processes and schedules). From a technical point of view, the software tools and methods needed to support knowledge systems across the spectrum of functions must be able to capture important information about both spatial and temporal reasoning.

An Example of the Design Step—Wellhead Configuration

The first application focuses on the first major step in the manufacturing process—design engineering. This application comprises two prototypes developed for FMC's Petroleum Equipment Group, which has as one product line petroleum wellheads. A wellhead is the equipment that sits above the ground on a producing oil well, as seen in Figure 12.1. The wellhead comprises valves and gages that control the pressure and the flow of oil out of the well. A typical wellhead configuration consists of 35 to 40 different parts selected from a catalog containing more than 10,000 different parts. A customer or potential customer—typically an oil company—requests a quotation for a particular wellhead configuration appropriate for the conditions of their well. The parameters of a well include location, operating temperatures, pressures, and properties of the material being pumped out of the well. So the operating environment for which a wellhead is specified can be tremendously varied and complex.

The sales department collects the requirements information and constraints from the customers and passes them to individuals in the quotations area. The quotations people will then design a standard wellhead configuration by selecting catalog parts. After the wellhead design is completed, it is checked by an engineer who decides whether or not that configuration is appropriate. If so, the cost of production is estimated and the price is quoted to the customer. That entire process generally requires one to two weeks. If the quotation required is not a standard configuration but requires a new part design, the request goes to the Engineering Department for a new part design to be included with the standard parts in the configuration.

The selection of materials for wellhead components can influence in a signifi-

Figure 12.1.   Petroleum Wellhead

cant way the correctness and the final cost of the quoted product. Different materials are appropriate for different operating conditions and also entail different production costs. In the petroleum industry, cost is a major purchasing criterion of customers; therefore, it is important to select materials that meet the operating requirements but minimize costs.

The business opportunity here is to reduce the time delay associated with generating a quotation and to eliminate the potential for human error in the final configurations. Errors in selecting parts or materials for the configuration can lead to equipment failures in the field that in turn can lead to dissatisfied customers and expensive repairs. The prototype systems we have developed automate portions of the configuration process, both the catalog selection of parts to be used in the configuration as well as the selection of materials that will be used to manufacture those parts. To the extent that we can quickly quote the least expensive materials and still adhere to the customer's performance specifications, we can obtain a competitive advantage at the front end of the design process by maximizing the value for the customer.

An Example of Process Development—Carrageenan Blending

Let me turn now to the second application, one that focuses on process development. One of FMC's chemicals businesses is the Marine Colloids Division, a business that produces about 200 specialty chemicals derived from a seaweed extract called carrageenan. An FMC plant in Rockland, Maine, receives shiploads of seaweed from all over the world. The seaweed is subjected to a treatment process to produce carrageenan. Differing molecular structure, pH, and viscosity result in dozens of different carrageenan classifications. From those basic raw materials the plant produces various custom-finished products for customers by combining specific raw materials from inventory with other additives. The finished products delivered to customers are used in their food and cosmetic product applications to achieve gelling or emulsification. For example, carrageenan is a typical additive in toothpaste to bind the paste to the water and to give the paste the proper viscosity. Similarly, carrageenan is used to bind chocolate particles to milk in chocolate milk to provide a consistent solution.

It is very important to produce finished customer products that are consistent in quality from shipment to shipment. A toothpaste manufacturer always wants toothpaste with exactly the same viscosity and color; therefore, the carrageenan that FMC delivers to the manufacturer for use in its toothpaste must be of consistent color, quality, and so on. The Rockland plant has one expert, an FMC employee of more than 20 years, who is the only person who knows how to juggle the various constraints on product formulation and inventory to fill current orders and prepare for future orders expected in the next 30 to 60 days.

The job of selecting and blending raw materials to produce a finished product involves knowledge of the different product formulas that can be used to combine the raw materials. The formulas permit a degree of latitude in which materials are used, and thus blending decisions are subject to discretionary materials selections. These decisions must take into account the customer preferences on viscosity, pH, color, and so on, as well as constraints in the raw inventory that is available now or likely to be available in the near future (see Figure 12.2). It is a very tricky job because the plant cannot control or accurately predict raw carrageenan inventory. There are various grades of carrageenan; some grades are highly valued in certain applications but may be available very infrequently. The expert has to consider how to protect his valued inventory in order to have it available for an anticipated order 30 or 60 days hence that he believes will need some of that raw material. Therefore, in addition to having to do product formulation and production scheduling, the expert has to do some hypothetical reasoning to anticipate the kinds of orders that will be coming along in the future to place demands on the material inventory.

On several occasions in the past unsuccessful attempts had been made to teach others how to solve the problem. Further attempts to automate various aspects of what the expert did using conventional data processing techniques had not succeeded.

We found that the kernel of the expert's problem solving was his ability to make intelligent decisions about how to draw from the raw resource inventory to

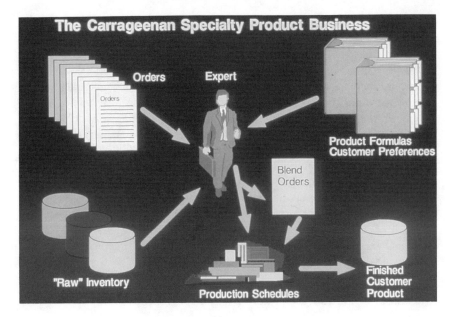

Figure 12.2.   Carrageenan Product Blending

produce final products that had the proper characteristics of viscosity, pH, color, and so on. The problem was to manage inventory cleverly by selecting one of the alternative formulations within a given general formula that made best use of available carrageenan. Our goal for automated support was to help the expert make these decisions more quickly and to enable others to perform the same task with the skill of the expert. This meant developing a system that could recommend a finished product that would satisfy the customer's need, would allow our expert to be responsive and flexible in meeting emergency or unscheduled orders, and would take into account costs of production and costs of the final product to the customers.

We are developing a series of systems that will be able to perform reasoning about product formulation under a number of constraints having to do with inventory, customer preferences, and the like. The first step involved building an extensive, customized database to hold the raw information needed to make product formulation decisions. We also developed a highly interactive human-machine interface that allowed the expert to experiment with blending decisions using the computer in exactly the same way that he previously solved the problem manually. His manual procedure involved taking about three dozen different manila folders from a file, opening the folders, pulling out piles of three-by-five cards containing various product formulas and information about the batches of raw material in inventory, spreading them out on a large table, and moving them around in order to build combinations of materials needed for product formulations.

We felt that the interface we provided had to permit our expert the same kind of physical manipulation of objects so that use of the system would not interfere with his reasoning process when he performed the task. The custom interface we developed, therefore, had the ability to support these manipulations of physical objects. Associated with the interface will be a series of intelligent assistants. Some will interact with a knowledge base of objectives, tactics, and strategies for producing product formulas. Others interact with a filing system containing information about inventory, forecasts, and formulas. Some assistants are designed to interact with a communications interface to obtain external data from sales and marketing regarding new orders, sales, forecasts, and shipping schedules. All of these assistants are or will be accessible to the expert through an intelligent user interface that allows him the same mode of interaction as he had previously with his paper files.

An Example of Production—Controlling a Phosphorus Plant

The third system addresses a production control problem that appears throughout FMC—process management of a dynamic, continuous process. The first implementation that we developed in this area is a process management system for optimizing the efficiency of a phosphorus-producing plant in Pocatello, Idaho. To produce phosphorus, three different raw materials are combined and burned in a large furnace to produce gaseous phosphorus. The phosphorus is precipitated and condensed into solid phosphorus for shipment to other plants within FMC, which convert it into phosphates sold outside the company as a bulk commodity product.

A by-product of this process is a slag that looks like volcanic lava and that is tapped out of the furnaces periodically. The slag contains two materials, both of which contain some phosphorus. To the extent that the slag material contains phosphorus, it is being lost in waste material rather than collected as product. Naturally, there is a desire to minimize the amount of phosphorus lost in waste material and maximize the amount collected as product.

One of the principal ways to control this process for efficiency is to alter the composition of materials flowing into the furnace. Throughout the plant there are approximately 60 different points where observations can be made that are pertinent to understanding the state of the process. Operators use these observations to diagnose what changes, if any, should be made to the composition of materials in order to maximize efficiency. Some of those observation points are indicated by dots in Figure 12.3. Some observations are available from computer-generated data (such as lab reports or process-control parameter values). But

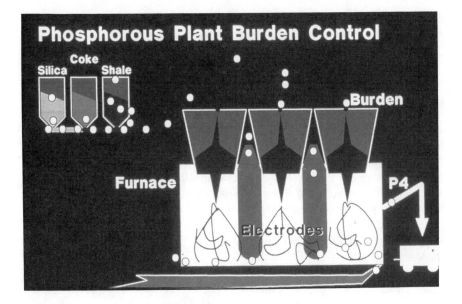

Figure 12.3.   Phosphorus Plant Schematic

other observations are made visually by operators who walk through the plant and look at the color and viscosity of the slag, feel the furnace vibration, listen to and try to infer from noises what is going on in the process, and a variety of qualitative measures that supplement the online quantitative data. The operator performing the diagnosis uses the current view of what is going on in the process and some historical data about what has happened over recent shifts to decide how to change the composition of materials (called the *burden*) that flows into the furnace.

Once again, this is an operation with a single acknowledged expert who has been with the company for many years. Whenever there is a problem with the process, this expert, if available, is called in to make a diagnosis and suggest actions. Unfortunately, the expert is nominally available only eight hours a day and five days a week, but the process runs 24 hours a day, seven days a week.

An interesting characteristic of this process is that the process changes fairly slowly over a period of hours or even days. Therefore, the knowledge that has to be brought to bear to make a control decision about the process may use data and observations from earlier shifts. But the plant operators change every eight hours. One operator may have a certain view of the process during his shift that he uses to make control decisions. When he goes off shift and another operator comes on, the new operator may be using a different subset of data to make decisions. There can be, therefore, inconsistency across shifts based on different operators' know-how and views of the process.

The system we developed collects and logs data continuously during furnace operation and uses a knowledge base of process expertise to provide advice to plant operators. The system was built using a tool specifically designed to handle real-time, knowledge-intensive, process management applications. The tool was developed collaboratively by FMC and Teknowledge, Inc. AI software engineers at FMC built the application using that tool. The system is able to monitor the process by collecting data from process-control computers, lab computers, and humans. It is able to use those data to come up with an assessment of the current situation and a prediction of future developments likely to occur in the process. The system then recommends actions be taken by the operators to bring the process back into optimal operating conditions. It helps control the execution of those actions by indicating at what points in the future those actions should take place.

An interesting characteristic of this process is that corrective actions spawn a process that interacts with the ongoing process. The system has to be able to predict how control actions will influence or change the process and then be able to compare the anticipated changes in the process with the actual changes that take place over the next few hours. The system is, therefore, constantly monitoring the actual unfolding of the process against the expected future that it predicted would unfold.

An Integrated Example Spanning Design and Production

The fourth application spans the design and production process in an attempt to reduce costly iteration through design and manufacturing. The application is in the discrete manufacturing domain and addresses the problem of gage generation. In the production of a mechanical part, the CAD specification for that part has certain tolerances associated with features of that part. In order to determine whether or not the part as manufactured is within the tolerances specified by the CAD model, a physical device is created called a gage. This gage represents the worst case mating characteristics of the part to be manufactured. For example, determining whether a metal plate with drilled holes is within tolerance requires inspection of the diameter of the holes, the distances between the centers of each of the holes, the size of the plate itself, and the relationship of the holes to the perimeter of the plate. In order to make those determinations, the Quality Engineering function designs a specification for a gage that is sent to the factory floor to be produced. The gage will be a metal plate with posts that can be matched with the holes of the metal plates on the part of interest.

If the gage is produced accurately, any part off the production line should mate with the gage by fitting onto the posts with the perimeter of the two plates aligned. If so, the part is within tolerance. There is, of course, variability in how a part can be manufactured but still be within tolerance.

In practice, it is more expensive to design and produce gages than it is to design and produce the actual parts. There are often several iterations through the design and production of a gage. Of course, a gage has to be accurate to detect a part that is out of tolerance. Further, if the part does not fit, one needs to know whether it can be reworked to bring it into tolerance or if it needs to be scrapped.

A project at FMC developed a software system that automates the major functions of gage generation and comparison of the manufactured part with the gage. Rather than being performed in a physical manufacturing process, gage generation and part inspection are carried out in software. The system is based on a technology called Computer-Integrated Gaging (CIG).

The part designer, interacting with ANVIL or other commercial CAD systems, designs his part. Then the CIG system will lead him through the specifications of the feature tolerances according to geometric dimension and tolerance standards until he has completely specified the part. It then generates in software the tolerance zones and the virtual gage that will be used to measure whether or not a part has been manufactured within tolerance. At that point the system then automatically generates a machine inspection path for how that part will be inspected to determine whether or not the tolerances are met for each of the features. The points at which a touch probe (shown in Figure 12.4) of a coordinate measuring machine (CMM) will measure the part are displayed graphically to the designer as the gaging program is developed by the system. The CIG system sends the inspection program to the CMM that it uses to collect measurements on part tolerances.

Figure 12.4 shows a particular coordinate measuring machine with a touch probe inspecting a part. The probe touches the features of the part to determine the various sizes and locations of the features. Then it will produce an output such as the observation that the diameter of a measured hole is less than the specified lower limit. Having noted that the part is not within tolerance, the system can mathematically drill out the hole to the proper diameter and re-measure the hole to see whether or not the hole would be within tolerance. "Within tolerance" in this case will mean that the hole has the correct diameter and is the proper distance from other part features. The results are then displayed for the user with recommendations on whether to scrap or rework the part. This, then, is a case where the system has performed computations in software to determine whether or not reworking would be adequate or whether scrapping is required.

This software was initially developed for use at FMC. But the success of the software led to an investigation outside the company to determine the commercial potential for a software product. Ultimately, a new company named Valisys was incorporated to focus on product development and marketing based on this

Figure 12.4.   Inspection by Coordinate Measuring Machine

technology. Today a family of products available through Valisys supports de-sign, quality engineering, and integration with shop floor inspection.

SUMMARY

Within most job functions, there is wide variability in the skills of the workers. Studies attempting to quantify the differences in the skills of workers have observed that the best 10 percent of the workers perform about 10 times better than the worst 10 percent of the workers and about three times better than the average worker. Our work in knowledge systems seeks to enable uniformly high performance across the entire spectrum of workers using a particular skill by capturing in software the expertise of top performers and making it available everywhere that skill has to be utilized. Closing the gap between performance at the top level and skill at the average performance level can have tremendous economic benefits for many companies.

In applying knowledge systems at FMC to create operation smoothing at the top end of the performance spectrum, we have seen a number of advantages. We have seen that knowledge systems technology is able to solve problems that have previously thwarted conventional data processing techniques, as in the carrageenan blending operation or in the phosphorus production application. In the latter case, process-control computers were unable to perform the knowledge-intensive reasoning required to evaluate qualitative data and manage the overall process. We have seen that knowledge systems technology provides the opportunity to capture and preserve perishable expertise. Such expertise can then be distributed throughout the organization, as in the case of wellhead configuration where sales and marketing offices around the world need accurate knowledge of materials and configuration options.

We have also seen that in some instances this technology allows managers to alter the way they think about our businesses and actually to conduct business differently. By exploiting this technology, we can organize our business functions differently, and we can provide different kinds of products and services. Integrating the design and manufacturing function can enable new organizational structures and new kinds of quality engineers. A system that can automate wellhead configuration offers the opportunity to make that software available to customers as a point-of-sale entry system—providing a new marketing tool. So the technology provides new ways to think about how to structure our business and ways to help us be competitive in our markets.

In summary, then, the vision I am working toward is one in which a business runs a highly automated and highly integrated manufacturing facility as illustrated in Figure 12.5. At the front end, "manufacturing" may begin with the

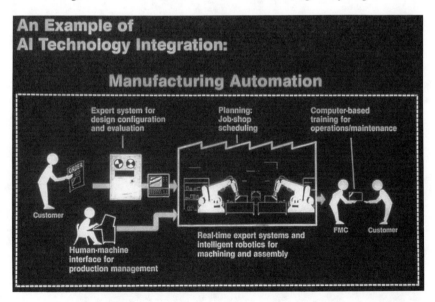

Figure 12.5. Vision of Highly Integrated Manufacturing Facility

customer specifying an order to an automated system able to perform design configuration and design evaluations. The design would be shipped electronically to a highly automated factory floor where teams of robots would be working together under the control of real-time process management systems and are able to produce and inspect a product. An intelligent human-machine interface operated by a production manager or supervisor would be able to inspect the status of the manufacturing process at various levels of abstraction or detail, depending on his or her interest. Out the back end of the process would come a product delivered to a customer, perhaps with some computer-based training on how to service that product or how to use that product. Portions of this vision are reality today, and the continued success of knowledge systems applications in the manufacturing sector will undoubtedly accelerate progress toward the ultimate goal.

13

Integrating AI for Increased Productivity: A Decade of Applications

Julie Wallin Kaewert

Digital Equipment Corporation

The author describes the successful integration of expert systems throughout Digital Equipment Corporation. Expert systems have become strategic to Digital where they have built on and leveraged existing information systems, applying AI only to problems that could not be solved with conventional tools and languages. Uses of expert systems with Digital include systems in engineering, sales, finance, field service, distributed resource planning, manufacturing, process control, diagnostics, materials handling, and job matching. The author cites many benefits of AI to the corporation: increased productivity, cost savings, increased communication, better information management, consistency, development of policies and procedures, greater customer satisfaction, and greater reliability of products and services. Additionally, AI has facilitated close communication among various organizations within the corporation, which has been an unexpected benefit and a strategic advantage. Through its wide use of AI, Digital has learned how to transfer expert systems technology to both customers and internal users.

INTRODUCTION

Digital Equipment Corporation has a history of increasing productivity through the use of technology. As we will see by looking at Digital's successful expert systems applications, AI technology plays a major role in Digital's approach to what the company calls the Intelligent Integrated Business—a business that uses expert systems integrated with conventional systems, networked and distributed throughout the enterprise.

Before looking at several specific instances of increased productivity through the use of expert systems, it will be useful to understand the Digital approach to AI. At Digital, AI builds upon and leverages existing information systems, and networking is indispensable.

Digital has never tried to apply AI to break new technological ground; instead, the corporation has tried to solve problems that couldn't be solved using conventional tools and languages. Along the way, it became clear that an expert system component was the best solution for some problems.

The first step in optimizing a system is to look carefully at the existing system to be certain that the foundation is solid enough to warrant enhancement. Next, Digital matches an appropriate technology to the problem. If it can be solved using an algorithmic solution, conventional technology will be used. If expert systems technology is appropriate, then it will be applied.

The results of expert systems at Digital have gone far beyond increased productivity and cost avoidance, although those would be adequate rewards. Unexpected benefits have accrued in the form of increased organizational effectiveness, central repositories for vital corporate expertise, more efficient information management, and reduced complexity of products and services.

The following are results of integrating over three years an expert system component with existing systems in Digital's Networking and Communications group:

- Revenue up 300%
- Revenue per person up 64%
- Space utilization up 144%
- $ inventory/$ revenue down 54%
- Gross margin up 20%
- Time-to-market down 20%
- Manufacturing cycle time down 30%
- Reliability up 285%
- On-time deliveries up from 85 to 99%.

This list does not take into account additional strategic advantages that are hard to measure, such as developing a set of policies and procedures to help solve problems consistently, or developing a central repository of knowledge for an application.

Customer applications developed by Digital follow the same strategy of optimizing existing systems: Integrating AI with existing systems and applying networking for efficient distribution of information. As Figure 13.1 shows, expert systems are at work at customer sites in petrochemical, airline, food service industries, and government, performing tasks including configuration, scheduling, diagnostics, and commodities trading. In the banking, investment insurance, and finance industries, Digital has built expert systems to perform transaction pattern analysis, loan applicant analysis, risk analysis, investment operations, and user interface tasks.

The successful transfer of expert systems technology throughout the company and to customer sites has become an art at Digital. The company has developed a

Customer AI Applications Developed by Digital:

Expert Systems at Work

Application Areas in Manufacturing

	Petrochemical Industry	Airline Industry	Food Service Industry	US Govt.	Printing
Configuration					
Scheduling					
Diagnostics					
Trading					

Customer AI Applications Developed by Digital:

Expert Systems at Work

Application Areas in Insurance/Finance

	Banking Industry	Investment Houses	Insurance Industry
Transaction Pattern Analysis			
Loan Analysis			
Risk Analysis			
Investments			
Operations (Underwriting and Contracts)			
Natural Language			

Figure 13.1.   Digital has helped customers build and implement integrated expert systems in a variety of problem types across applications and industries.

nine-week knowledge engineering and technology transfer curriculum to train project managers and knowledge engineers for expert system projects as well as a five-day management curriculum for upper-level managers. A two-day technology transfer seminar covers the issues of managing change in an organization with specific attention to the organizational and cultural changes brought about by expert systems.

One clear message all students take from Digital's training programs is that technical, business, and organizational issues must all be considered for successful expert system development and implementation. Often the technical issues are the least problematic; first, the real business issue must be determined, and organization issues, such as which group will own and maintain the system, must be settled. If business and organizational issues are ignored in the course of a project, it has been Digital's experience that the expert system will not succeed.

EXPERT SYSTEMS AT DIGITAL

An illustration of what Digital calls the Intelligent Integrated Solution can be seen in Figure 13.2. It is a snapshot of the corporation, showing how convention-

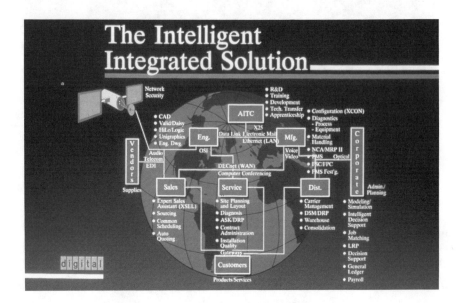

Figure 13.2.   The Intelligent Integrated Solution at Digital: Expert systems integrated with existing applications, distributed through networking.

al applications are integrated with expert systems and distributed worldwide through networking. In the areas of engineering, sales, service, manufacturing, and distribution, integrated expert systems provide us with a competitive edge.

Engineering

As an example of expert systems in computer-aided design (CAD), APES (Automatically Produced Engineering Schematics) is a logic synthesis tool that mimics the process an engineer uses to create a logic design for a computer chip. APES creates a design capable of being processed into an application-specific integrated circuit.

Early in the product development process for computer systems, a concept or behavioral model of the machine is developed. This model must be elaborated upon so that it can be captured by the CAD tools that will transform it into physical parts. During this design capture process, an engineer draws schematic diagrams of the individual gates on a graphics workstation. This work is vital but very tedious and slow. Typically, it takes an engineer about one week to design and enter a 200-gate section of the behavioral model. Five years ago, such a model contained 2,000 to 4,000 gates. Today, a model can contain 50,000 to 100,000 gates. The time required to enter them all is too great for Digital to spare engineers' time for the task.

The company decided it needed to mimic the engineer's decision-making process by using an expert system. APES enters logic gates quickly and directly, far more quickly than the fastest engineer. APES can design and enter thousands of gates per hour, far outstripping the engineer's best average of 200 gates per week. APES, built in VAX OPS5, first reads in the behavioral model with additional comments, establishing constraints and goals for the final design. Then it develops a logic design. Finally, it selects a set of logic gates and draws the schematic diagrams.

Sales

Because Digital custom configures computer systems to customers' needs, the sales person's task of ordering the correct configuration for a customer is very complicated. There are roughly 20,000 parts, 33 component types, and 63 attributes of computer systems that the sales person must master, and there are thousands of sales people worldwide. Achieving a consistent level of expertise worldwide is a nearly impossible task, yet it is very important that a consistently high standard be achieved in the timeliness and completeness of customer orders.

Digital decided to apply expert systems technology to the effort and built an expert system called XSEL (Expert Selling assistant) using VAX OPS5. XSEL is integrated with XCON and acts as an expert sales assistant. The system contains

manufacturing operations before they are implemented. With this information, managers are able to make better informed, more intelligent choices, thereby saving money and improving customer satisfaction.

MOC lets users answer three critical questions:

1. Are the supply and demand for each product well-balanced?
2. What are the critical resources needed to deliver the plan?
3. What is the financial impact of a proposed plan if it is implemented?

MOC captures the interdependencies of the planning process. Users consult one source for the data they need—for both financial implications and manufacturing options.

MOC is easy to use; it is menu-driven and uses icons and a mouse. Users can train themselves. Running in a VAX station environment, MOC's program logic is coded in the VAX LISP programming language, combined with the expert system building tool KnowledgeCraft from Carnegie Group, Inc. Because MOC is based on object-oriented representation and modular, frame-based technology, its database is structured to allow relationships between elements to interact and to change as the need evolves. Digital's networking and integration expertise is crucial and provides the infrastructure that enables such data sharing.

MOC gives Digital the ability to respond proactively to changes in manufacturing planning and sales forecasts faster and more accurately. Analysts can now prioritize product mix based on manufacturing conditions and address instances of shortfall before they occur.

Can Build. Digital found it had a significant amount of inventory remaining at the end of a product's life and set out to find the best way to handle this hard-to-manage asset. The first challenge was to identify what inventory was left and what should be done with it. Beyond that was a long-term critical need to maintain a competitive edge that could be addressed by a tool to help synchronize the inventory parts across the corporation, not just for each plant or each product.

Existing inventory control programs only looked at a single plant. Manual analysis of data across plants was time-consuming, subjective, and inefficient. Reports were issued independently by different plants on a quarterly basis, often in different formats.

Can Build was developed to address these problems. One goal of the Can Build project was to gain quick, easy access to current information on existing materials wherever the location. A second goal was to determine the costs of alternative uses of the inventory, perhaps utilizing it in other projects or even writing it off. Finally, Digital wanted to be able to make timely, consistent decisions based on a corporate perspective rather than on individual plant evaluations, and the business need was urgent.

The Can Build design incorporates several components. The integrated software solution included both conventional programming and rule-based technology, plus VMS utilities, such as mail. It used the best technology for each piece of the full solution. The interactive simulation aspect made the system easy to use because the menu, jargon, and displays were designed by the user team. Finally, the flexible, modular architecture meant the system could be easily expanded and changed as usage evolved.

The business impact of Can Build was immediate and extremely beneficial. Timely, consistent decisions—made possible by up-to-date, more easily accessible inventory information—facilitated a productivity increase. Knowing where excess inventory remained and what was likely to become a liability enabled better planning, and as a result, significant cost could be avoided. Can Build also provided a strategic contribution by facilitating corporate asset management and enabling the development of policies and procedures for a corporate "product phase down" model.

Can Build met the long-term need of synchronizing inventory by solving the immediate problem of where inventory remained and what should be done with it. Can Build paid back 60 times its cost within its first quarter of use.

Performance Analyzer. Management information systems are excellent vehicles for making manufacturing operation performance data readily available to managers. In many cases, however, the better the MIS system, the greater the amount of data managers have to analyze.

Digital decided to apply an expert system to the information overload problem as most of the expertise needed to analyze data in management reports is non-procedural, judgmental, and based on empirical experience and rules of thumb. It is difficult to automate knowing what is important to whom, under what circumstances, even with the help of sophisticated statistical analysis. Traditional programming methods proved to be inadequate, but the rule-based VAX OPS5 programming environment was ideal for capturing this type of rule-based, exception-based knowledge.

The Performance Analyzer expert system now analyzes MIS data to identify discrepancies between current and historical performance. Online analysis of performance lets senior managers interpret the impact of exceptions, recommend corrective actions, or make immediate adjustments as necessary. In addition to data on past performance, Performance Analyzer uses business objectives to analyze data and calculate exceptions.

Performance Analyzer's knowledge, in the form of control limits and rules, allows it to notice deviations from typical past performances or from a goal specified by the user. Special-case rules interpret the meaning of each exception in terms of impact and probable cause; it can even make a recommendation for corrective action.

The system allows management quickly to evaluate:

- Projection accuracy.
- Execution performance.

make these components and how they will be merged into a final system. An expert system, called Configuration Dependent Sourcing, helps determine which factories will supply which parts, depending upon the system configuration.

A project called DELPHI deals with quality control in manufacturing operations, isolating areas where there are problems, and identifying faults using expert diagnostics. Statistical quality control and fault diagnostics are now embedded in Digital's manufacturing processes.

IMACS deals with shop floor control and is a collection of cooperative expert systems. IMACS has remained in prototype stage, because implementing it would require replacing existing software that took considerably more resources to build and implement than it took to build IMACS.

Out of IMACS came the Matcher system that helped control work-in-progress by helping make use of a partially built system whose order had been cancelled. A simple rule-based system looked at the incoming order stream and matched attributes against the partially built system to come up with the best use of the system. The goal was to satisfy a future order with minimum change.

Another module of IMACS is Dispatcher that controls work-in-progress for a number of assembly stations. It dispatches the parts required to assemble certain components onto the factory floor with the help of robots.

The next functional block of the Knowledge Network is distribution, where an

Top CIE Expert Systems Applications

Dept.	Application	Description	Benefits	
			Primary	Secondary
Factory				
Locations: San Germane Puerto Rico and 10 Other Plants	Process Control	Wave Solder	Quality	Reduce Cycle by 10%
Hundson, MA and Other Plants	Diagnostics	Statistical Process Control	Cost of Qualtiy Improved by 10%	Improve Process Development Cycle Time
Burlington, VT	CTS	Configuration Tracking System	Time to Market	
Augusta, Maine and 3 Other Plants	DSM	Distributed Simulation/Modeling	Cost	Customer Satisfaction
Internal Data Centers	Task Schedulers	Computer Center Task Scheduler	Consistency of Data Center Operations	Cost
US Area Distribution	Transportation Routing	Dispatch Trucks	Reduce Cost	Customer Satisfaction
Worldwide Telecommunication	Security	Computer Security Inspection	Information Resources Security	Cost ($18M per Year)

Top CIE Expert Systems Applications

Dept.	Application	Description	Benefits	
			Primary	Secondary
Order Admin.	XCON/XSEL	Configuration	Ability to Sell What Customers Want Problem-Free Installation	$40M Annual Savings
Salem System Manufacturing Plant	OTP	Order Transaction Processing Model	Reduced Order Processing Cycle Time	Customer Satisfaction Reduced Inv.
Salem System Manufacturing Plant	CDS	Configuration Dependent Sourcing	Scedule Performance (3 Days)	Lower Overhead ($2.5M/Year)
Northboro, MA	Distribution Planner	Distribution Model/Simulation	Customer Satisfaction	Distribution Cost ($2M/Year)
Internal Data Centers	Task Schedulers	Computer Center Task Scheduler	Consistency of Data Center Operations	Cost
Corporate Headquarters Planning	Manufacturing Operation Consultant	Business Decision Support Systems	Reduce Planning Cycle Time 70%	One Ship Plan from Design to Manufacturing

Top CIE Expert Systems Applications

Dept.	Application	Description	Benefits	
			Primary	Secondary
Financial	XFCS	Financial Rollup and Closing System	Immediate Corporate Finance Metrics	$6.5M Annual Alternate Use of Capital
Personnel Westford, MA	Job Matching	Skill and Opening	Human Resource Management	Career Planning and Skill Matching
Field Support	SPEAR	Remote Diagnostics	Customer Response Time by 10%	$20M Annual Cost Savings

Figure 13.4.   Expert systems are applied throughout Digital manufacturing, field service, sales, operations, and engineering groups.

as the sole solution to all existing problems, because of their success outside of the laboratory a demand for new expert systems had arisen.

A common misconception held by many members of the corporate world is the belief that expert systems, in their many manifestations, are the sum total of artificial intelligence. While expert systems can often provide viable solutions to existing problems, an expansive view of artificial intelligence and its betterments should be explored by the corporate world. Research in the areas of speech recognition, user interface design, and natural language processing, for example, offer interesting and useful applications in the realm of telecommunications. The successful implementation of these and other artificial intelligent domains can be just as effective as expert systems and help with cost effectiveness, as well as future expansion of a business.

Finding the solution to a given problem can be as tedious as matching the glass slipper of Cinderella's foot. Sometimes all possibilities must be exhausted before the solution presents itself. Once discovered it becomes so natural that it appears as if there never were a situation of difficulty.

Though the perfect vision of hindsight, many problems were solved by what appeared to have been the obvious solution. However, the application of artificial intelligence discovered to create a solution is only achieved through the meritorious endeavors of visionaries who ride the wave of the future. This exciting wave of discovery that utilizes human resources coupled with artificial intelligence disciplines is one area where U S WEST Advanced Technologies places itself today.

Keep in mind, however, that "those who try to sell artificial intelligence seem to promise more intelligence than they can deliver" (MIS, 1988) and thereby create a feeling of hype that surrounds the artificial intelligence research laboratory. This nominal use of skepticism that's currently gone around AI organizations. What's the difference between a used car salesman and an AI engineer? A used car salesman knows when he's lying. Now, it's true that many people involved with artificial intelligence fall into this category, and that has resulted in the feeling of hype that surrounds the technology. But it is not true that all artificial intelligence is simply hype.

U S WEST attempts to avoid the hype surrounding artificial intelligence by illustrating market needs to guide its applied artificial intelligence research laboratory. Pure research, which may have no grounding in organizational needs nor potential applicability to meeting customer needs, can often contribute to the hype factor by promising claims that are long into the future. U S WEST has chosen to address this important area of basic research through the funding of laboratories at leading universities that are often better equipped to handle this research. Hype is often used to acquire funding and interest associated with basic research. Applied research typically is not placed in such a compromising position because of the necessity of the work. Additionally, this approach to performing applied and basic research helps defray some of the cost associated with as the sole solution to all existing problems, because of their success outside of the laboratory a demand for new expert systems has arisen.

A common misconception held by many members of the corporate world is the belief that expert systems, in their many manifestations, are the sum total of artificial intelligence. While expert systems can often provide viable solutions to existing problems, an expansive view of artificial intelligence and its outgrowths should be explored by the corporate world. Research in the areas of speech recognition, user interface design, and natural language processing, for example, offer interesting and useful applications in the realm of telecommunications. The successful implementation of these and other artificial intelligence domains can be just as effective as expert systems and help with cost effectiveness, as well as future expansions of a business.

Finding the solution to a given problem can be as tedious as matching the glass slipper to Cinderella's foot. Sometimes all possibilities must be exhausted before the solution presents itself. Once discovered it becomes so natural that it appears as if there never were a situation of difficulty.

Through the perfect vision of hindsight, many problems were solved by what appeared to have been the obvious solution. However, the application of artificial intelligence discoveries to create a solution is only achieved through the meticulous endeavors of visionaries who ride the wave of the future. This exciting wave of discovery that utilizes human resources coupled with artificial intelligence disciplines is one area where U S WEST Advanced Technologies places itself today.

Keep in mind, however, that "those who try to sell artificial intelligence seem to promise more intelligence than they can deliver" (*MIS*, 1988) and thereby create a feeling of hype that surrounds the artificial intelligence research laboratory. This reminds me of a witticism that's currently going around AI organizations: "What's the difference between a used car salesman and a knowledge engineer? A used car salesman knows when he's lying." Now, it's true that many people involved with artificial intelligence fall into this category, and that has resulted in the feeling of hype that surrounds the technology. But it is not true that all artificial intelligence is simply hype.

U S WEST attempts to avoid the hype surrounding artificial intelligence by allowing market needs to guide its applied artificial intelligence research laboratory. Pure research, which may have no grounding in organizational needs nor potential applicability to meeting customer needs, can often contribute to the hype factor by promising claims that are long into the future. U S WEST has chosen to address this important area of basic research through the funding of laboratories at leading universities that are often better equipped to handle this research. Hype is often used to acquire funding and interest associated with basic research. Applied research typically is not placed in such a compromising position because of the necessity of the work. Additionally, this approach to performing applied and basic research helps defray some of the cost associated with advancing research projects. A more in-depth discussion of the U S WEST applied research laboratory is given below.

To summarize, expert systems do not constitute the sum total of artificial intelligence. While some members of the corporate world acknowledge this and then ignore everything but expert systems, this chapter ignores expert systems and focuses on other fruitful areas of AI research currently being performed at U S WEST. This is not to deny the importance of expert systems to industry— that would certainly be foolish on my part.

TELECOMMUNICATIONS

Alexander Graham Bell's vision of telecommunications since its inception has remained virtually unchanged in that it provided what is commonly known in the industry as P.O.T.S., or "plain old telephone service." Speaking into a telephone at one end and having the spoken words produced at the other is "by far the most widely used method of person-to-person telecommunication" (Brewster, 1986).

From its inception, communication through the telephone has been enhanced greatly by technology. Enhancements include, for example, increased transmission quality, improved networking and switching, and universal reliable service. While developments in artificial intelligence may only claim a small fraction of the contribution to the development of the telecommunications industry, future artificial intelligence research will play a greater role in pushing the barriers of technology in an effort to better serve telecommunication subscribers.

In addition to the ever-increasing role of artificial intelligence in traditional telephone service, it will also become a major contributor to the shaping of telecommunications as we delve more deeply into the information age. As more people seek information and businesses arise to meet these needs, it will be necessary for a telecommunications company to satisfy both of these subscribers—the people providing the information services and the people subscribing to them. The telecommunications industry is "clearly moving rapidly toward providing more than voice communication, of becoming, in fact, a universal transmitter of information" (Hyman, Toole, & Avellis, 1987). The video gateway project outlined below is one example of advancing our capability to provide customers with the ability to transport information more easily from themselves to their customers.

U S WEST SCIENCE AND TECHNOLOGY

U S WEST Advanced Technologies is a wholly owned subsidiary of U S WEST, a diversified telecommunications holding company, responsible for directing the use of technology to meet the needs of the U S WEST companies and their

ods for evaluating software usability, and applications of new input and output devices and technologies.

Current research design approaches include investigation of the use of cognitive models in interface design and AI techniques for creating customized and adaptive systems, and techniques for consumer direct manipulation and symbolic description. Research on design tools is currently focused on expert system design advisors and tools that support rapid user interface prototyping and iterative design. To support iterative design of prototypes and research on evaluation methodologies, a test lab with video facilities has been constructed.

Advanced Software Technology

The Advanced Software Technologies department is currently focused on the exploration of emerging technologies and paradigms to improve software productivity and quality. Current software production processes tend to be characterized by the "waterfall" model (Boehm, 1981) in which distinct phases of requirements (specification), design, coding, testing, etc., occur in sequence. This 10-year-old model, initially developed for batch-oriented computing environments using expensive hardware, was a major step in the improvement of quality and productivity; however, new technologies and low-cost hardware are radically changing the future of software environments.

Emerging technologies affecting software development methodology include expert systems and knowledge bases, the object-oriented programming paradigm, and graphical (e.g., icon-based) programming environments, and a variety of high-level languages and shells. Members of the Advanced Software Technology group are exploring ways in which these technologies may be used to improve and optimize future software development and development processes. Both rapid prototyping and software production technologies are being investigated to improve the transition from rapid prototyping to software production.

Work currently in progress is aimed at the development and demonstration of an integrated prototype environment that would allow knowledge acquisition via graphical programming to generate object-oriented knowledge bases. Such knowledge bases could then form the basis for rapid prototyping using the object paradigm.

APPLIED RESEARCH PROJECTS

This section briefly outlines three applied research projects being investigated within U S WEST Science and Technology.

ods for evaluating software usability, and applications of new input and output devices and technologies.

Current research design approaches include investigation of the use of cognitive models in interface design and AI techniques for creating customized and adaptive systems, and techniques for combining direct manipulation and symbolic description. Research on design tools is currently focused on expert system design advisors and tools that support rapid user interface prototyping and iterative design. To support iterative design of prototypes and research on evaluation methodologies, a test lab with video facilities has been constructed.

Advanced Software Technology

The Advanced Software Technologies department is currently focusing on the exploration of emerging technologies and paradigms to improve software productivity and quality. Current software production processes tend to be characterized by the "waterfall" model (Boehm, 1981) in which distinct phases of requirements (specifications, design, coding, testing, etc.) occur in sequence. This 10-year-old model, initially developed for batch-oriented computing environments using expensive hardware, was a major step in the improvement of quality and productivity. However, new technologies and low-cost hardware are radically changing the future of software environments.

Emerging technologies affecting software development methodology include expert systems and knowledge bases, the object-oriented programming paradigm, and graphical (e.g., icon-based) programming environments, and a variety of high-level languages and shells. Members of the Advanced Software Technology group are exploring ways in which these technologies may be used to improve and optimize future software development and development processes. Both rapid prototyping and software production technologies are being investigated to improve the transition from rapid prototyping to software production.

Work currently in progress is aimed at the development and demonstration of an integrated prototype environment that would allow knowledge acquisition via graphical programming to generate objected-oriented knowledge bases. Such knowledge bases could then form the basis for rapid prototyping using the object paradigm.

APPLIED RESEARCH PROJECTS

This section briefly outlines three applied research projects being investigated within U S WEST Science and Technology.

Indus

Intelligent document understanding has recently emerged as a center of focus for a significant amount of artificial intelligence research and development (Norvig, 1987; Young & Hayes, 1985). Additionally, electronic mail environments and their relationship to information sharing in organizations has also received a great deal of attention. Indus is a mail targeting program that combines these two areas using recent developments in natural language processing, a heuristic rule-based paradigm, and research on information flows within large organizations and their relationship to documents found in these organizations.

Most of the management and administrative activity within nearly any large business organization consists of acquisition and sharing of information about the organization's business: its costs, customers, competitors, product plans, and business opportunities. The majority of an organization's visible activity, as reflected in the paper that it generates, is concerned more with the production and distribution of information to support executive, administrative, and personnel functions than with the execution of those functions.

In a multibillion dollar corporation, the costs of sustaining the interoffice mail flow may amount to tens or even hundreds of millions of dollars per year for the cost of paper, photocopying, and distribution (including preparation and verification of mail distribution lists, mail handling and sorting, and delivery) alone. More accurate targeting of interoffice mail that reduces mail volume by even a few percent can therefore save substantial amounts of money. Savings can also occur when more accurate targeting increases mail volume. This second type of savings comes from the increased flow of appropriate information between employees where no information exchange occurred previously.

From an artificial intelligence point of view, the symbols on an interoffice memorandum representing natural language have to be recognized by an "intelligent system." At some level, the meanings have to be interpreted or understood. This recognition process, for the most part, is still a research problem; however, significant progress has been made to date. After recognition has occurred, the decoded symbols need to be classified as to the type of document they indicate. The document type is then presented to a traditional heuristic rule-based expert system. In the case of Indus, the system must decide who within the corporation would be interested in the information contained within the memorandum.

A message similar to the one in Figure 14.1 is found in all organizations. This is an organization change type of notice distributed to employees informing them that Richard will be joining the company at a future date. Initially, it's necessary for the computer to be able to recognize this sentence.

So the first problem for Indus is the natural language processing problem in AI. "Natural language" might be better termed "common language," meaning to

without focusing too narrowly on any specific network domains, would offer significant power for building network-oriented models.

A good example of a network problem is the typical communication network; a hypothetical network is shown in Figure 14.3. Modeling on a computer makes sense because it is quite easy to perform tasks on the computer (for example, alterations to the network) that aren't very easy to perform to the actual network. For example, should a trunk line be run from node C to node G? A trunk line for purposes of this sort we can just think of as carrying more telephone calls than a nontrunk line. So should node C be connected to node G as opposed to the current depiction, as shown in Figure 14.3, which connects nodes C and G by going through nodes D and F. In order properly to process this type of information about potential network modifications, further research examining routing algorithms, such as dynamic anticipatory routing, are needed. With a computer-based model it's easy to test the hypothesized changes by simulating the traffic flow through the network.

Networks are interesting in that they are often recursive. Each node in a network can be expanded into a network in its own right—just as an icon is opened or closed. Thus, each of the nodes in Figure 14.3 has some internal structure within it. The internal structure for node B of Figure 14.3 is shown in Figure 14.4. This nested internal structure of networks must also be handled by a network modeling program.

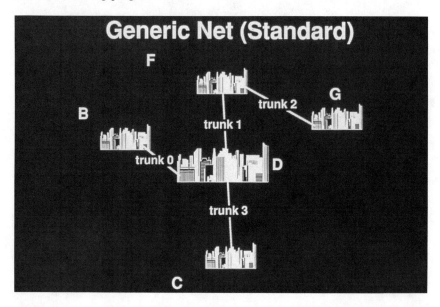

Figure 14.3.   Hypothetical Communications Network

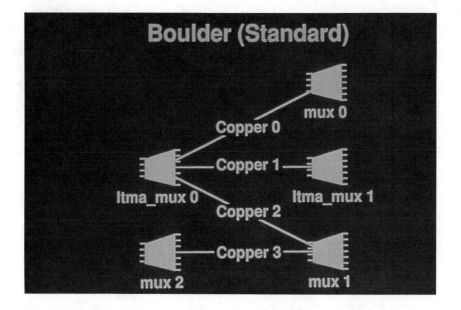

Figure 14.4.   A Network within a Network

Given such a "hierarchical network" model, it is then very interesting to use it to view problems at the right level of abstraction. For example, some network designers will only need to see the network from the Figure 14.3 point of view. Others will need to see only the Figure 14.4 point of view.

Another example of a network problem is diagnosing a communications network. For example, when an error or fault occurs in the network, it's very important to be able to identify quickly what's wrong and where it's wrong so that repair operations can begin. Indeed, identifying and isolating a problem is often the hard part—once that is accomplished, it is, typically, relatively easy to fix the problem.

The problems and technologies needed to do network modeling are in fact very complex. The means and technologies used to solve these problems begin to look like a list of AI problems: design problems, diagnosis problems, prognosis problems, and simulation problems are all amenable to network approaches.

The Generic Network Modeling System (GNMS) has been designed to capture the essence of network systems using an object-oriented approach (Laufman, Blumenthal, Sylvan, & Freeman, 1988). The GNMS project was initiated to address several fundamental design goals that may be grouped into five categories:

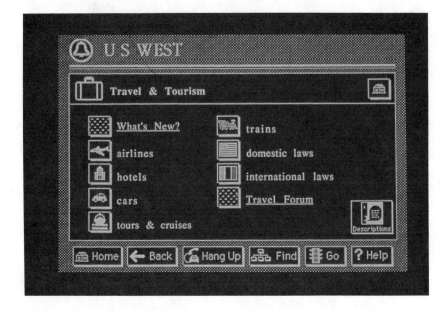

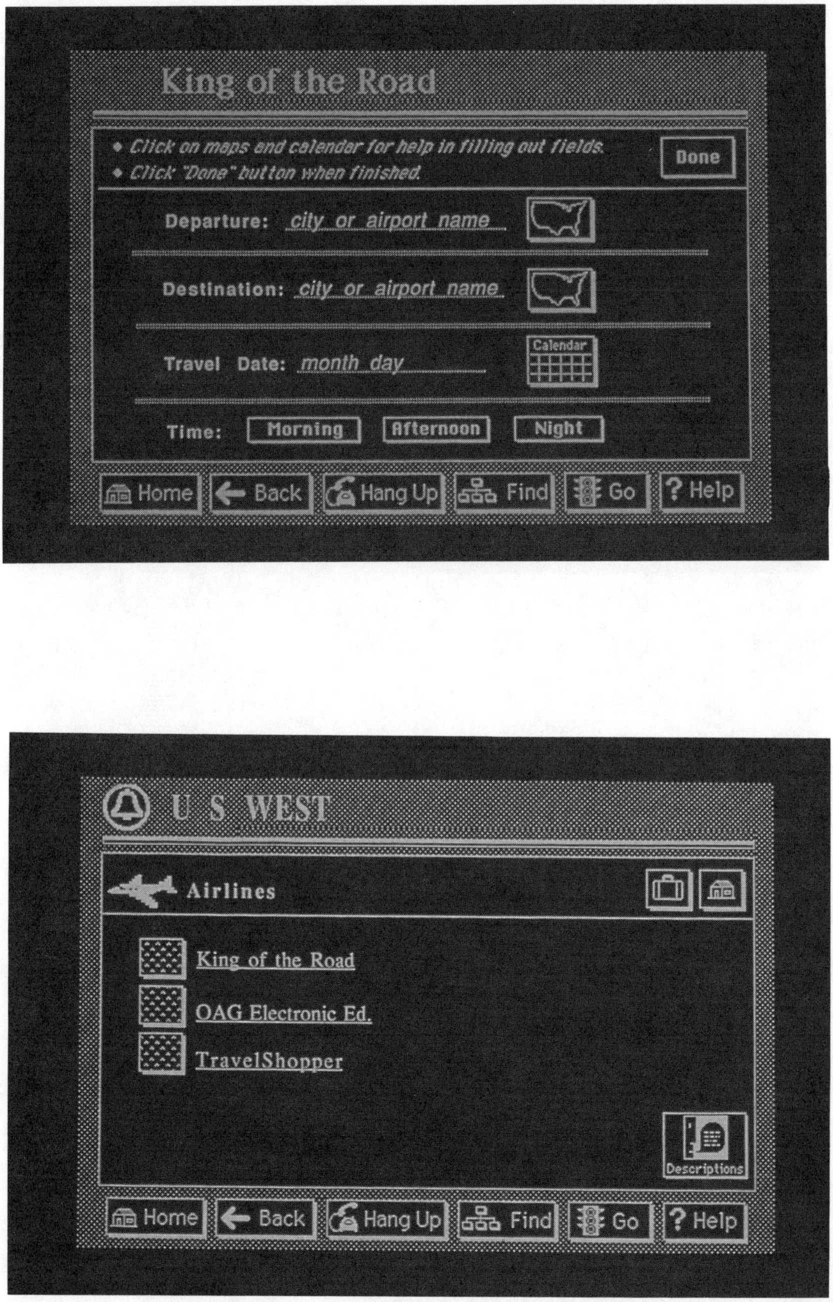

Figure 14.5. Prototype Information Gateway

15

Cargo Loading Expert System, New Efficiencies in Distribution and Inventory Control

J. Kenneth Klitz
IBM

The transportation industry of the United States represents eight percent of the Gross National Product. The loading of products into various modes of transportation involves variations in size, stacking requirements, rotation of orientation, packing material needs, and the differing dimensions per the same load. How to store and load into multiple vehicles is an excellent application for an expert system. This chapter depicts the expert system developed by IBM to accomplish the above for the purpose of reducing the staging and loading time, which in return can reduce inventory and improve the quality of the shipment and delivery.

OVERVIEW

The transportation industry of the United States represents eight percent of the Gross National Product. There is a significant reliance upon the global transportation network of air and surface. It is immense, complex, and continues to be an important part of international trade.

Over the past 20 years we at IBM have seen improved methods of how products are distributed through this global network of distribution. There has been a significant growth in cargo container shipping, rail transport of truck trailers, and air cargo. Much has been done in automating the way in which products are received, stored, packed, loaded, and transported.

Where there are discrete multiple diverse products we have relied upon an individual to determine how those products shall be loaded, arranged, and packed into the container itself. This chapter describes how an expert system can provide an assistance or an improvement in loading such products into containers that will move into the U.S. and global distribution networks.

15

Cargo Loading Expert System: New Efficiencies in Distribution and Inventory Control

J. Kenneth Klitz

IBM

The transportation industry of the United States represents eight percent of the Gross National Product. The loading of products into various modes of transportation involves variations in size, stacking requirements, rotational criteria, packing material needs, and the different destinations per the same load. How to stage and load transportation vehicles is an excellent application for an expert system. The chapter depicts the expert system developed by IBM to accomplish the above for the purpose of reducing the staging and loading time, which in return can reduce inventory and improve the quality of the shipment and delivery.

OVERVIEW

The transportation industry of the United States represents eight percent of the Gross National Product. There is a significant reliance upon the global transportation network of air and surface. It is immense, complex, and continues to be an important part of international trade.

Over the past 20 years we at IBM have seen improved methods of how products are distributed through this global network of distribution. There has been a significant growth in cargo container shipping, rail transport of truck trailers, and air cargo. Much has been done in automating the way in which products are received, stored, picked, loaded, and transported.

Where there are discrete multiple diverse products we have relied upon an individual to determine how those products shall be loaded, arranged, and packed into the container itself. This chapter describes how an expert system can provide an assistance or an improvement in loading such products into containers that will move into the U.S. and global distribution networks.

PROBLEM DESCRIPTION

Discrete products that are placed into cargo containers vary in size and weight. Furthermore, some products can be stacked and rotated in multiple directions, while some can be loaded by laying the product on its side. Others can be stacked only in one plane. The loading of products can be a combination of these various rules.

There also can be a variation in packing material required with different products. Restrictions in the handling and loading of hazardous products can be unique. Finally, the size of the cargo container itself can vary allowing a larger number of products to be loaded.

Given the above variations and nonuniform loads, the combination of ways in which a particular set of products can be loaded is significant. If the cargo being shipped varies over time, the training to complete the different loading tasks can be lengthy. One does not see a repeat of similar types of loads to obtain the required training in the desired short period of time.

Desired Effect

Again, where there is a significant product set (greater than 50) and the loads are not uniform (10 to 20 different types of products will be loaded into the container), the ideal or optimum solution is to load the set of products into the least amount of space. If there is a cargo container one is attempting to move, an imaginary line delineates the last row of products forward to the front of the container, having met all of the stacking rules for the products. Further, the load must have the correct amount of packing materials, and all rules relative to hazardous material must have been met.

Improvements

Some of the major improvements seen in providing an expert system assistant to the loaders of discrete nonuniform products are the following:

- Reduced loading time
- Reduced training time
- Improved container utilization
- Adherence to the handling of hazardous products
- Improved quality loading.

If the time is reduced in the loading of containers, the inventory pipeline can be reduced as well.

PROBLEM DESCRIPTION

Discrete products that are placed into cargo containers vary in size and weight. Furthermore, some products can be stacked and rotated in multiple directions, while some can be loaded by laying the product on its side. Others can be stacked only in one plane. The loading of products can be a combination of these various rules.

There also can be a variation in packing material required with different products. Restrictions in the handling and loading of hazardous products can be unique. Finally, the size of the cargo container itself can vary, allowing a larger number of products to be loaded.

Given the above variations and multitudinous loads, the combination of ways in which a particular set of products can be loaded is significant. If the cargo being shipped varies over time, the training to complete the different loading tasks can be lengthy. One does not see a repeat of similar types of loads to obtain the required training in the detailed short period of time.

Desired Effect

Where there is a significant product set (greater than 50) that the loads are not uniform (10 to 20 different types of products will be loaded into the containers), the ideal of one expert solution is to load the set of products into the least amount of space. If other factors render one as interruptions to move an in-sequence line delineate, the last row of products toward the front of the container, having met all of the stacking rules for the products. Further, the load must have the correct amount of packing materials, and all rules relative to hazardous material must have been met.

Improvements

Some of the major improvements seen in providing an expert system assistant to the loaders of discrete nonuniform products are the following:

- Reduced loading time.
- Reduced training time.
- Improved container utilization.
- Adherence to the handling of hazardous products.
- Improved quality loading.

If the time is reduced in the loading of containers, the inventory pipeline can be reduced as well.

PROBLEM DESCRIPTION

Discrete products that are placed into cargo containers vary in size and weight. Furthermore, some products can be stacked and rotated in multiple directions, while some can be loaded by laying the product on its side. Others can be stacked only in one plane. The loading of products can be a combination of these various rules.

There also can be a variation in packing material required with different products. Restrictions in the handling and loading of hazardous products can be unique. Finally, the size of the cargo container itself can vary allowing a larger number of products to be loaded.

Given the above variations and nonuniform loads, the combination of ways in which a particular set of products can be loaded is significant. If the cargo being shipped varies over time, the training to complete the different loading tasks can be lengthy. One does not see a repeat of similar types of loads to obtain the required training in the desired short period of time.

Desired Effect

Again, where there is a significant product set (greater than 50) and the loads are not uniform (10 to 20 different types of products will be loaded into the container), the ideal or optimum solution is to load the set of products into the least amount of space. If there is a cargo container one is attempting to move, an imaginary line delineates the last row of products forward to the front of the container, having met all of the stacking rules for the products. Further, the load must have the correct amount of packing materials, and all rules relative to hazardous material must have been met.

Improvements

Some of the major improvements seen in providing an expert system assistant to the loaders of discrete nonuniform products are the following:

- Reduced loading time
- Reduced training time
- Improved container utilization
- Adherence to the handling of hazardous products
- Improved quality loading.

If the time is reduced in the loading of containers, the inventory pipeline can be reduced as well.

PROBLEM DESCRIPTION

Discrete products that are placed into cargo containers vary in size and weight. Furthermore, some products can be stacked and rotated in multiple directions, while some can be loaded by laying the product on its side. Others can be stacked only in one plane. The loading of products can be a combination of the various rules.

There also can be a variation in packing material required with different products. Restrictions in the handling and loading of hazardous products can be unique. Finally, the size of the cargo container itself can vary, allowing a larger number of products to be loaded.

Given the above variations and nonuniform loads, the combination of ways in which a particular set of products can be loaded is significant. If the cargo being shipped varies over time, the training to complete the different loading tasks can be lengthy. One does not see a repeat of similar types of loads to obtain the required training in the desired short period of time.

Desired Effect

Cases where there is a significant product set (greater than 50) that the loads are not uniform (10 to 20 different types of products) will be harder into the container, the ideal or different solution is to load the set of products into the least amount of space. If either in a cross container one is attempting to move the magnitude to delineate the last row of products forward of the front of the container, having met all of the stacking rules for the products. Further, the load must have the correct amount of packing materials, and all rules relative to hazardous material must have been met.

Improvements

Some of the major improvements seen in providing an expert system assistant to the loaders of discrete nonuniform products are the following:

- Reduced loading time.
- Reduced training time.
- Improved container utilization.
- Adherence to the handling of hazardous products.
- Improved quality loading.

If the time is reduced in the loading of containers, the increasing pipeline can be reduced as well.

16
Intelligent Systems in Transportation

Michael P. Gelhausen

Andersen Consulting

Transportation industry deregulation has helped fuel the evolution of intelligent systems in the 1980s. In this chapter, the author ties the problems of the transportation industry to the information services industry. Andersen Consulting's views, advanced technologies, and specifically artificial intelligence as a means to solving some of the more urgent problems of the industry and achieving operational success. Several applications of AI are discussed, including two both in resource planning, vehicle scheduling, fleet planning and assignment, and route determination, and decision support (fault diagnosis and status evaluation). Benefits of the systems are spelled out. Systems integration of new tools, especially those coming out of the universities, is seen as a future goal. Advice is for the developers of AI systems. A section on how you'll approach job not started concludes this chapter.

INTRODUCTION

In today's business environment, companies in many industries realize the importance of utilizing evolving technologies to retain competitive in the marketplace. Each industry understands the need to improve business operations to meet the goals of enhanced customer service, improved resource management, and reduced operating costs.

The transportation industry is no different. In the face of a dynamic environment, the pace of change will continue to quicken as rising costs continue to apply pressure to corporate profitability, regulation of industry policies change, expanding market segments and increasing competition, and customers require means become more specific and demanding.

These factors place a great emphasis on the critical operating decisions that

16
Intelligent Systems in Transportation*

Michael P. Gelhausen
Andersen Consulting

Transportation industry deregulation has helped fuel the evolution of intelligent systems in the 1980s. In this chapter, the author ties the problems of the transportation industry to the information services industry. Andersen Consulting views advanced technologies, and specifically artificial intelligence, as a means of solving some of the more urgent problems of the industry and achieving operational success. Several applications of AI designed to improve productivity of operational areas of the transportation industry are discussed, including two each in resource planning (vehicle scheduling, load planning and assignment, and route determination) and decision support (fault diagnosis and status evaluation). Benefits of the systems are spelled out. Systems integration of new tools, especially those coming out of the universities, is seen as a future area of focus for the developers of AI systems. A section on how your company can get started concludes this chapter.

INTRODUCTION

In today's business environment, companies in many industries realize the importance of utilizing evolving technologies to remain competitive in the marketplace. Each industry understands the need to improve business operations to meet the goals of enhanced customer service, improved resource management, and reduced operating costs.

The transportation industry is no different. In the face of a dynamic environment, the pace of change will continue to quicken as rising costs continue to apply pressure to corporate profitability; regulation of industry policies change, expanding market segments and increasing competition; and customers' requirements become more specific and demanding.

These factors place a great emphasis on the critical operating decisions that

---

influence corporate profitability. The motor carrier, airline, railroad, shipping, and metropolitan transit segments of the transportation industry are all concerned with the efficiency of operations associated with meeting the goals and objectives set by the industry. Consequently, efforts are being made to facilitate the overall execution of the entire operations process.

Firms in the transportation industry typically seek substantial benefits in specific areas, including:

- reduction of overall operating costs
- efficient utilization of available resources
- improvement of the planning and execution of logistics activities
- operation of an effective maintenance system
- establishment of an integrated communications network
- reduction of equipment and stores levels
- improvement of management reporting on key performance factors and activity measures.

TRANSPORTATION AND LOGISTICS OVERVIEW

The Management Problem

Transportation companies typically deal in a reactive way to changes in the marketplace. Critical logistics and operating decisions are often made based on vast amounts of varying types of fragmented information. In order to be successful, management must recognize and understand the urgent need to manage their resources on a minute-to-minute basis. Carriers must recognize the importance of providing key personnel with the information required to make minute-to-minute decisions that affect profitability. They must understand the frustration that live operators feel while striving to plan and control performance without having the critical information they require.

The transportation function provides the vital link in the logistics services pipeline. That is, the applied level of transportation service effects all aspects of the business chain. In manufacturing, the chain begins with the movement of raw materials from supply sources to production facilities (physical supply) and ends with the movement of finished goods from the production facility to the warehouse and to the customer (physical distribution). For a freight distribution firm, the pipeline chain begins with the receipt of freight from the customer and ends with the delivery of the shipment to its intended recipient. For a passenger transportation company, the carrier's "cargo" is slightly different. However, the context of the logistics problem is basically the same.

The cost/service trade-off permeates the decision-making process involved in choosing appropriate courses of action by management. Improving the productivity of logistics activities is a very effective way for companies to improve their bottom-line performance. Moreover, improvements provide quick returns and require little capital investment.

Improving the productivity of transportation activities in operational areas of the industry is one of the most beneficial areas for management to focus attention due to a number of factors. First, productivity improvements provide an immediate impact on corporate cost savings. Additionally, favorable transportation activities offer benefits to all facets of the logistics pipeline (i.e., suppliers, manufacturers, and customers). Finally, improvements provide immediate relief to the planning and execution functions of management. Often, the greatest productivity improvements arise from limited capital investments.

The State of the Industry

As the marketplace continues to change and the consolidation of transportation firms continues, a focused strategic direction provides a carrier with the opportunity to effectively utilize available resources. In order to be successful, the executive management of transportation companies and those with the responsibility for executing the logistics activities face an enormous challenge. Competition for the customer dollar will be severe—even fierce—in the competitive sense.

The challenge of tomorrow will bring with it a great opportunity for operational success through corporate maturity and technological advancement. The need to present competence in all areas of the logistics process is real. The successful transportation companies and logistics departments are those who utilize established technologies today and invest in emerging technologies for the future.

INDUSTRY PERSPECTIVE

Past Advances in Applications Technology

In the more than seven years since government deregulation activities (over nine years for the airlines), transportation companies have made exceptional strides in the development of applications technology. This evolution has brought data processing to the forefront of management decision-making activities.

The computer has become a way of life in almost every business. Its use has infiltrated the operational and financial aspects of the transportation industry and is moving into the strategic planning and execution activities of the business. Management's task is to utilize this powerful tool's competence through skill and leadership.

The evolution of computer systems began with the need to manage the financial matters of the business. Accounting systems provided transportation companies with the information necessary for tracking the financial success or failure of business strategies. Accounts receivable and payable activities were tracked through small systems on hardware configurations with limited processing capabilities. These systems were well equipped for the limited information needs of small companies.

As the size and sophistication of transportation activities increased, the desire to monitor these activities evolved. The result was an automated approach to serve the informational needs of operating personnel. Operations control rose to the forefront of transportation information technology needs.

New systems offered the ability to monitor and control operating activities, such as maintenance and inventory control; equipment and stores tracking; resource dispatching; order processing and other customer services; and performance reporting of key activities.

One vital step in establishing a program to control the operational activities in the transportation industry was to improve the maintenance activities at major maintenance stations and remote site locations. Management recognized and understood this need. Internal data processing departments and independent consultants responded by providing computerized maintenance management systems to accomplish the following:

- to monitor historical costs for equipment and other assets
- to maintain and to control the inventories of spare parts required to perform maintenance activities
- to assist with the periodic scheduling of preventive maintenance activities
- to generate work orders for tracking all maintenance and logistic activities for all corporate resources.

Complex transportation infrastructures affected management's ability to provide better, more rapid, and reliable service to customers. The size and complexity of these structures required them to concentrate on the coordination of a number of disparate activities. As a result of this need to improve activity coordination, an intricate communications network was identified as the solution to the evolving problem.

Remote communication networks evolved from the need to improve service activities and to provide certain individuals access to vital information. This link between resources within the company coordinated a number of activities. Automating such activities as vehicle dispatching and load assignment through an integrated communications environment improved workforce productivity and enhanced many of the operational aspects of the business.

A further incremental step in the communications process was the emergence of Electronic Data Interchange (EDI). EDI refers to the transmission of data from one computer to another within the vertical levels of the market. Since its acceptance in the early 1980s, EDI has gained momentum in the transportation industry. Rapidly changing communications technology provided an answer to data flow problems between the different levels. This technology provides the benefits of improving operational efficiency as a way of cutting costs; differentiating the firm through customer service improvements; and providing accurate information on a timely basis.

By responding to customer and industry needs through conventional applications technology, transportation companies discovered a competitive way to retain existing accounts and preserve market share through positioning in the marketplace.

The Status of Intelligent Systems Today

While the concept of intelligent systems is relatively new, its acceptance by the transportation industry has undergone a rapid evolution. Prior to the 1980s, decision-support consisted of domain experts accessing and processing vast amounts of complex information on a manual basis. These experts utilized existing conventional systems to retrieve needed information. In the 1980s the evolution of intelligent systems was fueled by the industry deregulation and by advances in technology. Deregulation provided alternate choices and caused a focus on prices. In turn, the focus on prices led management to seek ways to control costs while maintaining an acceptable level of customer service.

Today, through advances in systems technology, management has the tools to facilitate the activities of their operating personnel. Transportation companies are realizing significant benefits in a number of areas through intelligent, decision-support systems. These areas include scheduling, load assignment, maintenance diagnostics, in-bound and out-bound logistics, inventory management, customer services, and performance monitoring.

Intelligent systems fill the "applications void." That is, those problems that were once considered too complex for conventional solutions are now being addressed with artificial intelligence (AI) technology. Knowledge captured from functional experts provides the opportunity to disseminate vast amounts of intelligence to large user audiences.

THE INTELLIGENT APPROACH TO TRANSPORTATION MANAGEMENT ISSUES

The Need for Intelligent Systems

Many decisions made in the transportation arena are made under extremely complex situations and in time-sensitive environments by first acquiring information about a particular problem and then by applying heuristics or "rules of thumb" and past experiences to provide solution alternatives. Intelligent (expert) systems capture knowledge about a particular domain in the form of a knowledge base and use the acquired knowledge to provide decision-support.

For years, artificial intelligence has been viewed as a theoretical solution to "futuristic" problems. This is no longer the case. AI has passed the buzzword stage to become a vital technological alternative for use by more and more companies to advance their position in the competitive marketplace. Intelligent systems are the cornerstone of this movement and are the most widely implemented and well-known applications of AI technology today.

Intelligent systems provide the opportunity to capture expert knowledge and make inferences about incoming information to solve critical problems that required significant human expertise to accomplish in the past. To solve a problem in transportation, an intelligent system might request initial information regarding a particular problem or occurrence from a variety of potential sources (e.g., existing systems or current users). The application then searches its knowledge base to find a reference that "fits" the information. Based on this knowledge evaluation, the system provides a conclusion to recommend management action or requests additional information to continue processing.

The purpose of this chapter is to tie today's transportation problems to the future of the information services industry. The "applications void" seen previously as the unsolvable problems of tomorrow are now approachable with advanced technologies.

There are two broad categories of applications within transportation where intelligent systems are well suited. First, monitoring and controlling critical resources provides the opportunity to plan various operational activities. Resource planning issues cover such intensive topics as vehicle scheduling, load planning and assignment, and route determination. Second, intelligent systems provide decision-support in the operation of day-to-day transportation activities. The need for an intelligent interface is evident where expert knowledge is required to perform fault diagnosis and status evaluation on vehicles and other equipment. These systems are also excellent for problems concerning the complexities of "split-second" decision making. For example, in an airline operations environment, all aspects of a decision to release an aircraft from its assigned gate must be considered in a tight time frame and the impact of such a decision evaluated against the remaining launch schedule.

The long-term benefits from the use of intelligent systems can be significant. Use of expert systems to manage routes, resolve scheduling problems, evaluate truck versus air decisions, improve maintenance diagnostics and other areas, could greatly improve overall equipment utilization and potentially reduce the need for expensive capital outlays.

Effectively reducing costs throughout the organization will be the determining factor in becoming the low-cost provider of transportation services.

Resource Planning Issues

Improving the productivity of corporate resources is a very effective way to improve bottom-line performance. For the transportation industry, the resource problem is addressed through an enhanced operations planning process.

We have focused on a number of resource planning issues for a variety of transportation clients. In doing so, we have addressed a variety of problems in two specific areas: scheduling and assignment. Scheduling covers the breadth of in-bound and out-bound logistics problems. To support the requirements of an effective transportation system, many transportation companies must deal with two types of assignments: load assignment and route-level assignment.

As a result of our activities in these areas, we have developed a number of operational intelligent systems. The following two narratives illustrate solutions to a complex ship scheduling problem and an interactive route assignment problem.

We call many of the systems we develop at Andersen Consulting *assistants* or *tools*, that is systems that provide answers and recommendations. However, people in the process still have a lot of knowledge that you are never going to get into the current generation of technology. For example, you still need people in the loop in most kinds of scheduling applications, such as the one described below. As projected results are presented to the user, there is an opportunity to modify them or to query the application.

Ship scheduler tool application. Conventional computing technologies have proven largely ineffective in supporting complex scheduling applications. Due to the nature of the scheduling task, current commercial packages are mostly restricted to providing information from which the scheduler can make decisions. Virtually no "intelligent" support is provided by these systems. However, artificial intelligence and knowledge-based systems technology have been identified as key technologies in providing intelligent support for the scheduling task.

At Andersen Consulting we have developed an integrated system to address the scheduling needs of a major overseas government's Transport Division. The overriding objective of the scheduling function is to efficiently and cost-effectively service the needs of the Transport Division.

We took a knowledge-based approach with the ship scheduling application relying on the experience of current scheduling experts to define the decision-making strategies to be adopted. The scheduling problem comprised two components:

- the establishment of a baseline schedule with a planning horizon that, while long enough to be operationally useful, was not so long as to make the schedule impractical
- the reactive regeneration of this schedule based on changing constraints in the environment.

While the decision-making approach to both tasks had some similarities, in reactive (as opposed to baseline) scheduling, the human expert makes more use of tactics that have evolved from past experience to modify the schedule. Indeed, capturing these tactics with the knowledge-based system was one of the project's longer-term objectives. The dissemination of this knowledge to other schedulers is the result of this system.

The principal automated aids available to the scheduler are a database of ship characteristics containing historical information on each vessel—manual scheduling processes—and a linear programming tool that is used to construct a "standard voyage." As the context of the environment changes, the system modifies the existing routes and provides new scheduling information. Preparing and regenerating these schedules is a highly complex and very specialized task, and the associated knowledge domain covers a breadth of operational issues.

The use of AI to solve this unique problem addresses certain critical issues. The in-bound and out-bound logistics of the ship transport process is managed providing the maximum utilization of available resources. Other benefits realized are improved coordination of logistics activities; cost-effective route combinations, with selection of many more possible routes than a human is able to consider; and providing the user with what appeared to be a simplified solution to a complex scheduling problem.

The truck routing assistant application. Many transportation companies that deliver goods to a large base of customers face the problem of designing delivery routes that make the best use of available resources. Constraints such as differences in customer requirements and vehicle types complicate the problem. Add decisions requiring pattern recognition—traffic flows and switchbacks, for example—and routing becomes a problem too large to be handled by a simple machine.

We developed as a prototype system the Truck Routing Assistant (TRA), as a "proof of concept" to demonstrate how AI techniques can be used to solve this type of resource planning problem. As an intelligent workbench for companies involved in the distribution and transportation of products, the Truck Routing Assistant illustrates the feasibility of various techniques that can be used to develop a complete customized system.

The TRA is used as a starting point for developing production systems to assist in designing efficient routes that save time, money, and energy. It has the ability to monitor performance at both the distribution center and route levels. The user may use this information to analyze different scenarios through "what if" analysis. The TRA is capable of detecting and informing the user of illogical routes (e.g., backtracking or crisscrossing routes), which the user may choose to act on or ignore.

How much control the user exerts over the TRA varies according to the user's needs. On the one hand, the Truck Routing Assistant may be used as a simple route editing tool, while on the other hand, it may be used as an advisor that determines the recommended position for a stop on a route. The user may do some manual rerouting based on other criteria that is known.

The intelligent system helps to identify and correct routing problems quickly and easily. The general framework provided by this solution can be changed and extended to meet specific business requirements. With a customized knowledge base, the Truck Routing Assistant aids the user in accomplishing the following tasks.

- It displays all delivery stops for a route, pertinent information about any individual stop or route, all current routes (in graphics or text mode), and all stops yet to be assigned a route.
- It creates, edits, or deletes stops or routes.
- It adds or removes a stop (manually or automatically).
- It resequences stops (manually or automatically).
- It examines the consequences of route modifications through "what if" analysis.
- It displays and updates performance criteria at the distribution center and route levels.
- It maintains dynamic information about closed bridges, traffic patterns, shortcuts, access status, and road conditions.

The ability to react to changes in the environment allows the scheduler to properly identify the appropriate solutions. Improved resource planning results in the benefits of increased router (dispatcher) efficiency, improved service levels, increased distribution center and router capacity, fewer total miles driven, and decreased distribution center costs.

Decision-Support Issues

The essence of an intelligent system is knowledge about a specific domain of interest. With the dynamic state of an everchanging environment, certain types of decisions are "mission critical" to many transportation companies. The ability to access a source of knowledge to support these decisions will provide companies with a competitive edge by disseminating the knowledge and experience of experts within the company.

Andersen Consulting has been very active in this arena. We have made a concerted effort to answer specific operational questions for the transportation industry. The following three narratives (micro-dispatch, aircraft maintenance/diagnostics, and in-air maintenance debrief) will discuss two specific decision issues:

1. Critical ("split second") decisions. This decision-support area covers those decisions that are based on the current state of a dynamic operating environment.

2. Diagnostic decisions. The support of maintenance activities through intelligent diagnostic procedures provides benefits in a number of operational areas.

Micro-dispatch assistant. In the truckload carrier market, operations are very dynamic. Thousands of trucks may be moving across the nation's highways simultaneously, and customers call in for shipment movements on the day of desired pickup. For those unfamiliar with the freight segment of the industry, *truckload carriers* are irregular route carriers who pick up an entire load of freight from a shipper and transport it directly to the destination point without transloading or combining it with other freight at terminal facilities. In this environment, it is very important to utilize whatever information is available to you—whether complete or not—to make the best operational decisions possible.

Experienced dispatchers and planners are generally able to do a good job of assigning drivers to trucks and trucks to loads. During a given day, 30 to 40 trucks may be delivering within a major metropolitan area, thereby becoming available for outbound dispatch. Each of these trucks has various characteristics, including the type of equipment (dry or refrigerated van), length and cubic capacity, number of drivers, driver domicile, and so on. In a balanced operating environment, there would also be 30 to 40 loads originating in that major metropolitan area on the same day. These loads would also have their own characteristics, such as equipment requirements, pickup and delivery time windows, and weight. The operational problem is to perform optimal assignment between the available drivers, trucks, and loads. Experienced dispatchers and planners have historically performed this task with fewer variables. However, new people and fast growth of the industry have made this task a very difficult yet key activity.

In order to assist the load planners, we developed an application that would assist the load planning function. The Micro-Dispatch Assistant (see Figure 16.1) takes as its primary inputs customer forecasts, known loads, and current truck locations. Its outputs are marginal load values and equipment movement plans. This graphics-driven interface shows many of the variables and situations to the load planner at a glance. Suggested assignments of drivers, trucks, and loads are displayed to the load planner upon session initiation. It is up to the load planner to modify or query the application to try to improve upon the answer. It is important that the load planner have this ability, as the dynamic situation frequently means that he may know more about the evolving situation than is in the system's database. The system is able to automatically check against 25 to 30 criteria for determining whether or not a recommended match is a good one for the system as a whole. Inappropriate matches, or those that could be done more effectively, have critiques that are presented to the load planner describing potential alternative courses of action.

This application provides several benefits to the motor carrier. In addition to increased load planner productivity, it is also possible to decrease the total number of miles driven, improve customer service through more on-time pickups

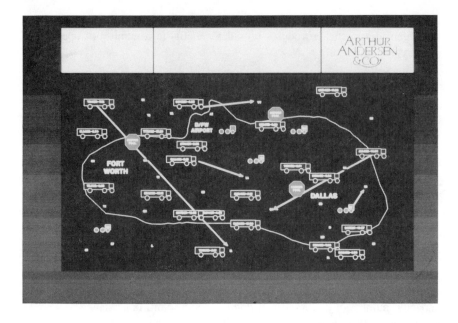

Figure 16.1.   Sample Screen—Micro-Dispatch Assistant

and deliveries, and improve the driver's quality of life by assigning drivers to loads that match their desires to return home periodically.

The aircraft maintenance/diagnostic system. Transportation companies understand the need to maintain low equipment maintenance costs while operating safely. Consequently, efforts are being made to facilitate the overall execution of the maintenance process. The airline industry, in particular, seeks substantial benefits in certain areas: reduction of aircraft "down" time; efficient utilization of the maintenance labor force; decreasing overhead costs; operation of an efficient maintenance system; lower aircraft component and stores levels; and management reporting on key performance factors and activity measures.

We have taken a significant step toward achieving productivity improvements in each of these areas. Using artificial intelligence technology and conventional application techniques, we developed an integrated diagnostics and fleet maintenance control system to address these needs.

The Aircraft Maintenance/Diagnostic System (AM/DS) is an interactive system that complements the flight technician. AM/DS is a diagnostic tool developed to analyze aircraft problems and the conditions under which each occurred.

It provides the technician with a comprehensive diagnostic path and offers corrective action solutions based on knowledge captured from experts in the field.

Inside the diagnostics module, complex reasoning tasks are performed using a rule-based knowledge structure that culminates in the production of a diagnostic maintenance path. The diagnostic path provides the technician with the information that is necessary to correct the particular aircraft problem and consists of three parts:

1. The *operational checkout*, which is the first set of procedures performed by the technician.
2. The *meter checks*, which are related to the specific operational checkout procedures performed.
3. The *corrective action list*, which provides the technician with the appropriate action to solve the specific problem.

The diagnostic process consists of the satisfaction of a series of related questions via a dialog between the maintenance technician and the flight crew. The questioning process allows the user to identify the particular problem, the conditions under which the problem occurred, and the appropriate action to solve the problem. The pilot or crew is involved in some of the troubleshooting exercise to actually come through the diagnostic process to direct the maintenance technicians how to troubleshoot the process more effectively.

AM/DS provides many features and capabilities. These include problem determination and identification, simple solutions through a structured diagnostic path, and graphic presentation of corrective action trends. Some benefits of this integrated maintenance diagnostic approach are lower vehicle "down" time, improved labor productivity, maintenance cost history tracking, and status (exception and performance report generation).

In-Air Maintenance Debrief System. The In-Air Maintenance Debrief System application was designed to be part of an overall Air-to-Ground Maintenance Communications System for a major commercial airline and was developed to capture the functionality of an in-flight diagnostician. The system is a tool that facilitates the flow of critical maintenance information between the flight crew and maintenance operations. Almost 70 percent of the problems that occur in the air are not repeatable on the ground. Thus, if the air crew says that they experienced a problem in the air, perhaps a hydraulic problem, and it is not apparent on the ground what the problem was, then the maintenance crew may have to replace the entire hydraulic system, which is time consuming and expensive, or they don't do anything because they could not replicate the problem. As a diagnostic tool, the in-air system provides the crew with a simplified approach to problem identification, an automated tool replacing search-and-find techniques required with cumbersome manuals, and an integrated communications system to forewarn operations personnel of pending aircraft maintenance.

In today's business environment, airlines understand the need to meet the goals of enhanced customer service, improved resource management, and reduced operating costs. One critical component of improving customer service is time. Time savings impact each operational aspect of a successful carrier.

As the pace of technological change continues to quicken, one area of increasing concern becomes the assimilation and communication of maintenance information from a carrier to a hub or remote-site maintenance location. For airlines, this problem is compounded by the complexity of an aircraft's design and the need to perform standardized procedures to locate maintenance problems.

When the flight crew utilizes an in-flight diagnostic system and notifies the receiving maintenance station, there are several previously time-consuming activities that are performed. Utilizing the fault analysis process eliminates the need for maintenance to perform these steps *after* the aircraft arrives. Also, early reception of the fault code by the receiving station before the aircraft arrives permits maintenance to pre-plan the necessary tasks to eliminate the fault and reduce delays due to unnecessary maintenance activities. Figure 16.2 is a sample screen of the diagnostic system.

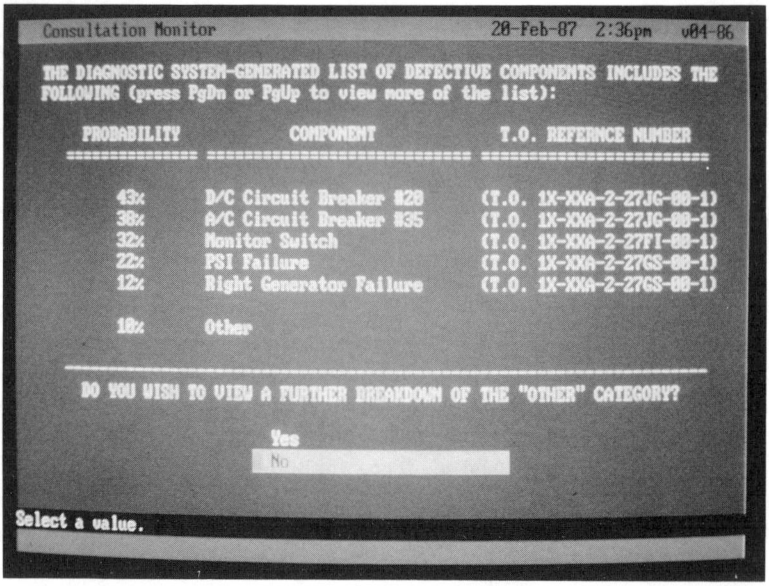

Figure 16.2.   Sample Screen—In-Air Maintenance Debrief System

The benefits of in-flight diagnostic systems are several. They include increased aircraft reliability, reduced aircraft down-time and lower maintenance costs. By utilizing the flight environment, the flight crew can perform the system fault analysis utilizing an on-board system and transmit the results to maintenance operations with a standard code prior to the arrival of the aircraft. This provides the flight crew with an automated diagnostic tool and maintenance with a direct "troubleshooting" entry, and avoids duplicating flight crew efforts in fault analysis. Other benefits are improved aircraft turn-time and improved customer service; enhanced revenue due to the reduction of passenger rescheduling and cancellations; decreased impact on maintenance activities at remote sites and hubs; increased available operational hours; and improved productivity of the maintenance workforce.

The Future of AI in Transportation

Artificial intelligence has entered the mainstream of applications technology and established itself as a viable solution for a number of problems in the transportation industry. Where do we go from here?

As our understanding of the technology improves, so will our perception of the use of intelligent systems in the business arena. In the few short years since its emergence into the commercial market, our view of AI as a stand-alone decision-support tool has changed. There has been a concerted effort to integrate intelligent processing with conventional applications. This trend will continue. In the future we will see embedded expert systems as the norm. One of our partners who is in charge of our advanced technology practice in a worldwide basis believes that 70 percent of all of our projects within the next five years will have some form of artificial intelligence activity imbedded within them. This will be a radical change for us as well as for our clients. We have already started to see this prediction borne out.

The ease of maintenance and flexibility in design will facilitate the acceptance of AI technology. We will see improvements in a number of operational activities. One such activity is the integrated maintenance environment, where the coordination of the activities of the maintenance function will involve tying together such areas as maintenance history and equipment diagnostics. Another activity where improvement will occur is in the integrated control facility, where the integration of decision support and resource planning systems with general operations control application will result in improved productivity.

CONCLUSION

The acceptance and support of artificial intelligence techniques by the management group is crucial to its success. We must focus on the business needs of carriers in areas previously unsolvable with traditional systems technologies.

What is the approach to applying AI technology to your company's situation? From a conceptual standpoint, this involves five major steps:

1. Problem identification
2. Initial prototype development
3. Development iteration
4. Systems implementation
5. Knowledge-base tuning

Customer service, resource management, and operating activities are key to the success of companies in the transportation industry. The constraints of operating in the dynamic marketplace will continue to challenge each of us. With the potential for significant cost savings and productivity improvements, intelligent systems will most certainly continue to be commercially accepted as a solution to a number of transportation problems.

17
Corporate Management Considerations in Moving Toward the Implementation of a Knowledge-Based System

Ron Roberts

Federal Express Company

This chapter is an overview of how one corporation, motivated by the desire to realize its corporate mission of 100 percent performance efficiency, has moved toward implementation of a knowledge-based system. The chapter explains how Federal Express progressed from the realization that an opportunity for an AI application existed within its scheduling operations through the process of defining a goal and strategic plan to its approach, including design perspective and development considerations. Included is a discussion of the operational environment for the knowledge-based system.

INTRODUCTION

Artificial intelligence may very well prove to be the most significant influence in how a business utilizes automation since the original invention and introduction of the computer itself. Whether or not the computer programs and systems developed with this technology can truly be said to be intelligent, even artificially intelligent, may be an issue that invokes some controversy, and no doubt those who have the time and inclination will engage in the debates pertaining to that subject for some time to come.

For those of us more concerned with decisions that are related to justifying and employing these systems, the time, energy, and focus of our efforts might better be on the bottom-line results that can be attributed to their use. In that context, the philosophical discussions, technical jargon, and marketing "hype" surrounding this increasingly well-publicized technology can probably all be reduced to a simple question—"Does it improve my operation, and if so, to what extent relative to the required investment?" The answers to those questions are not in this chapter. Indeed, I think it would be presumptuous even to attempt to answer the questions as they relate to one's business or endeavor, because we at Federal Express have not even fully answered the questions relative to our own interests at this juncture.

IDENTIFICATION OF POTENTIAL APPLICATION

One of several aspects of operations at Federal Express, where a potential for improvement through the use of AI technology has been identified, is in real-time dynamic rescheduling in some of our critical base business operations. It has been determined that some other organizations have been successful in applying this technology to address similar opportunities, in specific, the application of knowledge-based scheduling systems. The potential for success and the effort at Federal Express is seen as sufficient to justify some risk in proceeding. We have found a way to minimize that risk by approaching the total scheduling opportunity through incremental steps.

The application in question is not the kind that differentiates between corporate success and failure. What Federal Express is seeking is more like a fine-tuning of an operation that already works at an amazingly high level of performance efficiency. At present, the best internal measures of performance indicate that Federal Express is consistently successful in meeting our service commitments between 96 or 98 percent of the time. It is that remaining 2 to 4 percentage points, as shown in Figure 17.1, that *elusive* 2 to 4 percentage points, that are the target of the effort I address below.

A series of scheduling applications have been identified, proposed, and are now being pursued within Federal Express. What I share with you below is a corporate overview of the overall process experienced thus far by the corporation in its pursuit of knowledge-based scheduling applications. Some detail will be shared about how the task is being approached. We won't throw the covers completely back, as we have to attempt to protect any proprietary operational magic that we may have conjured up or devised over the years. Hopefully, however, you will be able to judge if and how this utilization of technology in our corporation may apply to your own opportunities.

OPERATIONAL ENVIRONMENT

First, let us look at the operational setting within which this development is taking place at Federal Express. Our corporate mission statement reads in part that Federal Express will provide totally reliable, competitively superior, global air-ground transportation of high-priority goods that require rapid, time-certain delivery. At present that entails movement of one million packages and documents each day. The majority of those items enter the system after 1:00 pm and

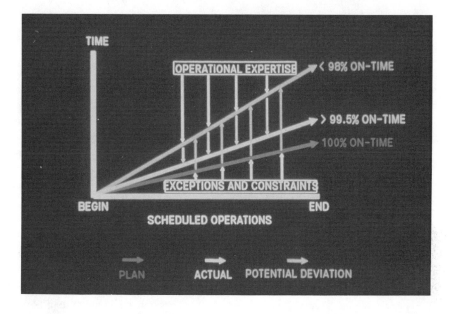

Figure 17.1. Federal Express's performance in meeting service commitments

are committed for delivery by 10:30 am the following day. To accomplish that mission, the company employs almost 60,000 people, operates about 20,000 surface vehicles, and flies more than 100 airplanes in an increasingly complicated hub-and-spoke transportation and distribution network.

Each consigned package and document must flow through a minimum of three, and frequently more, of the company's globally dispersed facilities enroute to its final destination point. During that journey the item may be sorted and consolidated with other packages headed for the same intermediate or final destination. All the people, trucks, airplanes, sort equipment, and other resources and activities have to work together in a highly interdependent, tightly scheduled environment. In that environment, delays of only a few minutes in any single activity has the potential to adversely impact our service commitment to literally thousands of customers in a given day.

Federal Express allocates tremendous levels of human and computer resources to the modeling, planning, and scheduling function supporting operations groups responsible for ensuring optimization and efficiency of those critical resources. The result, generally, is a finely orchestrated daily, weekly, and monthly operating plan, or set of plans and schedules. Theoretically those plans and schedules define what it takes to successfully perform the corporate mission. In any particular operational window, there are dozens of separate exception conditions and constraints that can and do manifest in thousands of combinations, all pressuring toward schedule delays.

Those factors that cannot be planned beyond general anticipation of their occurrence have to be handled as they happen. Many times that has to happen in only seconds to minutes from the time the exception situation is recognized and identified. Examples of the kinds of influences involved are equipment failures, adverse weather, traffic congestion (both surface and air), as well as unanticipated freight volume. Other constraints (e.g., cost, government regulation, time, distance) frequently complicate the problem resolution process by eliminating the viability of what would otherwise be logical or obvious alternatives for resolution.

When the projections are accurate, plans well-executed, and the schedules are met, the operation runs truly at very near perfect levels of precision. It is when those scheduled activities begin to be affected by unforeseen events that the operation begins to drift downward from the 100 percent reliability standard set as the only acceptable level of performance for the corporation. For those that might scoff at that goal of perfection, Federal's CEO is likely to point out that no one would very likely accept 98 or 99 percent reliability in their banking transactions or telephone service. It is understood that the people who entrust their high priority goods and documents to our company for delivery expect and deserve nothing less than absolute assurance of on-time delivery every time they use the service.

THE OPPORTUNITY FOR KNOWLEDGE SYSTEMS

Traditional scheduling, modeling, and planning techniques generally fail to produce the needed ability to respond in operational real-time with new, optimized schedules based on conditions that can change anywhere in the system at any time. Even sophisticated, conventional operations research methods and tools may take more time than is available to present the required output reschedule in the real-world operating environment. To provide the needed problem resolution and exception-management capability, numerous monitoring and control functions have been established throughout the corporation's critical operations organizations. These functions are supported by a number of manual and automated communications and information systems. The systems are designed to supply timely status updates and narrowly focused aspects of the overall package transfer operation.

The people who receive the status information collectively possess the knowledge required to compensate for any known potential schedule-delaying event. They also have the authority to initiate necessary schedule adjustments and resource diversions as required to respond to the exception situations. That human knowledge base and the cooperation of all the people who possess and apply it, frequently are the ultimate guarantors of the service commitment that is the cornerstone of Federal Express's success in the overnight express freight market. It is within this particular domain that knowledge systems technology is seen to present a unique opportunity for both operational and productivity enhancements.

In many instances the people tasked with providing alternative courses of action must do so not only within very short time frames but also without visibility to the potential downstream impact of their decision. Often the result is selection of the best alternative considered that effectively addresses the immediate concern. In such cases, the proper resolution of one problem may introduce additional factors into other aspects of the operational cycle or into subsequent operations, which, in turn, must also be handled as exception situations. The size, complexity, and dynamics of the operation, exacerbated by the time constraints under which the decisions must be made and actions initiated, expand the relevant decision factors significantly beyond the number that the human mind can consider concurrently.

Post-operational analyses performed each morning following the nightly turn through our main work facility in Memphis, Tennessee, reveals some instances where other-than-the-optimum available alternatives were chosen or selected to resolve plan irregularities. The comparison may show that unnecessary expense in incurred by actions taken to restore the plan to within bounds required to meet service commitments. In some situations, it may have been possible to both spend less *and* avoid a service failure that ultimately occurred in spite of the implemented recovery action.

At the same time, the Monday morning quarterbacks seldom determine that the decisions made reflect flawed logic or judgment in context with the information and factors considered. Nor is it often determined that it would be reasonable to expect the decision makers to consider additional information or factors in the amount of time allowed to respond to the situation, given the available decision-support tools. In short, Federal Express has demonstrated the capability to plan and schedule the most efficient and reliable system possible for providing its marketed services. Further, the company has acquired and developed the necessary operational expertise to consistently execute those plans and schedules with very near-perfect precision. However, that expertise currently exists in a somewhat fragmented aggregation of organizational control units. Within those organizations, it is inventoried primarily in the individual minds of people who are in key personnel positions. When called upon to apply that expert knowledge, it may not always be possible to consider the global operational perspective—the "big picture."

Since no single person or group individually possesses all the knowledge, it is difficult to ensure that all of the decision factors are incorporated in any given exception response. Even if such person or group did exist, the dynamics and time restrictions mentioned previously could prohibit effective application of knowledge within human limitations.

GOAL, STRATEGIC PLAN, AND APPROACH

The goal of this application of knowledge systems technology is a fully interactive complex of dynamic scheduling and planning systems, as shown graphically in Figure 17.2 linking individual operations control functions in the various operations groups. The embedded knowledge-base components of the system's complex can advise control personnel concerning available alternative actions for recovery in what we sometimes call "irregular operation scenarios." When fully implemented, the system will present a networked series of knowledge bases separately capable of reasoning about particular scheduling activities. Collectively, the network can shift the knowledge and information concerning interdependencies among the individual operation functions. In this way, the advice given in response to any specific exception condition will incorporate relevant considerations pertaining to subsequent critical path activities.

The strategic plan (design, development, and deployment) of these applica-

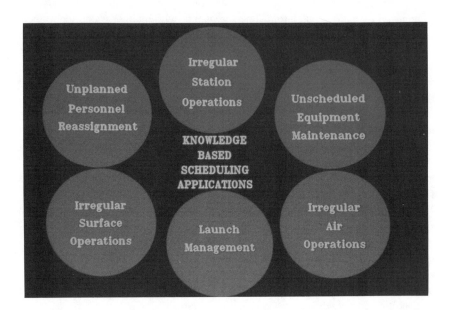

Figure 17.2.   Knowledge-based scheduling applications

tions recognizes that the ultimate objective of the effort cannot and does not need to be accomplished in one step. It is fully expected that as the effort progresses, additional applications opportunities will surface. An incremental, iterative process can break the total effort into manageable development projects and facilitate rapid delivery of valuable functionality at the same time. As a general guideline, we target completion of each increment in about 4- to 6-month time frames. The goal is to deliver functionality that is perceived as valuable from the end-user's perspective in each of the represented organizations in those time frames.

Both the goal and strategy of the effort emphasize a business rather than a technological focus. While that perspective is arguably prudent in any considered use of automation, it is particularly important where new or advanced technologies are involved. In these cases the tendency may exist to justify use of some exciting technological advancement by rationalizing development of less than high leverage applications. It is here that the question of relative improvement versus investment has to be asked and answered.

From those functions within Federal Express that have been identified so far, a representative application is being considered for the initial development effort. That effort will be augmented by contracted assistance from a qualified external supplier. The contract support may help both to ensure success with the project and at the same time aid in the acquisition of needed skills and transfer of technology. The experience of the supplier may also bring to the table the ability to facilitate development of program code and modules that will be able to be reused in subsequent development applications in the same domain of scheduling activities.

Concurrent with that initial development and transfer of technology, a slate of applications-specific development tools will begin to be constructed and applied. This will allow us to take some of that front-end investment and further leverage it into the future as other applications are developed. As the effort progresses, internal staff may assume a greater share of the development responsibility with the obvious intent being to eliminate dependence on third-party support as quickly as possible.

We think that if we can demonstrate success and value from the initial application and leverage that through internal publicity to secure increased involvement and support from other areas in the corporation, these efforts will support our need to branch into parallel development projects as we are ready internally to do. As the expansion occurs, we will continue to maintain our focus on the high-value applications and emphasize that approach.

DESIGN PERSPECTIVE AND DEVELOPMENT CONSIDERATIONS

The final point that should be understood in this case overview is that these applications under consideration within Federal Express are neither stand-alone nor exclusively AI technology–based systems. Analyses conducted thus far indicate that knowledge systems development will represent really only a relatively small percentage of the total development effort as shown in Figure 17.3. Similarly, automated reasoning is expected to account for substantially less than half the total computing resource required to operate the systems in a production environment. Other technologies, including those related to communications, computer graphics, and conventional database transaction processing will consume the lion's share of both the development and computer resource allocations.

It seems increasingly apparent to us that this relationship with conventional data processing technologies is much more likely to be the rule rather than the exception in practical business applications of so-called intelligent systems. Unfortunately, that realization has been somewhat slow in dawning on many of the corporations and companies pursuing commercialization of artificial intelligence. The reason for that oversight may be traceable to the origins of many of those companies in the academic community where for over 30 years the technologies were developed in relative isolation from the realities of business-oriented data processing. Here again is possibly a topic worthy of some extended discussion and debate for some and of little or no practical concern for others.

What is of concern is the result of an abundance of marketed tools that may

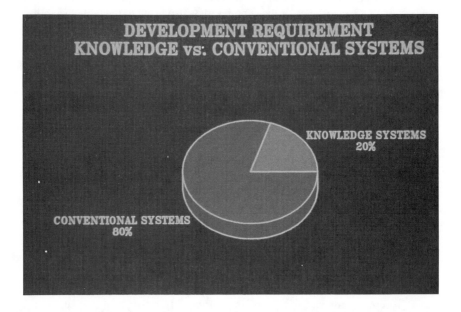

Figure 17.3. Development requirement: Knowledge vs. Conventional systems

work for knowledge systems development, but may also restrict or prohibit access to other electronic environments where needed data and information resides. It is also often difficult when using these tools to incorporate use of other development aids, such as graphics packages, with many of the software tools commercially available for use in development of knowledge-based systems. On the other hand, the AI technology market environment, particularly in business applications, is still in its infancy. It is evolving at an increasing pace in response to the pressures from an extremely demanding corporate customer base.

Recently, the AI market is also responding to the competitive thrust of major computer heavyweights who are entering the arena at a full charge to capture leadership positioning. This latter influence includes both the business savvy and the awareness of the importance of systems integration that have been characteristically absent in the strategies of most of the early marketeers of the technology. We are beginning to see the results of those influences in the form of tools that seem to be much better suited for use in the business computing environment. At present, however, I think I would say that the caution "buyer beware" continues to be sound advice for those who are looking to acquire development tools or shells for their use in facilitating introduction of this technology into their operations.

SUMMARY

What I have discussed above with respect to Federal Express's internal assessment of need and subsequent development of a strategic plan for implementation of knowledge systems technology is really quite simple to understand. Once plans and schedules have been implemented and the associated activities are begun, any number of constraints and exceptions may develop anywhere in the system. It is the objective of this effort to programmatically capture and apply the available corporate knowledge about how to recover from those situations through an integrated network of knowledge bases. Individually, these knowledge bases may contain information and expertise concerning only a very narrow facet of the scheduled operation. Together, they can share the knowledge related to the interdependencies among those activities. That shared knowledge should enable the systems to present recovery alternatives, including both broader and longer-term schedule and plan considerations than might be possible within the limitations of human reasoning alone. Of course, it will remain the responsibility of people, who can apply judgment as well as knowledge and information that the systems may not contain, to either accept or reject the machine-generated alternatives.

At this juncture, it is still too early to evaluate either the benefits or the challenges that may result from the application of knowledge systems technology at Federal Express for the scheduling opportunities presented by the company's operation. It will take another year or two to realize any results. I do know that suddenly there is a great deal of anticipation and enthusiasm associated with the applications, both in the development and user communities. This enthusiasm may be tempered by perhaps something more than a modicum of apprehension having to do with the notion of computer systems that mimic human reasoning abilities. Overall, I think the feeling of those most aware of the risks and potentials is probably best characterized as hopeful expectation—hopeful expectation that the technology will support achievement, both of those remaining couple of percentage points of service and performance as well as in a significant reduction in the costs associated with those levels of operational excellence. With respect to the latter, if only as much as half the improvement reported by others using this technology in similar applications could be realized at Federal Express, the result would literally be tremendous savings in operation cost each year.

A lot of the publicity to date about the use of knowledge-based or expert systems in the business environment has focused on relatively small tactical applications. Certainly there are an abundance of opportunities in that regard for use of the technology in almost any organization. Many of them can return significant value. The message I would hope to leave with you from this overview is that there is also a great potential for employing the technology in much larger strategic applications, including those that may center directly in the heart of one's operation and for which there is no other practical automated solution. I would certainly encourage anyone who has not already done so to, at the very least, investigate the possibility that those opportunities may exist in your organization. If you find that they do, I would challenge you to be bold in championing an aggressive pursuit of knowledge systems solutions. The return certainly may prove to be worthwhile and far exceed the risk that you have to encounter initially.

18

A Unique Use of Expert Systems in Scheduling Complex Personnel Assignments

Claude McMillan

Management Robotics

The author provides in the introduction a general description of the components of commercially available development systems for building an expert system, or general problem solvers: the largely decoupled inference engine and knowledge base. The difference between knowledge-based systems and the traditional mode of producing information systems is described. The subject of this paper is a unique knowledge-based system for employee scheduling, in which the inference engine is closely coupled to the knowledge base in contrast to the decoupled development systems. This expert system has been developed to make complex personnel assignments and functions to replace operations managers in the performance of the scheduling function. This system provides an example of how expert systems may be used to solve complex scheduling problems. Chosing to use a decoupled or a closely coupled system is dependent upon whether a problem is ill structured or well defined.

INTRODUCTION TO EXPERT SYSTEMS

In his book *The Sciences of the Artificial*, Nobel laureate Herbert Simon suggests that the difference between a real expert and a novice is not so much in the quality of his "inference mechanism" as in his "knowledge base."

Each of us has a rather adequate capacity to observe facts and relationships and to make inferences—to reach conclusions. However, some of us have stores of knowledge that are substantially richer than those of others that equips them to solve more complex problems and frequently to produce better solutions. Our personal inference mechanisms have something in common with the inference engines supplied by those firms in the artificial intelligence (AI) business that provide their customers with development systems, systems for building expert systems, or knowledge-based (KB) systems, as we will refer to them in this chapter.

Many of these systems are readily available today on the commercial market—they are computer software systems that help their users to build KB systems. Examples of development systems are KEE (supplied by Intellicorp), S.1 (Tecknowledge, Inc.), ART (Inference, Inc.) and PC Plus (Texas Instruments).

The typical development system comes equipped with two major components: an inference engine and a rather highly interactive component to help the user build a knowledge base (Figure 18.1). Since much of the skill required to build a knowledge base is built into the development system, we find many prospective users of knowledge-based systems—people in business and government— building their own knowledge bases rather than employing experienced knowledge engineers, systems analysts, or software engineers.

Once the knowledge base has been constructed, the user then needs only to turn to the inference engine that comes with the development system, using it to interact with the knowledge base much as he might interact with an expert (Figure 18.2). These two components—the knowledge base, constructed by the user, and the inference engine, supplied with the development system— constitute the KB system that development systems are designed to help their users construct.

The inference engine proves to be a relatively modest part of the ultimate KB system. The real powerhouse in most KB systems is the knowledge base, confirming in a way Simon's conviction that in human beings the inference mechanism may be pretty much there for each of us. However, for the experts among us the associated knowledge base in each expert's field of expertise may be truly unique.

Like the development system of which it is a part, the inference engine is software—a computer program. Three things about the inference engine are particularly interesting:

1.   It is nonprocedural in design (unlike traditional software systems)

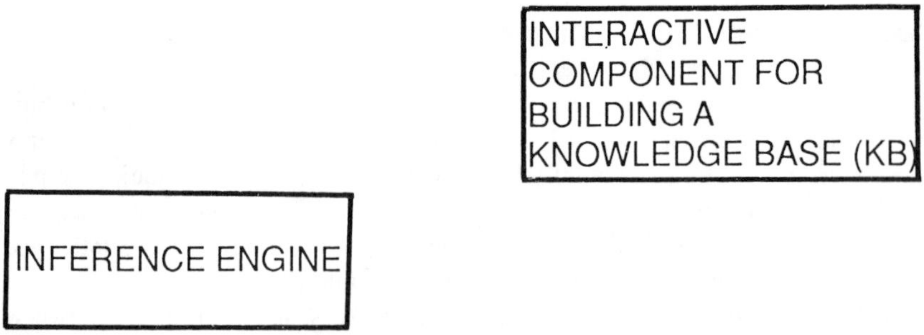

INTERACTIVE COMPONENT FOR BUILDING A KNOWLEDGE BASE (KB)

INFERENCE ENGINE

Figure 18.1.   The Basic Components Supplied by Vendors of Development Systems

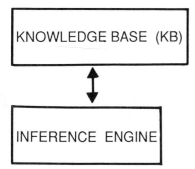

Figure 18.2.   The Basic Components in a Knowledge-Based System

2. It is rather fully decoupled from the data it processes (that is, from the knowledge base)
3. It is a kind of general purpose problem solver.

The inference engines supplied with development systems are very commonly written in the LISP programming language rather than in traditional procedural languages, such as COBOL, FORTRAN, PASCAL, and C. When programming in a procedural language, software engineers are very explicit in telling the computer precisely how to do things at every step in the processing of the data.

When programming in LISP, the software engineer tells the computer *what* is to be done but is not explicit in specifying *how* it is to be done, leaving that for the system to decide. This implies that the inference engine must be more intelligent than traditional, procedural systems, and indeed that is frequently the case. The inference engine is also different in that it tends to be so designed as to be relatively independent of, or decoupled from, the data it processes. That is, it is independent of the knowledge base (Figure 18.3). Change the knowledge base and the associated program needs no modification.

In contrast, traditional software systems are not independent of the data they process but instead are intimately coupled to that data, for example, a payroll system whose purpose is to solve the payroll problem. Typically the nature and structure of the data files that the payroll system must process to produce a payroll have a heavy influence on the design of the software that produces the payroll. If the structure of the files is changed the payroll program must be changed. The payroll system and the data it processes are closely coupled.

Programmed in a nonprocedural language such as LISP, and decoupled from the data it will process, the inference engine becomes a general problem solver. To create a new KB system, designed to address an entirely new problem, one simply builds a new knowledge base, then calls into play the general purpose inference engine. For example, given a KB system designed to diagnose diseases, we simply supply a new set of facts and rules relating to financial risk

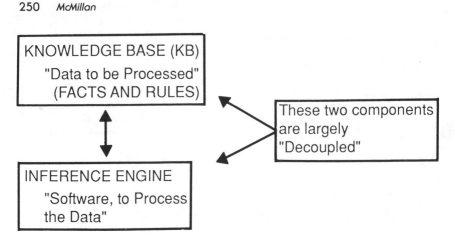

Figure 18.3. The Inference Engine as Software and the Knowledge Base as Data

analysis (that is, we build a new knowledge base) and we have a new KB system, an expert for doing risk analysis. Our general purpose inference mechanism is suitable for either domain of expertise (Figure 18.4).

The importance of this innovation should not be underestimated. In some ways, the real distinction between producing information systems in the traditional mode and producing information systems in the symbolic logic mode (the mode employed in the development systems we speak of), is that the software produced in the symbolic logic mode (the inference engine) is more intelligent, more independent of the data to be processed, and it serves as a kind of general problem solver.

An additional distinction merits a comment. In the knowledge base associated with a KB system (that is, in the data that the inference engine processes) some information has been made more explicit. Therefore knowledge bases tend to

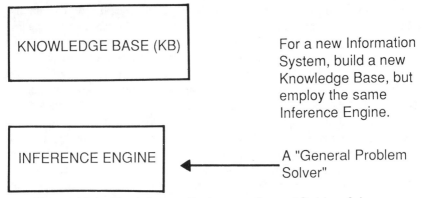

Figure 18.4. The Inference Engine as a General Problem Solver

have a larger semantic content—to be more intelligent—than do routine administrative databases. Therefore, both the program and the data are generally more intelligent in KB systems.

Does this mean we can produce new information systems without programming? If that were generally true it would be a great boon to management; programming is tedious, labor-intensive, and expensive. While in the past 30 years we have made extraordinary strides in productivity in the development of new hardware systems, productivity gains in producing software have been relatively insignificant.

Happily, as we have already implied above, development systems do equip us to produce new information systems without programming. However, we can avoid new programming as we construct a new information system only where the problem the new system is to solve is relatively simple. For more complex problems, users of today's development systems generally find it necessary to do some programming, generally in a language like LISP. For this reason the assistance of the knowledge engineer and the software engineer may be required.

For another reason the help of specialists may be desirable. Where the management problem to be solved is relatively well structured, well defined, and the factors to be considered are largely quantifiable, it may be that the need for efficiency in data processing calls for sacrificing generality in the inference engine and calls also for closer coupling between it and the data to be processed. And for these things, specialists can be especially useful.

Thus, while the concept of a general problem solver is an important one—a concept that may grow in importance as general purpose inference engines are made even more powerful—nevertheless we should not automatically assume that the development system approach to building new information systems for addressing management problems is always the proper one.

In the next section of this paper we will cite an example of a class of well-structured management problems for which the development system approach has thus far proved unpromising. We will see that by sacrificing generality, in the inference engine, and by more closely coupling it to the knowledge base to be processed, we were able to build an intelligent system that performs considerably better than experienced human experts.

A KB SYSTEM FOR EMPLOYEE SCHEDULING

In many administrative offices each employee works the same shifts as all his fellow employees each day of the week. In such settings scheduling employees involves little more than dealing with the exceptional cases: employees on holiday, attending official meetings, or temporarily indisposed. But in other settings assigning work shifts to employees can be quite involved. When the job is done badly the employer experiences an inflated payroll during some portions of the day and poor customer service during others. An inbound call center is such a setting.

Inbound call centers are service centers manned by personnel who respond to incoming phone calls. Call centers are especially prevalent among the scheduled airlines, the telephone companies, credit firms, insurance companies, hotel and retail merchandise chains, banks, and others. In these settings the number of employees required during the day and week may fluctuate greatly. In some centers, at the peak of the day as many as 600 or more persons are required to handle the call traffic while at other times no more than a dozen employees may be kept busy.

Since their labor requirements change from week to week, many call centers produce a new schedule each week on the basis of a forecast of the volume of telephone traffic that can be expected. Typically the forecast specifies how many persons should be on duty by quarter-hour periods throughout the week and which work stations they should staff, when they should take breaks for rest or lunch, and when they should be off duty attending training sessions or meetings.

Heavy Reliance on Part-Time Employees

With each new census a larger percentage of the American work force consists of part-time employees. This is especially true in call centers. Many part-time employees like being able to specify the minimum and maximum number of hours they want to work during the week, which days of the week they prefer to work, and what ranges of time they prefer to work on those days. With the flexibility that the use of part-time employees makes possible, call center managers may better accommodate the rather great fluctuation in labor requirements from quarter-hour to quarter-hour during the day, by assigning shifts of varying lengths and by carefully positioning breaks within those shifts. Where the number of employees is large (60 or more), where the availabilities of individual employees are varied and limited, and where the labor requirement fluctuates widely, producing a really good schedule by hand becomes exceedingly difficult and time consuming.

Operations researchers view the employee scheduling problem as a problem in combinatorics, a search for the right combination of things, especially human skills, work tasks, and time periods. With the development of the computer in the early 1960s, many researchers endeavored to employ solution procedures that would assure an optimal schedule. But, as AI specialists have long recognized, the scheduling problem may be combinatorically explosive, involving too many possibilities for an optimal schedule to be readily manageable. To produce a demonstrably optimal schedule for 60 employees for one week may require solving a problem involving over 20 million integer variables—a goal totally out of reach, in a reasonable period of time, for even the most powerful mainframe

computers. The coveted Lancaster prize several years ago was awarded to a team that produced an optimal solution to a problem involving fewer than 4,000 integer variables!

When those of us in Management Robotics began to address the general employee scheduling problem we abandoned the search for a demonstrably optimal solution and instead sought a near optimal solution via heuristic search in the symbolic logic mode of the AI community. We began by first observing how managers who produce comparatively good employee schedules produce those schedules, what rules of thumb or heuristics they employ. Our intent was to embed those rules in a knowledge base that would then be processed by an inference engine to produce a schedule—the usual practice in building KB systems.

A knowledge base consists of facts on the one hand, and rules about those facts on the other hand. In call centers the rules in the knowledge base remain relatively stable from month to month but each week many of the associated facts change, especially the labor requirements by quarter-hour periods (reflecting the new forecast for the coming week), and the employee availability for the coming week (in some centers about 20 percent of the employees change their availability to work each week).

It soon became apparent that even the best human schedulers were unable to approximate very closely the number of employees assigned on duty with the number wanted each quarter-hour period, while still respecting all the various labor and management specifications, specifications such as those that follow.

1. Some minimum time must elapse between an employee's quit-time one day and start-time the next.
2. Short shifts should provide rest breaks, longer shifts both rest and lunch breaks, all falling within reasonable time windows.
3. Employees should be assigned work only during the days and within the time ranges they have specified as their time availability.
4. A part-time employee with more seniority is entitled to more work if there is not enough total work to go around.
5. Some minimum specified skill mix must be provided each quarter-hour period, and the mix may vary with the total number of employees called for and with the time of day.

In many settings a well-paid manager may spend one or two days each week doing manual scheduling yet be obliged to violate employee preferences or labor/management rules, or to tolerate heavy shortages and overages during the day and week, because of the size of the problem. It was apparent to us that building a KB system that does as well as a human expert was not enough. Tricks going beyond those developed over time by even the best managers were clearly called for if humans and machines were to perform as well as our intuition led us to believe possible.

Over a period of several years Dr. Fred Glover, U S WEST professor of system sciences and a member of the professional staff of the Center for Applied Artificial Intelligence, developed rather extraordinary insights into the combinatoric problem of labor scheduling. Glover discovered a number of techniques for containing the combinatorically explosive problem of labor scheduling. But it soon became apparent that Glover's techniques (clever heuristics) could not be fully exploited without more discipline and control than is possible through the use of the various inference engines that we find in commercially available development systems.

In the employee scheduling problem, efficiency is of paramount importance. It is imperative that we produce a new schedule for the coming week in a matter of minutes, frequently on a small microcomputer. Speed in producing a schedule permits the manager to reschedule at the last minute to accommodate changes in employee availability and changes in the requirement forecast and to refine the scheduling process through the exercise of "what-if" analysis.

We therefore rejected the concept of a general problem-solver inference engine, largely decoupled from the knowledge base, and we constructed our own. Our inference engine is constructed using the C programming language, a procedural language. It is rather closely coupled to the knowledge base it processes. And to produce a new expert scheduling system—one for scheduling maintenance personnel in manufacturing operations, for example—it is not always possible to avoid modifying the inference engine. Therefore our inference engine is not a general problem solver.

The gains we enjoy by reducing the generality and independence of our inference engine are impressive. For scheduling problems involving 100 or more employees, using our system, all labor/management rules are accommodated, and we achieve a remarkably close approximation between employees assigned (by quarter-hour periods) and employees wanted, in minutes of execution time on an IBM PS/2 microcomputer or equivalent. Figure 18.5 shows graphically a schedule produced by our system, a schedule for only 18 employees on a particular day. The numbers along the top of the graph represent time: The day starts at 5:00 and ends at 24:00. Each horizontal bar with an arrow on each end represents an assignment (a shift).

Note the fluctuation in the number of employees required, by quarter-hours during the day, as indicated by the curve at the bottom of the figure—rising from a minimum of two employees at 6:30 to 10 at 17:00, the dropping again to 2 at 23:30. By assigning shifts of different duration, as shown, and by the skillful placement of rest periods within those shifts (indicated by "B" for break, and "L" for lunch), the number of employees assigned each quarter-hour almost exactly matches the number required.

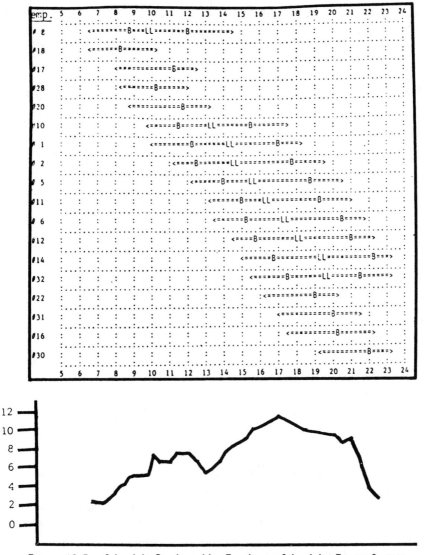

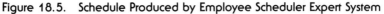

Figure 18.5.   Schedule Produced by Employee Scheduler Expert System

How the System Works

The search process by which the system produces a schedule (solves the scheduling problem) is somewhat similar to that employed by persons who produce schedules by hand. Imagine that you were obliged to produce a schedule for a pool of employees for the coming week, to specify the start-time, quit-time, breaks, and work station assignments for each employee, each day, during his work week. The data you have to work with can be classified under employee data, shift-type data, requirements data, and labor/management rules. Examples of each of these is provided in the following sections.

Sample Employee Data

1. Jones, William: part-time employee; available to work only Monday through Friday before 2:00 PM; has 4 years of seniority; qualified to work only work stations 2, 7, and 9; prefers to (but does not insist upon) the same start time each day of the week. Maximum hours for the week, 40; minimum hours, 20.
2. Hanson, Mary: full-time employee; available to work any day of the week after 3:00 PM; has 7 years of seniority; qualified to work every work station; insists on long shifts (no fewer than 7 hours). Maximum hours for the week, 40; minimum, 40. For the coming week only: unavailable on Tuesday.

Sample Shift Type Data

1. No shift may be shorter than 3 hours in duration nor longer than 8 hours.
2. Shifts from 4 to 5 hours in duration require one rest break with the break coming no sooner than 1.5 hours after the shift-start time and no later than 3 hours into the shift.
3. The ratio of short shifts (4 hours or fewer) to long shifts (6 hours or more) must not be larger than 2 to 3.
4. Longer shifts should start earlier, whenever practicable.

Sample Requirement Data

1. 7:00 AM to 7:15 AM on Mondays. Number of persons required: 2 at work station 1, 1 at work station 2, and 3 at work station 3.
2. 7:15 AM to 7:30 AM on Mondays. Number of persons required: 2 at work station 1, 2 at work station 2, 4 at work station 3, and 1 at work station 4.

Sample Rules Data

1. At least 8 hours must elapse between an employee's quit-time one day and start-time the next day.
2. If employee A starts before employee B on a particular day, then employee B must not get his first break sooner than employee A.
3. If there is insufficient work to go around, then part-time employees with more seniority get their minimum hours of work at the expense of employees with less seniority.

Additional rules may abound, such as, other things being equal, the rules below.

1. Give more hours to the employees with the lower pay rate.
2. Rotate less desirable shifts (late at night, the weekend) so that the same employees do not get them every week.
3. Do not assign work to an employee on his birthday.
4. If other rules are not violated, give the work to the employee with the highest skill level, especially at work stations 3 and 4.

Given this raw material to work with, you would probably choose, arbitrarily, a day to start with, perhaps Monday. You might then find that period in the day when the requirement is highest (perhaps 10:00 AM to 2:00 PM); design a shift (specify its length and position its breaks, if any) and fix its start time. For each quarter-hour of that shift during which the employee is *not* on break, you would then reduce the requirement by 1.

You would then design a second shift, position it, reduce the remaining requirement by 1, and continue this practice until the requirement approaches zero, in each quarter-hour period throughout the day. As the requirement approaches zero you would be obliged to design shifts with special care, and to position breaks with care so that in reducing the remaining requirement you do not create overages during certain quarter-hour periods—employees assigned in excess of the requirement.

To approximate a perfect fit—the remaining requirements all equal to zero in every quarter-hour period—you might find it desirable to modify the duration, break position and start-time for shifts designed earlier during your scheduling. As in the game of chess, you cannot make the current move without consideration of subsequent moves, many plays deep. You would then proceed to invoke the same process for the other 6 days of the week.

In fact, the procedure above would be risky. Designing shifts without regard to which employees will get them risks having shifts that nobody is available to take. Perhaps it would be best to assign a shift at the time you design it, and before the next shift is designed; that is, to specify the employee to get that shift. It should be apparent that the number of possible schedules is virtually infinite. But some schedules are better than others. And it is important to produce the schedule within a reasonable period of time and with a modest investment of managerial effort.

If one studies this well-structured problem with care, one begins to discover clever means for exploiting its structure, to conceive of techniques that may be translated into rules that guide the search process as that ideal combination of people, time slots, and work stations is approached. It is in the design of such heuristics that a good automated scheduler differs from a mediocre one. The techniques (heuristics) that enable our approach to produce remarkably good schedules in only minutes on a microcomputer constitute the proprietary features of our scheduling system and will not be elaborated further in this chapter. The speed with which this system produces a schedule could not have been achieved by use of one of the general purpose inference engines supplied by those who produce AI development systems. As suggested earlier in this chapter, we have found that close coupling of the software and the data is essential, if efficiency in the search process is to be enjoyed. And to contain the combinatorial explosion, efficiency is indeed essential.

In the paragraphs that follow I speak of the attributes of those problems that discourage full reliance on one of the ready-made, general-purpose inference engines that generally accompany development systems.

PROBLEM STRUCTURE FOR DECOUPLED OR CLOSELY COUPLED SYSTEMS

General purpose inference engines are especially attractive for dealing with problems that are ill structured and that are essentially diagnostic or evaluative in character. Examples are systems that diagnose infectious diseases, find faults, for example, in high technology equipment, evaluate risks, or identify areas that are promising for finding petroleum deposits. These tend to be ill-structured or ill-defined problems. The playing of chess, on the other hand, is a well-defined problem. The options at each move may be many, but the nature of each possible move is clear and unambiguous, and its payoff can frequently be quantified.

Determining which supplier to employ for replenishing stock of a particular item of inventory is a well-structured problem. Designing a corporate policy for promoting good public relations is an ill-structured problem. Given a well-structured problem one can generally define or specify what constitutes a good solution in unambiguous terms—and frequently in quantitative terms. Life is not so easy with ill-structured problems.

KB systems in which the knowledge base and the inference engine are decoupled are especially powerful for dealing with ill-structured problems, particularly those that are essentially diagnostic in character. For relatively well-structured problems, closer coupling is desirable (Figure 18.6).

The employee scheduling problem, like many others at the operations levels of management, is a well-structured, management planning problem, one in which the time dimension must be dealt with explicitly: Work must be assigned by quarter-hour periods throughout the week. And there are linking constraints that must be considered: An employee cannot be assigned to work one period without consideration for the rest of his schedule, for the week, and for those schedules of other employees. The number of possible combinations is explo-

FOR ILL- STRUCTURED PROBLEMS:

> KNOWLEDGE BASE (KB)
>   (Facts & Rules-- mostly Rules)
>
>
> INFERENCE ENGINE
>
>   (Written in a non-procedural language
>   such as LISP or PROLOG).

These two components
are largely
"Decoupled"

FOR WELL-STRUCTURED PROBLEMS:

> KNOWLEDGE BASE (KB)
>   (Facts & Rules-- mostly Facts)
>
> INFERENCE ENGINE
>
>   (Written in a procedural language
>   such as PL/1, PASCAL or C).

These two are more
intimately "Coupled"

Figure 18.6.   Features of System for Ill-Structured Versus Well-Structured Problems

sive, and *efficiency* in the process that searches for a good schedule is of paramount importance.

Advice for Operations Level Management

In addition to call centers, supermarkets, fast food restaurants, and other businesses find that producing really good employee schedules manually may be arduous. We have produced versions of our basic scheduler—each with its own inference engine—to accommodate settings other than call centers. In each case we found it appropriate to tailor the inference engine to meet the needs of the particular application. We might have avoided this need for new programming by utilizing one of the standard development systems. But the gains enjoyed in increased efficiency more than compensated for the added programming effort, given the combinatorically explosive nature of the scheduling problem.

Our advice to those considering building intelligent systems for addressing operations level management problems—especially well-structured and largely quantifiable problems—is that they employ the development system approach during the early stages of the project for exploring the attributes of the problem and perhaps for capturing the expertise of the experts, as they build the initial prototype, but that for routine operational use they may find it appropriate to build their own inference engines as we have, using a traditional procedural language.

Thoughts on Management Robots

Much management literature today speaks of decision support systems (DSS). These systems supplement managers in making certain types of decisions. In that respect they constitute technology that differs from that employed in industrial robots. Industrial robots *replace* craft workers. The systems that replace those workers are not support systems, they are replacement systems.

The employee schedulers described above do not just support or supplement managers. They replace them in the performance of the function for which our schedulers were designed. They permit the manager to intervene in the scheduling process where appropriate—to change assignments and to swap shifts between employees to accommodate last-minute changes. But fundamentally our systems replace managers in the same sense that an industrial robot replaces a craft worker on the assembly line.

Just as added intelligence is being built into cameras, automobiles, and data access systems, so also increased intelligence is being built into systems designed to serve managers. The greatest opportunities for gains in productivity may well be in the front office, in the administrative superstructure of the average enterprise, rather than on the shop floor. There is a substantial place for management robots in well-managed business operations today. I advocate a healthy respect for management robots as mechanisms for increasing productivity in American business: machines that replace managers in dealing with relatively well-structured, largely quantifiable problems.

Management has been traditionally critical of labor leadership for opposing the introduction of labor-saving devices. It will be interesting to see if managers prove receptive to the introduction of devices whose purpose is to replace operations level managers in the performance of certain management functions that can better be performed by intelligent machines.

19
Application of Expert Systems to Field Services

Barbara L. Braden

Bull HN

Bull HN's corporate experience in building three expert systems in the field service domain is presented. Scarcity of expertise is a primary characteristic of the field service problem. Project selection criteria are presented, followed by detailed descriptions of the experience and issues in building and fielding three expert systems—two for hardware maintenance, one for software maintenance. The chapter closes by focusing on the future of expert systems in field service—the inevitable trend toward integrating expert systems with the overall information systems of a field service organization and embedding diagnostic expert systems within the hardware and software to be maintained.

INTRODUCTION

The competitive advantage of the field service organization of a computer manufacturer lies in its unique skills and knowledge. An absolute requirement of a successful field services organization is to respond immediately with the right solution on the first customer call. With the increasing complexity of products, the networking of multivendor products, and customers scattered across 50 states, this requirement is becoming more illusory. The field engineer who has the appropriate knowledge to diagnose the problem quickly is not always immediately available.

Some Typical Field Service Problems

Troubleshooting the wide range of products and systems that we service requires access to a diverse, and often scarce, expertise. For example, one problem is maintaining the mature products or "old" technologies that nobody wants to support. Service technicians are bored with them; they want to go on to something new and exciting. However, these technicians cannot be reassigned just yet since they are the only ones who have the knowledge. A repository for knowledge, available on demand, could free talented personnel to move on to new challenges.

The systems and products we maintain are becoming even more complex and sophisticated, and the need to troubleshoot interconnected, multivendor products increases. There may not be one expert but rather many experts and sources of information that must be tapped efficiently and immediately.

As a final example of scarce expertise, higher standards for reliability and quality ensure that more products simply do not break down. If two years hence such a product has a problem, where is the experience to diagnose the problem? Scarce expertise is probably the biggest factor that prompted the field services organization to invest in expert systems technology.

Project Selection

In 1984 the Customer Services Division of Bull HN began to explore the feasibility of the expert systems technology with its promise of capturing scarce expertise and making it broadly and immediately available to all field engineers. On paper, expert systems and field services seemed to make an excellent marriage. The project was initiated by the general manager and vice president of the division, an important factor in introducing a new technology with a bit of mystique.

Fortunately Customer Services had access to relatively experienced knowledge engineers in the corporate research and product development organizations for the initial study and support. Subsequently we created our own knowledge engineering group within Customer Services.

We quickly learned that for the first project we would not only be learning a new technology in an R&D mode but also that success would be measured by the standards of an operating division with profit and loss goals. Hence for the initial projects we established these minimum criteria for project selection:

1. The domain must be well bounded and self-contained.
2. A recognized expert must be willing to participate and to take ownership.
3. The domain should be sufficiently complex to test fully the technology.
4. Implementation of the system would satisfy a real requirement for better service at less cost.

Other criteria began to emerge in a relatively short period of time. For example, we learned that each development effort could become the foundation for a family of systems; therefore, a longer view of the potential payback and evaluation had to be factored into the more immediate development efforts.

The range of possible candidates for the first projects was extensive and paralleled the activities of a field services organization. The types of projects fell into four categories: diagnostic problems, configuration problems, predictive maintenance, and intelligent searches of large databases (electronic and paper). Diagnostics and configuration problems became the primary focus (Figure 19.1) since the technology at that point did not support integration with traditional databases and in-depth expertise was not available for predictive maintenance. In fact, one hoped-for side benefit for expert systems development was the ability to identify patterns for predictive maintenance.

Even though we could not address intelligent search of databases in our initial efforts, this area continues as a high priority. Considerable data, documentation, and techniques for existing products have accumulated over a long period of time. Needless to say, immediate access to the right answer to almost any question from any location would empower the field engineers to tackle any task.

In the first year two diagnostic projects, PAGE-X and PERMAID, and one configuration project, ISC, were developed and made ready for limited testing in the field in 1985. PAGE-X, which actually includes three systems, was developed internally within the Customer Services Division and the other two by Bull HN product development organizations.

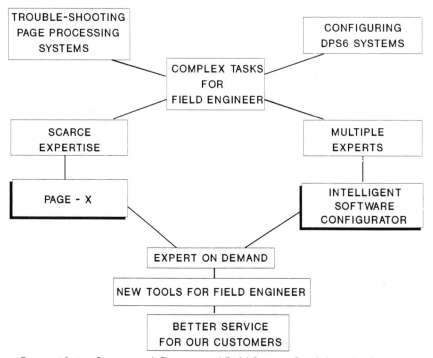

Figure 19.1. Range and Character of Field Service Candidate Applications

PAGE-X

The Target System

The first project, PAGE-X, is an expert system to assist the field engineer in troubleshooting two models of the nonimpact, high-speed Page Processing System (PPS) printers. These are the very large printers that produce at the rate of 20,000 pages a minute all that paper the computer revolution is supposed to dispose of. This product contains about 25 subsystems and 2,000 replaceable components and combines several technologies—hydraulics, electronics, chemicals, printing.

The Subject Matter Expert

A fully qualified PPS field engineer is a scarce resource. From the very beginning the PPS expert has been the most enthusiastic supporter of this project since he was the one with the greatest demand on his time at all hours of the day. He desperately needed assistance. A consultant on call 24 hours a day, seven days a week, would free him for other activities all within a normal work day. This was also a measure of the success of the project.

One requirement instituted in the initial stages was that the expert would become responsible for the expert system, for its maintenance and validation, in

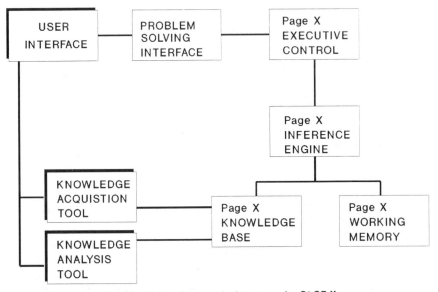

Figure 19.2. System Architecture for PAGE-X

effect, have total and complete ownership. The underlying rationale was to take advantage of the incremental growth in system maintenance knowledge. Over the life of a product the kinds of faults and symptoms change as the product ages. If a separate organization for the expert systems maintenance were to be created, the ability quickly to update and change the knowledge base could easily be lost. Field engineers need the most current and accurate information.

Since responsibility for the knowledge base would reside with the expert, knowledge base editing tools for the expert became a mandatory requirement in the system development.

User Interface

The most interesting aspect of this project was the user interface and the view to problem solving. Figure 19.2 graphically illustrates the system architecture for PAGE-X. The user interface on PAGE-X takes up almost 65 percent of the expert system.

We found the user interface had to be adaptable and relatively flexible. The actual diagnostic process is very subjective. The range of problems can be trivial to some and difficult to others. Moreover, individuals have different approaches to troubleshooting. PAGE-X captured one person's approach and view of troubleshooting. Some field engineers wanted the information contained in the knowledge base but did not necessarily want to follow the same diagnostic process. As users became more expert at using the expert system, they grew more impatient with detailed procedures.

To be adaptable we were concerned with the issue of how detailed problem solutions should be. As illustrated in Figure 19.3, at one end of the spectrum, we could go down to the level of detail needed by trainees. Almost any PPS problem they would encounter could be difficult. At the other end we did not want to make it so easy that those with more expertise would not find value in the system. Balancing sufficient information content with user skill levels required multiple reiterations of the user interface and the symptom-fault structure.

We resolved some of the user interface issues by incorporating multiple modes of access in terms of experience with PAGE-X: beginner, intermediate, and advanced. Moreover, an engineer could begin by selecting one or more symptoms from a list, do a key work search on symptoms, or go directly to causes of the symptoms. (PAGE-X has the ability to solve multiple faults.)

Hence, the user interface became the most important and largest subsystem in PAGE-X in order to strike a balance between too much detail for those who had more experience with PPS, capturing perceptual information without too much clutter, and accommodating different diagnostic styles.

As a final note on the user interface, a rather interesting phenomenon evolved around PAGE-X. Those who used the system on a regular basis developed a somewhat personal relationship with it—as though a real consultant were on the

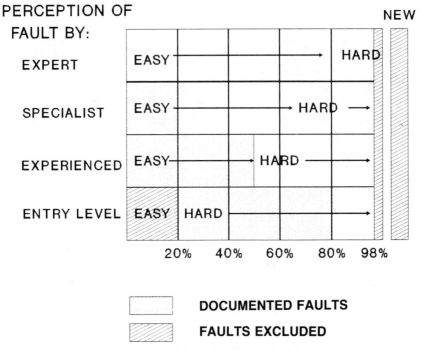

Figure 19.3.   PAGE X—Domain of Problems

other end of the line. They began to ask, "Well, can you change it so that it reflects more my way of doing business or my concerns." Since the system can be easily modified, the net result was the appearance that problems could be approached from several different perspectives and the system could quickly reflect an individual's concerns.

The Knowledge Base

PAGE-X is a relatively large expert system. The knowledge representation is in terms of frames, which we estimated to be equivalent to about 2,500 to 5,000 rules.

One interesting issue regarding knowledge representation is how to represent clearly perceptual knowledge. Printer diagnostics depend in large part on visual and aural descriptions. Without a detailed inquisition, a cursory description can easily lead to the wrong conclusion. Moreover, when the field engineer describes a perceptual problem, he may not use the same terms as the expert. To the expert a smeared page and a smudged page have very different causes. Different noises are almost impossible to describe. This is an issue that has not been adequately resolved. Over time, however, the language of Page-X is becoming a defacto standard for describing faults.

A knowledge base is not a static entity. The field engineers who made a habit of using PAGE-X were frustrated when a new model of PPS was announced but no expert system was available. Although this could be considered a measure of success for PAGE-X in terms of acceptance, it also meant that PAGE-X almost lost its most dedicated users. Unfortunately, one limitation of a diagnostic expert system is the inability to build a knowledge base when there is no diagnostic history, particularly for a product that is substantially different from its predecessors. The problems the product developer anticipates are not necessarily the problems the field engineer encounters. Fortunately, because of the editing tools built into the original system, the second PPS expert system, PAGE-3, equal in size to PAGE-X, was developed and implemented four months after the product was shipped. Moreover, the expert was able to assume responsibility for about 80 percent of the development alongside his regular responsibilities.

A diagnostic knowledge base parallels the life of a product and requires consistent updating. The problems encountered when a product is introduced in the first six months are quite different from the problems two years hence, three years hence, or in its last days. Diagnostics require a body of knowledge for each of these phases. Hence, the ability to easily update and maintain the knowledge base is a mandatory requirement.

Deployment and Integration

The underlying technology became a persistent issue. Tools and facilities that could have strengthened the project seemed always to come on the market a year too late. PAGE-X was developed on a Xerox 1100 series computer using LOOPS. No off-the-shelf software products met our requirements and the Xerox object-oriented environment allowed more rapid development. However, stand-alone workstations are not appropriate for a geographically dispersed field organization that requires access to the system preferably at customer sites. With a PC front-end to two Xerox 11XX's, the field engineer had a TTY (text only) access, but each machine could accept only one call at a time. Moreover, the field engineers wanted to use PAGE-X to include information found on the traditional internal systems. For large expert systems, until the technology is part and parcel or at least complementary to ongoing data processing and communication systems, actual growth in the deployment of large expert systems is limited.

Utility of Expert Systems in Training

We underestimated the power of PAGE-X as a training tool, probably one of the most powerful training tools available, particularly for the experienced field engineer who only occasionally troubleshoots a PPS system. Typical comments include, "I had completely forgotten about such and such" or "I didn't know that you could fix it this way." New solutions and tricks of the trade as well as obscure and rare problems can be quickly and easily made available to any one in the field.

Attempt at Natural Language Interface

As a footnote, we did prototype a natural language front end to PAGE-X in an effort to address language problems—not only the semantic issues in English but also the use of the same diagnostic tool in other native languages. We did not, however, have sufficient power or storage to support a full-blown natural language front end. Since then Bull HN has constructed a tool called MAGIC that permits much easier language translation of the knowledge base as well as even more powerful editing tools for the expert for both deep and shallow systems.

INTELLIGENT SOFTWARE CONFIGURATOR (ISC)

The Problem Domain—Handling "Worst Case Configurations"

A persistent problem for the Customer Services Division's software support specialists is to build a special operating system file, called the CLM file, for the Bull HN DPS6 minicomputers. This file manages all the components that affect memory requirements. The physical construction of the file is tedious and an error-prone clerical task. The ability to create the file, however, requires knowledge of communications, the operating system, peripherals and software products and all of their interdependencies. This knowledge must be for the most current releases as well as earlier versions resident at a customer site.

Unlike most expert system configurators that aim for optimal systems, this configurator had to be capable of figuring out how to make the worst possible configurations work. The way the expert described it is that this particular system made the salesmen's mistakes work.

The software specialists accepted the system almost immediately because a one-to-three day largely clerical task was reduced to about 10 minutes. They could now use their special skills to fine-tune the configuration file, rather than consulting several different experts or ten feet of documentation to understand all the possibilities.

Multi-Expert Knowledge Acquisition

The knowledge acquisition process for the ISC was quite different from PAGE-X. The knowledge and cooperation of seven or eight experts in different fields had to be elicited and coordinated. Because each was an expert, available time for the project was scarce nor could some understand why the configurator was necessary. Fortunately, the operating system expert took ownership, was the primary expert in terms of coordinating and integrating all the pieces, became the primary user, and validated the knowledge base. Her word was the final word.

On PAGE-X we had one expert and with the lead expert approach with ISC, we had for all practical purposes only one expert for each project. I strongly recommend having only one expert to avoid one-upmanship as to who's way of doing things is better. Other experts can play an important role in validating the content through a peer review process. Having one expert also promotes a stake in the success of the system and ownership over the longer term.

Hardware Environment—Moving Towards the PC

The ISC was also developed in the Xerox 11XX environment. The workstation was resident in the Customer Services Division's Technical Assistance Center (TAC) as an aid to the TAC software support personnel. Since the field did not have direct access to the system, ISC was never as fully developed as PAGE-X. The user interface was not as flexible and the requirement for editing tools for the expert was never fully implemented. In part this was a factor of using knowledge engineering personnel outside the Customer Services Division with multiple priorities and the limited number of users.

Since access to the ISC needed to be broadened and the editing tools enhanced, the system was completely rewritten to run on a 286 PC. In effect, the technology was beginning to catch up to our requirements. Also underlying the change from an AI workstation to a PC-based solution was the demand for configuration systems for more complex problems. Hence, the first requirement for the PC development was to construct a configuration shell as well as rehosting ISC. The shell would become the foundation for future configuration and planning type expert systems.

PERMAID

Permaid is a diagnostic system for disk subsystems. PERMAID addresses, in part, a unique problem and that is the problem of no apparent fault, except the disk drive was not working correctly. If a field engineer cannot quickly isolate the fault, he may only compound the problem. The easiest solution is simply to order a replacement subsystem, an expensive proposition. Thus, PERMAID is the only system we have which we mandated be used.

Similar to the ISC, PERMAID is an aid in the Technical Assistance Center (TAC). In this situation, before a field engineer begins to repair a disk subsystem, he or she must call the TAC to receive instructions on the correct procedure for isolating the fault. From this process PERMAID has paid for its development costs and then some. A side effect of having PERMAID in the TAC is that the people in the TAC have become almost too confident in their new-found knowledge and do not always consult PERMAID, thus missing the obscure fault that may resolve the problem.

Another strength of expert systems technology is the ability to build on previous work. PERMAID had PAGE-X as a base upon which to build. In turn PERMAID is now the basis for a comprehensive family of peripheral maintenance and diagnostic systems. From the accumulation of diagnostic information, a major emphasis is now being placed on predictive maintenance.

For broader access in the field, PERMAID is now being rewritten in C to run on Bull HN's large systems (GOOS8). Bull S.A. in France has rewritten PERMAID using its proprietary object-oriented language KOOL in a UNIX environment.

THE FUTURE

From the success of these initial projects the Customer Services Division continues to support expert systems development. The systems I have described have been in the field for three to four years now and other expert systems have been deployed. We have not yet, however, reached the critical mass of expert systems where we can say that they are a valuable asset to the company—in part because of the current state of the technology.

Three Applications Directions

Three distinct directions for the application of expert systems in field service have emerged (Figure 19.4). The first is for a very few large systems solving very complex problems that require substantial specialized knowledge. PAGE-X is an example of this type of system.

In a field services organization, there is a much greater need for small expert systems, or, for lack of a better term, intelligent databases. Because of the explosion of the number of products to be serviced, the field engineer must have a broad, but not necessarily in-depth, knowledge. For example, in one situation a device is controlled by any one of 75 controller boards. One controller board is not difficult to troubleshoot, but someone experienced with all 75 boards is virtually nonexistent.

With the development in PC-based tools and the power of 286 and 386 machines, the direction towards small systems is more easily persued. One issue that needs to be addressed, however, is how to manage the distribution and version control of intelligent databases in the field as well as access to the large geographically dispersed organization. The field engineers who were using PAGE-X wanted to integrate it with electronic mail, a forum for information on products and new releases and add access to parts lists, and logistics management systems.

Given the complexity that the field engineer has to face every day, whether his or her support system is a knowledge base or database is totally irrelevant. But integrating knowledge-based and database systems in an overall intelligent communications system is a vision that remains just beyond our reach. Until we can achieve this, our successes will be channeled into relatively narrow, focused, controlled arenas. As a consequence, today's expert systems are not as yet an integral part of customer service business.

SUMMARY

Despite any current limitations, the expert systems technology should be fully exploited by any field service organization. Our original proposition—that field services and expert systems would make an excellent marriage—has certainly been validated, and benefits we did not anticipate have been realized.

When embedded systems, expert systems technology for networked products and integration with more traditional support systems has been achieved, then the technology will achieve its full potential for a field service organization.

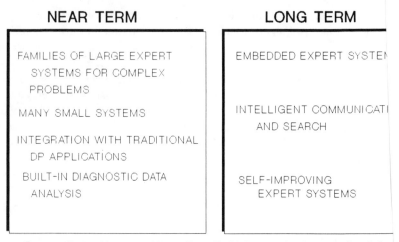

NEAR TERM

FAMILIES OF LARGE EXPERT
SYSTEMS FOR COMPLEX
PROBLEMS

MANY SMALL SYSTEMS

INTEGRATION WITH TRADITIONAL
DP APPLICATIONS

BUILT-IN DIAGNOSTIC DATA
ANALYSIS

LONG TERM

EMBEDDED EXPERT SYSTEM

INTELLIGENT COMMUNICATI
AND SEARCH

SELF-IMPROVING
EXPERT SYSTEMS

Figure 19.4. Near- and Long-Term Field Service Application Candidat

expert systems and core applications. An infrastructure running on a large c
host is now in place for downloading and uploading of files to field office
for control. This system now supports a system for the sales force and cou
expanded to include small systems.

A third direction and the most significant opportunity is to embed an e
system within a product. To change from a troubleshooting mode to preve
and predictive maintenance would not only reduce substantially the costs
field service organization for labor and spare parts but would also incr
customer satisfaction. We are now working on systems that can be embed
that can handle complex diagnostic repair and recovery, and can antici
problems. Embedded systems are a much better solution for delivering expe
on demand at the customer site. When this is achieved the real value of ex
systems can be measured.

With one exception, the requirements for separate large expert systems
for intelligent databases may be largely eliminated if the expert systems
embedded. The one exception, at least for the near term, is the application
expert systems technology to managing, configuring, and troubleshooting a w
variety of interconnected products, subsystems, and applications. The techno
gy is not ready to support this level of expert systems development and, parti
larly, knowledge acquisition.

The Need to Integrate

The expert systems technology must be integrated with information manageme
systems in order to realize the full benefits of this technology, particularly in

20
Expert Systems in Field Service Planning

Dennis West

Motorola Corporation

To those unfamiliar with expert systems and knowledge engineering, it may be hard to conceive of what kinds of expert system applications might yield benefits that justify development costs. Further, it may be difficult to imagine what "knowledge" makes up an expert system's knowledge base and how to go about getting this knowledge. Also, once cost/benefits are justified and kinds of knowledge are identified, how does one proceed? This chapter clearly illuminates these issues with a case drawn from field service planning—the development of the Service Planner expert system by Motorola.

INTRODUCTION

I am a field service man. I started as a hand-carrying tool-bag electronics technician in 1951. After attending some technical classes, by the late 1950s I was was servicing machines, such as Univac I and II, walking into a 1K memory unit and plumbing, and so on, on the Reader's Digest computer in Pleasantville, NY. A service technician lives on the leading edge of field service technology, for example, maintenance tools that tie into computers and analyze failures or exercise diagnostics that tie into a remote system under test. At this point in my career, I believe I am an expert in field service where the objective is to lower the cost and increase the quality of service to the customer. For the past three and a half years I have been Motorola's manager of service technology.

I got involved with expert systems as a natural extension, an evolution, or a progressive step in the long history of field service technology. It's a new tool, and we investigate new tools for their potential without needing to know whether we're going to get a benefit. But we could see that expert systems would allow us to do a higher quality job in handling the knowledge involved in field service.

FIELD SERVICE PLANNING

The objective of service planning is to prepare long-range plans that analyze cost of maintenance and the detailed requirements to provide field support for a device throughout its life cycle. The analysis involves these as variables: replaceable units, cost to repair, failure rates, operational hours, part hours, quality of diagnostics, field operation costs, training costs, and technical support. An expert service planner is expected to answer questions such as: How do we staff and support the product? What skills are required? How much inventory?

Support involves both hardware and software. While it is said—"Software doesn't fail"—at Motorola we release new software about three or four times a year. With every new release, we experience bugs, design errors, and feature errors—all of which require field support.

Methods of servicing software and hardware are different. We organize our technical people into a central area where we staff high capability software support. With hardware it is usually necessary to go to the site to replace parts, or parts must be removed and brought into a service center for repair.

Knowledge involved in the task includes the following: How does the equipment fail? Can you describe the failure mode? Can you determine which parts will be ordered a lot? Can you determine the cost of repair? Can you project a reliability and service availability? Can you project the quality support? What benefits are we going to get out of this service plan? Can you describe the service activity?

Variables are often handled by different departments within the field service organization: repair center, logistics, field operations, training, parts support, and spare parts inventory. Each variable keys an area of expertise, and personnel in each area know their own field well.

Input to service planning comes from product marketing forecasts, engineering, fixed operational support costs, service activity for a particular product, and warranty support cost. The objective is to produce a detailed summary report that we use as the basis of detailed planning once a new equipment model and production run are available. Using the rough service plan, executive management can decide whether or not to support a new product in light of the long-range support costs. So a service plan is a decision support tool for management.

ABOUT EXPERT SYSTEMS

Expert systems offer new programming techniques that allow the structuring of knowledge in a form that can be handled by the computer. To develop an application, expert system programmers, for example, knowledge engineers, take the knowledge they have and name it in the form of objects, which are described and organized. Information related to objects is recorded, and this information constrains the knowledge.

A natural fear is that expert systems in general will lower skill levels of people. But the increasing complexity of technology will require higher-level skilled personnel and increased need for high-quality information. This is the progression I've seen in field service. An expert system is a tool that can partition knowledge and store it away and make it easy to retrieve. With expert systems, we now have a way to collect and disseminate more knowledge than we have been able to handle with traditional approaches to technical documentation.

Since 1985 Motorola has been getting involved with AI applications in field service. In 1985, costs were high—a development system ran $30,000 and training cost $5,000 to $10,000. The tools, compared to what we have today, even in the PC world, were archaic and simple—primarily backward-chaining, rule-based systems. Software is better today; hardware is better. In a few more years, chip manufacturers, including Motorola, will be making LISP coprocessors, Prolog coprocessors, and a variety of other chips to support this new AI technology. It will become much easier for computers to support the language, text, and symbolic processing that we do in our minds. Looking toward this end, at Motorola we have implemented about 10 expert systems, including a service help desk that has been beta tested.

In spite of hardware advances and the promise of more advances, institutionalizing our expert systems at this time is not feasible. Having to put into a response center 25 workstations, each of which costs anywhere from $25,000–$50,000, was a problem; the low-cost software support center could not afford this expense. Moreover, even with the workstations, we have had trouble getting adequate response time; one or two seconds in a phone conversation with a user is a long time, especially when you have to say, "Ah, I'm waiting for the computer to respond." Response times are slow because in field service we need to display so much information to the technicians—block diagrams, schematics, illustrated part breakdowns, and so on. I think the help desk application will be more feasible within the next couple of years when hardware costs come down.

About Getting Started in Expert Systems Programming

I think it takes about six weeks to master a shell and get going on knowledge base development. The strategy is to start programming right away. Don't just read and study a book or go to training school. Get involved. Get a problem to work on and start up the learning curve. In perhaps six months it should be possible to transfer a significant amount of expertise to a working model.

WHY AN EXPERT SYSTEM IN FIELD SERVICE PLANNING

In field service planning, the issue is long-range planning for new or current products to support maintenance throughout the product's life cycle. Expert systems help management develop life cycle support plans by making knowledge more readily available and interfaceable to other sources.

Help in Managing a Shorter Product Cycle

In the past we were concerned with only single product releases per year rather than the multiple product releases we support today. A product's life cycle is about five years; years ago it used to be 10–20. We still have machines in the field that were built in the 1950s and especially the 1960s. I know of machines built in the early 1970s that are still running and still need field service support. With today's shorter product cycle, there is less time to do service planning.

Planning for Modern, Complex Equipment

Modern, complex equipment is harder to plan for. We have very high reliability equipment today compared to when I worked in the field. I experienced failures from every two hours to once a day. Then we went from once a day to once a week to once a month to four times a year. Today's hardware, a hundred, even a thousand times bigger than yesterday's machines, has failure rates that are just a fraction of what they used to be. But developing the field service plans is a much larger task than formerly.

Supporting Sharing of Expertise

Service planning requires the collaboration of many experts. An expert system can help in the sharing of information. In the past, service planning was done primarily by a single expert with many years of in-the-business service knowledge, using a spreadsheet designed by the expert and specific to a particular product's variables. We needed to enhance our planning capabilities in order to improve our business planning cycle. The advantage of the Service Planner expert system is that more people are involved in the planning process and made aware of the elements and reasoning of the service plan.

Expert systems are a means of helping us communicate better. They help compile and retain knowledge. With knowledge stored, it can be used when needed to trigger the rules put in before. The exercise gets shorter and shorter every time.

Gaining the Competitive Edge

When expertise is important, perhaps an expert system can give a competitive edge. Service planning is important to an electronics company. It plays a big role in profit margin analysis because field service is a significant cost factor in a system's life cycle. Field service in today's business can run anywhere from 20 to 25 percent of a company's revenue. We can't hire and support field service personnel (who are considered career personnel and who look to long-term life employment) unless we make a profit.

Improving Experts' Own Understanding

Building an expert system helps in understanding a field better. In the process of doing the knowledge engineering for the Service Planner, I found out that there are many, many subjects involved in service planning. When I started compartmentalizing the knowledge, I realized that there is a lot to know about service planning. This knowledge involves many cause and effect relationships and tradeoffs—if this is done here, it is paid for there. The service plan analyzes the costs and benefits of what might seem to be good ideas. The good idea may be at the head of a string of cause and effect that leads to unforeseen costs. In service planning, it is important to 'understand the negative as well as the positive impact of all the scenarios.

Backing Information Up with Explanations

Our modeled number would be a rule-of-thumb number, and we would be off only by a few millions of dollars. More important, if we did get the bid, we would know how to implement the project because we would have all the details from the Service Planner.

As an example of Service Planner's value, consider this example. We had spent 7$1/2$ million dollars on spare parts to support a new product. When Service Planner analyzed sparing, it indicated we only needed 2$1/2$ million dollars of parts. We ended up negotiating with engineering manufacturing to buy back these parts from field service since we are a separate business unit within Motorola and we needed to compete with the other business units to save the cost to us of this overstocking of spare parts.

The oversparing arose because someone said, "The last cycle we went through, we were short parts. Let's order a lot of parts this time." In order to satisfy marketing's whim, or in order to satisfy my peer at the meeting table, 5 million dollars were spent that didn't need to be. Of course, it's good business sense to reduce reactionary decisions that are not backed up with sound rationale. Today's business environment is very competitive, and anyone might lose a bid because we couldn't back it up with expert knowledge.

Avoiding Hasty Decisions

Expert systems help avoid hasty decisions. Past methods of planning were seat-of-the-pants quick calculations made under the pressure of writing a winning bid.

When the bid was won, the in-depth knowledge upon which the service plan was based was absent. There is a pressing need to support the quick generation of service plans. Often, in the press of contract binds, there are just too many questions, too many answers, and not enough time. Because of pressures in the preparation of a bid, it might be impossible to communicate effectively with the service planning experts. Technical know-how often gets left in the tracks when there is a need for a marketing decision. "Let's decide now. Let's get on the road with selling the product," even if we do not have answers to problems such as field support. This press for action often leads to the perception that experts can't communicate. The problem, in fact, is that there is too much to communicate. This is where expert systems can prove invaluable—making information available at a pace more in tune with marketing activity.

Expert systems methodology allows building small draft plans backed up by detailed analysis in a period of three hours for a simple computer product and up to three days for a medium-size product. For a large product an expert system planner might take one to three weeks to complete the full planning cycle, including several iteration runs. It is possible to develop a plan and run it back and forth between the field service organization and marketing several times because the expert system has the rules of all the various expertise groups in the field service organization. In the system I built I have encoded reliability rules, the operational hour rules, logistics rules, rules for supporting warranties, rules for allocating budget costs to various departments, margin requirement rules, and others.

Dealing with Employee Turnover

Expert systems help deal with employee turbulence. Trained operators are an important field support consideration. Attrition—as personnel move to different positions within the customer site, are promoted, or leave—requires training. Again, I emphasize software. We need to know where our staff belong and what to do with them, and we just can't make an arbitrary decision that we don't need these people any more because the machine's not feeling that way. But when it does, if they're not there, we're stuck. We have to know what we're doing. We can let a man sit, or we can let him go somewhere else, but we need to know where our staff are.

A Tool That Fits With How We Think

Finally, a major advantage of expert systems is that they make us think—as experts. They force us to consider the knowledge that comprises our expertise—to become aware. With expert systems, you can state your knowledge in your own terms—not in a programmer's terms or in Lotus 123's terms. This frees us to program or represent our expertise the way we think.

A Challenge

Here's a challenge. If there are any experts in your company willing to take this challenge, let them write an expert system. There are many tools available that they can use to write it. Just the learning that comes from structuring their knowledge in an object form will be beneficial. When they are finished, they have their knowledge all categorized and logged away. Their whole mindset will have changed. Having categorized and organized their knowledge in a formal, explicit way, they will do things differently in the future. Given this, they will be in a position to start broadening their knowledge.

THE SERVICE PLANNER EXPERT SYSTEM

My goal was to see if we could generate service plans with expert systems, and structure the knowledge in the form the various departments use to determine such things as budget allocation, spare parts ordering requirements, marketing forecasts, service activity, high failure rate parts, total service man-hours required for field support, hiring requirements, and skill requirements.

The objective of this service planner was to encode an expert's knowledge. A service plan is often formatted like a spreadsheet; data are organized in tables. To develop an expert system, I used this same spreadsheet-type format, formerly supported by APL or PL1 programs or lately Lotus 123-like shells.

The expert system I built is not in concept very different from the spreadsheet approach I formerly used. The problem with the spreadsheet approach was that it only compiled sets of numbers, lacking the knowledge behind those numbers. Even the formula in cells lacked the kind of support knowledge that would have helped me recollect how I got them in there in the first place. Through use of the symbolic language provided through an expert system's rules, the knowledge behind entries in cells can be called back, especially since it is easy to store the knowledge using common and familiar terms.

In the design of the Service Planner, we had to consider: Should the Service Planner be able to handle multiple components? Can it support analysis of anything from a large to a single unit configuration? Can it determine spare parts stocking levels? Can it determine manpower requirements? Will it provide a service contract pricing? Do we need to come out with a competitive pricing analogy for each replaceable part?

The Service Planner needed to be able to conduct its analysis given variations in several field service options or parameters. For example, pricing schemes would vary—spares pricing may be based on annual, quarterly, or monthly projections. Or, as another example, service contract type.

The Service Planner has been used in Motorola on both small and large modeling tasks. We took a large model plan, a major bid for $400 billion in service over the next eight years. This involved a major network employing every type of PC-type of arrangement, laser scanners, a complete network of information workstations, power backup, software support, and so on. The bid was in a very competitive race with other major companies, such as IBM, DEC, and Univac. In order for us to have an advantage it was important that we pay attention to detail.

In getting started I was helped a lot by Dr. Carmen Parsay's book *Expert Systems for Experts*, which conveys a good idea of expert systems. It is a very well-rounded book and is used at the University of Southern California and UCLA in some of their AI courses.

Development Shell

Service Planner was built on an IBM PC, using Intelligence Compiler, called IC, available from a company located in Los Angeles.

The architecture of Intelligence Compiler offers an interface manager, predicates for queries, a good tracer, and a debugger. The debugger is very helpful in developing expert systems, because it takes you right to the failure, be it in a predicate, in syntax, or in something else. IC also offers an editor for building knowledge bases, a spelling checker, a parser, a knowledge manager, frame manager, comment manager, and so on. IC has a group of predicates that allow creating of text and explanations and help within our expert system. It uses almost all of an IBM PC-AT's base 640 K of memory, leaving little room to write rules or manage facts. More memory is recommended.

Having a shell that takes care of memory management is important. This frees developers from low-level hardware concerns and allows them to be more concerned with the evolving rule base. In writing the expert system, one gets more ideas. You realize you can use a piece of information in a new way. It is often interesting to compute something and go back to see what the relationship of the result is to the knowledge computed a few seconds ago.

Speed of execution is also important because often one needs a response from a user in order to progress. With the user in the loop, it is important to minimize computing time. It is interesting that the Intelligence Compiler system, at $500, provides what a $30,000 product couldn't offer in 1985.

Service Planner's Architecture

At a high level, Service Planner orchestrates rules from several knowledge bases: serviceability rules, maintainability rules, reliability rules, organizational rules, and logistic repair rules. Interacting with a database of facts and a database of objects, IC builds output tables. The output reports include contract forecast, service activity, service cost, part order requirements, service pricing, parts and labor cost, reliability, availability and serviceability data, and an executive report.

Information is shared between the 10 knowledge bases, just as information is shared in the service planning activity between the various parts of the organization that have service responsibilities. For example, the reliability knowledge base computes the reliability of a product. It uses information about how many times a part will fail (stored in the frames representing each replaceable part) and the structure of the product, say a computer (hard disc, keyboards, display, scanners, parts within scanners). The reliability knowledge base implements a reliability engineering analysis. As the service plan evolves, each knowledge base passes information on to the next. The field engineering module, for example, computes field support manpower. It will burden the manpower cost and come up with the overall cost for field support. The output from field engineering goes to the logistics knowledge base. Here are computed parts distribution, service schedules, sparing levels, and so on.

The Service Planner runs a set of data past a whole series of experts and generates the information contained in a service plan. The knowledge bases do tasks that people—the home office, the finance group, the controller, the training group, the documentation group—would normally have to do.

Payoff

Our general manager and our vice president in charge of field service in Motorola are totally committed to this project. They believe we have captured the expertise involved in the task in Service Planner—we can now do service planning analyses. We have not just done a superficial study, an ad hoc collection of rules of thumb. What we have done is much more in depth.

SUMMARY

Service Planner provides an in-depth, financial, and long-range service plan for new products. It achieves a three-to-one productivity improvement. But more important, it backs service plans with a higher degree of information and knowledge than older methods.

21
Object-Oriented Programming: An Alternative to Expert Systems for Project Management

Robert A. Dwinnell

5thGen Technology Inc.

In the early 1980s, after more than two decades of scholarly research, artificial intelligence (AI) began to get a great deal of attention as a means for solving some of the problems of our technologically complex society. For business it was claimed that great cost savings could be realized by the automation of human expertise. The publicity surrounding AI's emergence aroused great expectations that have been only partially realized. There is, however, hope that second-generation AI technology will, in domains such as project management and resource allocation, fulfill some of the early expectations.

DIAGNOSING VS. PLANNING

In the early 1980s the message rang out loud and clear that artificial intelligence (AI) was ready to take its place as a tool for assisting society in coping with its increasing complexity (*Business Week,* 1982; Alexander, 1982a, 1982b, 1982c; *Dun's Business Month,* 1981). It was a message eagerly embraced by a public fascinated by the notion of machines that could think. Industry quickly mobilized the necessary resources to exploit this new technology. These initial steps were disappointing because of a mismatch between the claims that had been made for AI and the problems for which business was seeking solutions. More recently, however, some exciting new tools have emerged from AI research labs that show promise of fulfilling some of the early claims.

Human beings excel at problemsolving. Any technology that can demonstrate the ability to enable machines to solve problems will have an enormous impact on business. Machines are tireless, consistent, and, in the case of electronic machines, usually economical. The new tool that inspired the heightened interest in AI was an approach called knowledge engineering. The concept advanced by the adherents of knowledge engineering was that expertise was expressible as if/then rules, for example; IF your automobile engine won't start and the fuel gauge is on empty THEN you're probably out of gas. These if/then rules were used by the expert to structure his domain knowledge. It followed that, if the expert could be interviewed and these rules extracted from him, his expertise might be duplicated in a computer. By combining the rules with a mechanism for meaningfully searching and evaluating them into a computer program, a clone of the expert could be created.

The problems that business needed to solve were those involving the automation of human expertise. Problems such as scheduling, production control, and crisis management are performed by humans with alacrity, as long as they are small. As these problems grow very large, humans cease to do well with them. What AI had offered was a splendid tool for a large number of diagnostic problems. Would that suffice for the problems just mentioned? Were the problems business was interested in best solved by diagnosis or by planning?

A large number of the problems humans are asked to solve can be broadly classified into two categories: diagnostic and planning problems. The diagnostician, working from experience, examines a problem and notes which elements in the environment could be expected to cause such an affliction. If more than one possible cause exists he may run some tests to further narrow the field of possibilities. Finally, he tests the one remaining candidate by rectifying it and observing whether the problem has been eliminated. He can be confident that one and only one cause has resulted in the incapacity. Once the cause is eliminated all will be well with the world.

A different kind of problemsolver, the chess player, sits at his board confronted with one goal, to win. An astronomical number of solutions exist, many of which will allow him to reach his goal while others will not. In order to cope with this dilemma he must have a plan. He first decomposes the problem into an opening, middle game, and end game. Within each of these settings he considers the opponent's position on the board and his own. He ponders similar positions he has seen, read about, or actually encountered. He considers what his opponent's plan may be, recalling any knowledge he may have about his adversary. This example of strategic problemsolving is the sort used by humans to solve the previously mentioned business problems.

OBJECT-ORIENTED PROGRAMMING

AI can be defined in many ways. For the purposes of this discussion it's best thought of as a collection of tools. One of those tools is knowledge engineering, a good tool for solving diagnostic problems. For dealing with problems involving planning another tool exists, object-oriented programming (OOP). OOP shows great promise as a means for coping with project management and other problems involving the allocation of resources. OOP has its roots in the programming language Simula (Dahl & Nygaard, 1966). It has, however, been enthusiastically adopted by the AI community (Bobrow, Kahn, Kiczales, Masinter, Stefik, & Zdybel, 1986; Goldbert & Robson, 1983; Moon & Keene, 1985) and bears little resemblance to its ancestor. Object-oriented programs differ from conventional programs in that their fundamental building blocks are objects instead of procedures. These objects are little packets of behavior and information about the state of the object.

An early example of OOP is the spreadsheet. The broad acceptance of spreadsheets has come about, in large part, because of their simplicity, intuitiveness, and ease of use. This popularity stems from their object-oriented underpinnings. A typical object in a spreadsheet program is the cell. Two behaviors associated with a cell are edit and display. Editing the cell's value may or may not change other cells. Similarly, the cell may display itself as 100, $1.00, or 100 percent. Information about the state of a cell might include whether the value of another cell is computationally linked to this cell's value or an indication that, although the cell's value has changed, it has yet to be redrawn. Other object types might be formulas, pages, or even spreadsheets.

The way a spreadsheet works is by sending messages. A keyboard entry sends a change-value message to a cell. After the value is changed, a redraw-value message might be sent. Finally, if the value of another cell depends on the newly changed cell, a recompute-value message would be sent to it. The ease of use of the spreadsheet is further enhanced because the human interface also exploits the object metaphor. The abstract cell object is represented to you with a cell image object, a rectangle with room for text to be written inside of it. Similarly, the spreadsheet object is a special kind of window object that has cell images written on it. The design leverage gained by using the same metaphor for manipulating both the data structures in the computer's memory and their graphical representation on the screen allows for writing much "smarter" programs.

The success of this approach has not gone unnoticed. If this technology works so well at representing groups of mathematically related values and their images on the computer screen, why wouldn't it allow you to model the behavior of objects that are not only mathematically but also logically related? Attempts to do this are currently being made in the area of project management and other resource allocation problems.

OBJECT-ORIENTED APPROACH TO PLANNING

In order to see how we apply the object metaphor to this class of problems, let's define a plan for producing something as a series of precedence-related activities that result in the production of something. Furthermore, we define each of these activities as the allocation of resources to the transformation of the product to prepare it for the next activity. What we have just defined can be viewed as a domain of three object categories. The processes for creating products are de-

fined by production plans that specify the ordered activities and the appropriate resources for the transformations specified by those activities.

Most workplaces can be thought of as a collection of resources knowledgeable in the creation of a set of products. During the course of work, demands, yet another group of objects, are made for the production of these items.

The problem is to meet those demands in a timely, correct, and cost effective fashion. If the numbers of demands and resources are of any interesting size, the correct solution to the problem is impossible to find. Programs exist that will provide satisfactory solutions; however, they consume large amounts of computing time and aren't able to do the rescheduling that, almost certainly, will be necessary when a resource ceases to function or an unforeseen demand arises. In that instance it almost always falls to a human to provide a solution. These solutions usually involve a small perturbation of the master schedule in the locality of the crisis. In short, if the guy at the next desk goes home sick, the boss asks you to work late.

AN EXAMPLE

Consider a simple example of a workcenter, your neighborhood service station. It has resources, products, product plans and demands. In OOP the products might be organized in a graph such as in Figure 21.1.

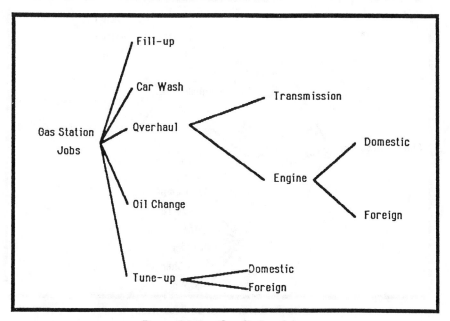

Figure 21.1.   Gas Station Jobs

We will take up the reasons for the hierarchy in a moment. For now, let's consider a similar graph, Figure 21.2, that contains the resources available for the completion of the tasks in Figure 21.1.

The graph in Figure 21.1 represents the hierarchy of tasks one expects to have performed at a gas station. They vary in complexity from filling up a gas tank to overhauling the engine of an expensive foreign car. The hierarchy in which the task objects are arranged is one of OOP's great strengths. For instance, all of the tasks have some characteristics in common. Each task, hopefully, will be completed in a predictable period of time, it will have a cost associated with it, and a plan for its accomplishment will exist. Where better to define these characteristics than at the GAS STATION JOBS node of the graph? The existence of these characteristics is inherited from left to right. The value for a characteristic is unique to each node unless an ancestor's value is appropriate, in which case it would be redundant also to place the value at the descendant. The same sort of inheritance occurs for aspects of behavior. Further down the graph other "branching" or specialization might be helpful. For example, it could be said that the overhaul of a domestic car engine is the same procedurally as that of a foreign engine, but a more skilled technician is required for the foreign car. The procedure for doing the overhaul might be defined as in Figure 21.3.

The bold font indicates that only Otto, a German mechanic, is capable of doing an engine overhaul on a foreign car. Similarly, the task times for this type

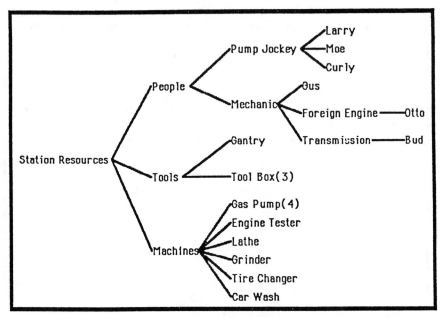

Figure 21.2.   Station Resources

Foreign Car Engine Overhaul

Activity	Material	Machines	People	Tools	Lead Time	Task Time
Remove Engine	Supplies	None	Mechanic	Gantry	1 Day	2 Hours
Disassemble	Supplies	None	Otto	Tool Box	1 Hour	8 Hours
Diagnose	Supplies	None	Otto	Tool Box	1 Hour	2 Hours
Order Parts	Supplies	None	Otto	None	1 Hour	2 Hours
Install Parts	New Parts	None	Otto	Tool Box	4 Hours	6 Hours
Reassemble	Supplies	None	Otto	Tool Box	1 Hour	6 Hours
Install Engine	Supplies	None	Mechanic	Gantry	1 Hour	2 Hours
Adjust Engine	Supplies	Eng. Tester	Otto	Tool Box	1 Hour	2 Hours

Figure 21.3.   Foreign Car Engine Overhaul

of overhaul are also different. Only the bold data become a part of the foreign engine overhaul object. The rest of its plan is inherited from ancestors in the graph. The general flow for an engine versus transmission overhaul, at this level of granularity, is very similar; therefore, most of the plan could exist at the OVERHAUL node. Any differences between engine and transmission overhauls occur at those nodes, respectively. Any arc (line) in the graph implies some specialization of a child node from a parent with only the differences recorded at the child.

The amount of classification and degree of difference are strictly under the control of the user. In OOP the amount of this detail is often referred to as the level of abstraction. The way a CEO, division VP, plant supervisor, or shop foreman view a machine shop is very different, but they must all be able to see it at an appropriate level of detail. OOP provides us with a powerful means of carrying out these varying levels of abstraction.

Assuming we had fully defined each of the plans for the tasks represented in the task graph, we could now apply some demand to our model and see what happens. Figure 21.4 represents a selected set of demands.

For each task type we've defined a number of demands to occur between the *from* and *to* dates. We'll generate them randomly to model the unpredictable demand pattern one associates with a service station. If desired, one would be free to concentrate gasoline demand around rush hour and lunch time to mirror more accurately the real world. We've chosen to close the garage for the weekend but to leave the pumps open.

Demands for Week Beginning 8/21/1988			
Demand type	Number	From	To
Fill-up	800	8/21/1988	8/27/1988
Transmission Overhaul	2	8/22/1988	8/26/1988
Domestic Engine Overhaul	3	8/22/1988	8/26/1988
Foreign Engine Overhaul	1	8/22/1988	8/26/1988
Oil Change	30	8/22/1988	8/26/1988
Domestic Engine Tune-up	20	8/22/1988	8/26/1988
Foreign Engine Tune-up	8	8/22/1988	8/26/1988
Car Wash	150	8/21/1988	8/27/1988

Figure 21.4.   Demands for Week Beginning 8/21/1988

Assuming that a suitable event-driven simulator has been written and the procedures that implement the object's behavior exist, the model is ready to run.

The earliest demand object would send a message to the plan for producing the item demanded. The message would ask for the first activity to be executed. If the task were a fill of gasoline, the availability of a gas pump and a pump jockey would be checked by sending messages to those resource objects. If the resources were available the activity would take place, followed by the window-washing, fluid and tire pressure checking associated with a full service station. During that period of time, the pump and pump jockey would not be available for a subsequent demand. The simulation would continue until all demands had been met or time had elapsed. All data relevant to the simulation are easily captured at the objects themselves. Larry "knows" which cars he filled and when. Similarly the more abstract object, pump jockey, has the composite data for Larry, Moe, and Curly.

The task plan in Figure 21.3 indicated a plan time of 30 hours for the overhaul of a foreign automobile engine. Figure 21.5 shows the time assumed for each of the other tasks.

The model would demonstrate very clearly that we're well balanced except in

Task Execution Times	
Task	Time
Fill-up	8 Mins.
Transmission Overhaul	20 Hrs.
Domestic Engine Overhaul	30 Hrs.
Foreign Engine Overhaul	30 Hrs.
Oil Change	30 Mins.
Domestic Engine Tune-up	2 Hrs.
Foreign Engine Tune-up	2 Hrs.
Car Wash	10 Mins.

Figure 21.5. Task Execution Times

the area of domestic engine work. Even with Larry, Moe, and Curly doing oil changes, we have a shortfall. One can arrive at these numbers in a few minutes with just paper and pencil, but without OOP you can't radically modify the model and get new results quickly. If we had chosen to identify the costs associated with the various resources we could have evaluated the tradeoff between 10 minute car washes with a pump jockey/car wash machine combination or 45 minute car washes with just the pump jockey. What's the impact on our mechanic bottleneck if we allow Moe to remove and install engines and transmissions? OOP models are excellent for doing this type of what-if analysis.

ENHANCEMENTS TO THE BASIC OOP MODEL

The integration of an OOP interface with the model allows for an intuitive, easy to use tool. The combination of object-oriented interfaces and models allows workers who aren't computer scientists to use them. It can't be emphasized enough that people must believe in a model or they won't use it. OOP takes a big step toward meeting this need by organizing models out of pieces of the domain being observed. It makes more sense to bend a computing paradigm to fit the problem than to make the problem unrecognizable to satisfy the paradigm.

Useful extensions to the Spartan model discussed here are easily implemented. The addition of animation is straightforward because the program objects themselves are the items to be animated. They "know" where they should be because they're privy to their location. Issues like work shifts can be described by assigning work-shift calendars to nodes in the resource graph. The objects then quit and resume work under their own control. Breakdowns can be incorporated by assigning time between failure and time to repair values to resources. The objects will then take the responsibility of breaking when appropriate and resuming work when they're repaired. Probabilistic, as opposed to deterministic, behavior is made possible by assigning a tuple rather than a single value to the characteristic in question. The real value then becomes a value between the two elements of the tuple.

Further model sophistication can be made possible by the introduction of user-selectable heuristics. Some of the behaviors a resource exhibits can be carried out in a variety of ways. When an object is confronted with multiple demands for its services, how does it decide what to do first? If it's Curly and they are gas demands, the rule he should use is first-in, first-out. Bud, on the other hand, should always work on the transmission if his choice is between a transmission and other mechanical work. Besides customer service and scheduling heuristics, quality and profitability rules of thumb might serve as a basis for resolving contentious demand. Other object behaviors could be implemented similarly. With OOP the user's ability to mirror the real world is more a challenge to his imagination than to the tool he's using. That is as it should be.

CONCLUSION

In the future, OOP is positioned to be at the center of intelligent decision-making systems. In order to accomplish this, some obstacles must be overcome. The objects need to be able to access information about themselves in conventional business databases. The greatest problem here is not enabling the object to do such a thing but arriving at database standards. It's unreasonable to expect the object to cope with the idiosyncratic nature of a particular firm's database. Similarly, having the object in touch with its real world counterpart would make the model even more accurate. With those issues resolved we could write systems that make management decisions after testing the decision on the model itself.

To summarize, early attempts to apply artificial intelligence programming techniques have met with mixed results. Attempts to exploit rule-based programming in complex domains have met with failure. The linear nature of if/then logic runs counter to the structure of the knowledge it intends to embody. Object-oriented programming, on the other hand, provides additional degrees of freedom for capturing the richness and complexity of this domain knowledge. OOP tools will be more widely used because they look and feel like the environment the user is familiar with.

REFERENCES

Alexander, T. (1982a, May 17). Teaching computers the art of reason. *Fortune*, pp. 82–92.

Alexander, T. (1982b, May 31). Teaching computers the art of reason. *Fortune*, pp. 139–145.

Alexander, T. (1982c, June 14). Teaching computers the art of reason. *Fortune*, pp. 148–160.

Bobrow, D., Kahn, K., Kiczales, Masinter, Stefik, & Zdybel. (1986, October) CommonLoops: Merging common lisp and object oriented programming. *OOPSLA*.

Business Week. (1982, March 10). Artificial intelligence, the second computer age begins, pp. 66–75.

Dahl, O.-J., & Nygaard, K., (1966, September). Simula-an algol-based simulation language. *ACM Communications*, *9*, 671–678.

Dun's Business Month. (1981, October). Computers that "think" are here, pp. 111–113.

Goldberg, A., & Robson, D. (1983). *Smalltalk-80: The language and its implementation*. Reading, MA: Addison-Wesley.

Moon, D., & Keene, S. (1985, December). *Flavors: Object oriented programming on symbolics computers*. Paper presented at the Common Lisp Conference.

22

Effective Information Management Through Artificial Intelligence: Maintaining Quality Customer Service at The Balsams Grand Resort Hotel

Stephen Barba

Balsams Grand Resort Hotel

This chapter presents a verbal testimonial about how dedication to customer service made The Balsams Grand Resort Hotel prosper and survive as one of the few remaining American plan hotels. The extraordinary information management task involved in providing detailed and individualized customer reservations service is described—it was a nightmarish pressure cooker of tape on a reservations board, duplicated effort in entering and reentering client data, and paper files overwhelming the confined spaces of the 19th-century office space. Mr. Barba characterizes an information processing challenge many will relate to, and then testifies as to how artificial intelligence enabled them to improve greatly customer service while getting rid of the paper shuffle.

INTRODUCTION

I am no expert on artificial intelligence other than I've been living with it in our operation for the last four years. I am, however, an expert on The Balsams. I started at The Balsams in 1959 as a caddy. I worked there the first several summers through junior high school and high school until I was old enough to work on the golf course greens-keeping crew. Eventually I became a bellhop, a bar boy, and then a busboy in the dining room; then a bar waiter, a bartender, and a waiter in the dining room; and then a doorman. I operated the elevator one season and then served as pool boy in the summers during college. I was actually teaching at Michigan State University in the Department of English. I had intentions of making that my career when the University went on strike in 1970 with the invasion of Cambodia. So I went back to where I always went during semester breaks, The Balsams. This place had had a rough history. I don't think it was because of me in those early years. There used to be hundreds of places like The Balsams throughout the Northeast and now, to tell you the truth, The Balsams is the last of two. The Mount Washington Hotel and The Balsams are still operating basically as they have for some time.

THE BALSAMS—HISTORICAL AND GEOGRAPHICAL SETTING

The Balsams started in 1873. It is the only four-star, four-diamond resort hotel in the Northeast. In 1971, a friend of mine and I told the owner that we wanted a chance to operate the hotel. Even though neither of us had had any formal management experience and we were both very young, he gave us that chance. Now that tells you about how bad off the hotel was. There had been a succession of managers there whom I had worked for many, many years, and each one had been succeedingly worse. The business of the place had dropped to almost nonexistence. There were 60 guests a day during the summer months, and a final-ditch effort had been made to open the resort in the winter to see whether or not it could survive as a winter hotel where it might not be going to make it as a summer hotel. And that did improve things, for it brought new guests for the first time in a long time. When I had worked there as a kid, we'd always said that the guests were either newlywed or nearly dead. The newlyweds never came back, and the nearly deads couldn't come back.

When we took over, we did so with a great deal of enthusiasm—no expertise but a great deal of enthusiasm. And it worked; the enthusiasm worked. We took a place that was doing no business and promptly started doing more business by showing up, by keeping the place clean, by having good food, and caring about the place. We built a clientele in a place that had no clientele. Eventually, we were able to improve the physical appearance. We were able to make improvements: to buy furniture it didn't have, to buy silverware, and to dress up the place, to make it a grand hotel once again. In 1976 the hotel made a profit for the first time since it was purchased out of bankruptcy in 1954.

And at that point the owner gave it to us with a very kind lease arrangement. The chef, the general manager, the maintenance superintendent, and I are now Balsams Corporation; since 1977 we have owned the company that operates this hotel. We have made millions of dollars in capital improvements to the building and to the property as a whole which has 15,000 acres of land. It is a wonderful, exclusive, private place—two golf courses, tennis courts, a winter operation with its own ski area and cross-country ski area, accommodations for 400 guests, and 450 employees, 200 of whom we house. The town of Dixville Notch has a population of 38. You may know Dixville Notch as being the first town in the country to vote in all national elections. We vote at midnight on the eve of elections. By everyone's gathering at midnight, by having individual voting booths for every voter, by opening the polls when we think it's midnight and closing them once everybody's voted (which is about two minutes later), our little town is always able to be first in New Hampshire and thereby first in the country in election returns reported.

We're in the northern White Mountains of New Hampshire; we're in a place that has no real support from a metropolitan area nearby; we are a destination resort. Our guests come primarily from Boston and New York. Boston is a 4½-hour ride away (I can attest to that because I did it yesterday late at night), and New York is 8 hours away. Montreal is only 3 hours away, but the Canadian exchange rate has been an impediment to our doing a lot of Canadian business.

This is an American plan hotel; one rate covers everything. That's important to understand. When our guests come there and agree to pay the rates that are being charged, they are not charged for anything else other than incidentals. There is no additional charge for any of their meals, three meals a day. There's no charge for any use of the golf courses or skiing in the winter; lessons are included. It's a very, very comprehensive plan, and it is not a package. I would resent it ever being called a package. A package involves multiple entrepreneurs, each in his own little business and each with his own little piece of the pie, putting their pieces together and making a whole. This has never been pieced apart. The traditions of the American plan started in New England and came right from the rural homes that were on the frontier. When travelers came along those old dusty roads trying to make their way between two very remote communities and they came at the end of their first day's stay to the home of someone who was living out there, homesteading on the frontier, they had the conventional courtesy of knowing that they could go right to that homeowner and ask for protection and for food. And in exchange for chores or liquor or tobacco or whatever else they might have with them, hospitality would be offered. And the hospitality was the hospitality of the host, the hospitality of the house. These people, these travelers, became house guests. They ate when the family ate, they ate at the family's table, they ate what the family did. That's what the American plan is; that's what we are still today. We would never understand how to charge for individual items. We welcome all guests in, and we take a very personal attitude toward the hospitality that we are trying to provide. It is not like other places. I don't know of any other place like this. Even the one other place that remains in New England has modified the American plan to the extent that their guests do pay for the incidentals—for golf and for lunch and for other packages that are being offered. Ours is not that way at all. I think it's imperative you understand this in terms of ever comprehending why we have an artificial intelligence system at The Balsams.

THE BALSAMS FACILITIES

Figure 22.1 shows the hotel, and Figure 22.2 shows the town. When Stephen Geer from ABC News was there to report on the elections, he wanted to know

Figure 22.1.   The Balsams Grand Resort Hotel

Figure 22.2.   Dixville Notch

where the town hall was, and I said, "Well, it's probably here in my office in the lobby." Then he wanted to know where the school was. Well, we're an unincorporated town so we don't furnish schooling to our children; that's done through local towns. We have a fire department. We supply all of our own energy by burning sawdust and bark in lieu of what would be 200,000 gallons of fuel oil a month. We supply our electricity. We own our own telephone company. We have our own TV cable for the people who do live in the town. Thirty thousand flowers are brought in bloom because we really are just two seasons there, winter and the Fourth of July, so all of the flowers are grown in Boston and then planted in the spring. The hotel was not intended to be a large place when it was first built in 1873; in fact, it originally offered only 25 guest rooms. It was enlarged in succeeding years until our *new* wing, the stone building on the left, was built in 1916.

We have on staff a doctor of archaeology who conducts our nature programs. We have the trails, the golf fairways, the ski slopes all marked with natural history signs. There are natural history walks that guests can take, and we're about to start an archaeological dig. This part of America is the oldest land mass above water on the surface of the earth. There have been Indians living where we are for the last 12,000 years, and there is archaeological evidence of this. There are children's programs galore. All of the children are privileged to participate fully in the facilities of the hotel along with their parents.

One of the golf courses is 2½ miles from the hotel (see Figure 22.3). There is

Figure 22.3.   Golf Course at The Balsams

a magnificent Donald Ross golf course, rated the toughest in the state. Because golf is free and unlimited, we get lots of golfers and lots of people who want to play golf, even if they've never played before. And there's an easier golf course should they be just starting off. There are tennis courts, a tennis pro, golf pros, and lots of activities and events scheduled every day.

The food is incredible. We operate a professional culinary training program in the kitchen; we have 55 chefs in the kitchen, including 15 apprentice chefs who are on a 6,000-hour, 3-year program to become certified by the American Culinary Federation and the U.S. Department of Labor as Journeymen Cooks. Every meal is different. The Balsams menu changes every day; the menu does not repeat itself. Guests who are there for a month never see the same selections, and guests have their choice of the menu.

There are three rooms with live entertainment in the evening. Figure 22.4 shows one of the cocktail lounges where there's a top 40-type combo. There's a ballroom here with nightclub shows six nights a week, and then we have another patio lounge. This happens to be the original hotel, the original section of the hotel that first operated in 1873.

The bedrooms do not have television, and they are traditional in their New England style. We're fully operative in the winter. We are right on the Canadian border in northern New Hampshire.

Figure 22.5 shows the ski-area base lodge with the mountain private to the hotel guests. It's a thousand-foot vertical drop with 12 trails, and facilities include

Figure 22.4. Cocktail Lounge at The Balsams

Figure 22.5.   Ski-Area Base Lodge

a full ski school, a full ski shop, beautiful base lodge, and luncheon counter. There are also 50 kilometers of cross-country trails (all part of our natural history program) with wonderful skiing—250 inches of snow is our snow index. That's the last figure. I think that will give you a perspective on where I come from. Having come from there and only there, I don't know much else other than what The Balsams is about.

MANAGEMENT STYLE

When we first went into management there, we prized every guest. Our office is in the main lobby, and we could meet them personally. We had to assemble a staff to work almost without pay because the hotel could not afford to pay very much, and there were not enough guests to provide very much in the way of gratuities. But an *esprit de corps* built up between the guests, the staff, the owners, and managers. It worked. The spirit of the American plan took over. And in American-plan places, in the original frontier places, the guest was just as responsible for having a good time as was the host. And guests could be judged by the way they accepted hospitality just as they can be today. Ben Franklin said,

"House guests are like fish; they begin to stink after 3 days." There is a certain truth to that. When every aspect of a guest's stay is being taken care of, the guest has no other options. He can't go to another restaurant; there aren't any others. He can't play any other golf courses; there aren't any. He can't go to any other nightclub shows; there aren't any. He has to enjoy every aspect of what we are including in the plan, and every aspect has to be of comparable worth from the guest's point of view. What good does it do if we have wonderful food, exquisite rooms, and lovely entertainment if the guest is a skier who does not like the ski area. He can't ski anywhere else; there's nowhere else around; and because of our isolation, that is the case. So everything has to be of comparable quality, comparable attraction.

The hospitality industry in and of itself is a very complicated business. If you think about it, and The Balsams is typical of this, we are dealing primarily with a staff (450 people), many of whom are not trained managers. These are people who have all been brought up within the business. Many of them don't have extensive formal education. Many of them are local people, which is part of where our genuine hospitality comes from, and some of the staff are transient; we offer lots of entry-level jobs. We have lots of exit-level jobs for people who are retired or semiretired and want to work a season. Many kids are going to college, and they work seasonally. We have lots of training. We are in and of ourselves an institution for training. We have a training program with four culinary schools. We have a training program with the Bahamian Tourism College; we have a training program for Irish college students; and we have a training program to place high school dropouts. We have lots of kids. New Hampshire has an unemployment rate of 2 percent and our hotel employs 5 percent of all the working people in northern New Hampshire. The Balsams supplies the State of New Hampshire with 1 percent of all the room and meals tax that is collected in the state. We are a big player in this scene; we are a leader in a number of ways, other than being wrong on most of our political predictions. So we have a changing staff and a dynamic environment as well.

Our business is seasonal; it depends on the season. The seasons have to be good, whether it's raining or snowing or too hot or whatever; we don't have air conditioning. There are a lot of variables in what affects our business—the stock market, the economy, the availability of gas—all of these things affect us, and we have to respond quickly in our decisions and our programs. Forming bonds with past guests is the most important aspect of that. Eighty percent of our business is with past guests; the other 20 percent comes from referrals from those past guests. It's a highly competitive business although we don't feel as though we have any competition, and we don't compete against ourselves. We have no time-sharing; we have no condos; we have no townhouses nor second homes. Our 15,000 acres is completely dedicated to the hotel and its guests. We have a large number of employees, a large number of guests, 100,000 guest names. In order to furnish the 450 positions which we maintain in our open season, it sometimes takes 700 different people. This is Labor Day weekend; a lot of our college students are going back to school. Those who work the front desk and the new people we're able to find all need to be retrained—right in the middle of our season. The house counts don't drop; it's a busy time. It's a very dynamic, changing world, with lots of conflicting or competing details. In addition, each guest room is different. We're an old hotel with wing after wing built in different eras under different conditions and different standards, and each room we wanted to treat individually, not as a unit within a block.

Our guests return, and they want the same room, they want the same furniture arrangement, they want it the same week each season. They want to make the same reservations, but their family changes. They no longer have the same size family. The ages of their family change.

We have an inventive system for charging for children that has worked wonderfully since our very first year. We were trying to build individual, personal relationships with our guests, and they were lying to us about their children's ages because at the age of 12 they were charged adult rates. It was a classic instance where one could almost say at the front desk, "How old are you?" and the child would say "12." "When will you be 13?" "As soon as we check out." So we have a rate that is $5 times the age of the child. It includes everything, but a 10-year-old pays $50 for the day and a 12-year-old $60 a day so long as they stay in the same room as their parents. That means that we average more than two people to a room. We are a family hotel. We indeed can sleep 400 people. If you take the average collection of individual single people, couples, and families, 400 people is full.

THE RESERVATIONS CHALLENGE

On our own, with a manual system of taking reservations on a chart, we have been processing these reservations each year, trying to remember everybody's name, trying to be personal, trying to be friendly, trying to give all past guests a gift of maple syrup when they arrived, trying to give all 10-year guests a silver pitcher that was personally delivered, giving plate after plate of fruit plates to all notable guests, and making sure that their starting times on the golf course and that their tables in the dining room were reserved. It was an incredible task; and through the tremendous accomplishments of our very dedicated people, we succeeded during our peak season, which is July 4 through Labor Day; we achieved 102 percent occupancy. We averaged 410 people a day. The next year the most that we could do was maybe 412.

We had to make more money. We saw there were holes in the system. In our chart there were days, in fact 500 of them during those 60 days of July and August, 500 room-days that were available for only one night because we didn't have guests who drove by. They all came to us on purpose. When we tried to accommodate their preferred schedules, they left us with 500 empty nights. So we said we've got to figure out a way to fix that.

CONSIDERING—AND REJECTING—SOLUTIONS

We tried all kinds of marketing programs, but they didn't really work. To attract guests for one-night stays is very difficult; we're a long way from anywhere. Then one day a guest of ours walked into my office. He said, "This is an incredible place." I had known him; he'd run for president. He'd been there to campaign. And he said, "I'll bet that with all the menus that you're preparing, changing every day, you've got to have recipes galore, ingredients galore, purchasing problems galore." His partners and he had had a company, called Fast Facts, which had dealt very successfully with such problems. Apparently they had invented the first cash register which could keep records of food in terms of the price, the ordering, the taking out of inventory, and the delivery to the customer. They had done very well with it.

He'd now been dabbling with artificial intelligence, and he said, "We could take your kitchen operation over and really do a job on it." He told me what he could do. Actually he went to the chef first, my partner. The chef got all excited because it was going to eliminate all of his problems.

I had just come back from the resort meeting of the American Hotel & Motel Association, 60 of the finest resorts in the country, including the Broadmoor, the Del Coronado, the Greenbriar, the Homestead, and The Balsams. One of the sessions at that program had been the discussion of computer programs being used in these resorts. Sixteen different reports were made by the chief executive officers of those hotels. Fifteen of them complained about their system; fifteen said it didn't do what had been promised, didn't do it in the time predicted, cost more money than it was worth, and wasn't working.

We, in fact, had tried to meet with representatives from the major computer companies, and I never could understand what they were saying. They constantly wanted us to change our system to fit these computers, to be a more commercial hotel. We're not so much a hotel as we are a community of people who care about a place and want to be there. So I couldn't see our ever addressing our problems with these standard systems. The one hotel owner of the sixteen reporting who said he loved his system has a 40-room hotel on the coast of Maine; he has a Tandy which he said worked perfectly for his resort. He has never used it in the reservations office, however; he has just used it for his mailing lists. He paid high compliments to the computer system.

So my first encounter with artificial intelligence systems came in the person of Bill Hunscher. He didn't have a company, but I said to him, "If you can do that for the kitchen, why don't you go take a look at reservations because reservations are where the money is. It's the only thing we charge our guests anything for in the first place." He said, "Yeah, but there are so many systems that do hotel and hospitality." I said, "None of them will work for us." So he studied our system, and he convinced us that artificial intelligence would make a difference. Eventually we signed on.

The Balsams has been inventive in a number of ways; we've had to be independent. It was a very scary thing. Everybody in the world told us not to do it. Hunscher started a company, Eloquent Systems, to build this artificial intelligence system for The Balsams.

DETAILS OF THE RESERVATIONS CHALLENGE

We wanted a front office system. We were suffering with our reservations chart. I don't know if you understand what that means, but it's a chart of our entire season, 140 days laid out on a wall with the 232 rooms of the hotel lined down one side and one space for every day of the season. Then a piece of tape, different colored tape for different sorts of guests or a different status of guests— whether the guest is tentative without deposit, whether he has been here before, whether we can change the guest or can't change him—would go on that chart. There would be reservations people from the office rushing up to the chart, and, especially after we started getting very busy, people booked in advance so that by the time July came around we were 95 percent sold out anyway. It became a war to try to find space on the chart. Tape would mysteriously be missing from the chart and so would people. If someone by the name of Smithsonian was staying two nights, we couldn't write his name on the chart, so we had to make an S and party of 5 and refer back to paper charts or paper files to figure out who this person was. It was a constant going back and forth, a constant retyping of names, a constant being at a complete loss of what we were doing. It was completely hit or miss, but we didn't make many mistakes. In fact, we ran at 102 or 103 percent occupancy. Our reservations staff are wonderful; they dedicated themselves entirely to this task. It did work, but it was like recreating a mountain every time.

We had to type the name and address of incoming guests 11 times before we got them checked in. We had reams of papers and duplicate forms, and this is an old hotel; it wasn't built with large office space. We had file cabinets galore, and we were so busy that the file cabinets themselves couldn't hold the papers from one season. We had two or three drawers filled with papers on one particular issue. It was a very hard time. The pace was frenetic. A new person, however, couldn't figure out who was a past guest without asking, "Have you been here before?" He had to know this to determine whether or not the guest was to receive the complimentary bottle of maple syrup. If we failed to give a former guest the bottle of maple syrup, that guest felt slighted.

If a guest were to call only two weeks in advance of his reservation, the only way he could stay for a week was to move his room every night. There were up to 30 room changes a day. Trying to move guests from a room with a beautiful view to a room that looks over the back of the kitchen and then the next night to a corner room, each move involving a rate change, is almost impossible. We were crying for help. We needed help, and it came.

THE ARTIFICIAL INTELLIGENCE SOLUTION

Eloquent's solution was to deal with the extensive information that we already had about our guests. We did, however, exclude from guest files anybody who arrived with a convention. We had no time to write their names and addresses down, type them, and put them in the card file. We had no time to put them in the IBM word processor; it was too busy. But we did have extensive information about our social guests. We had a thorough understanding of our management strategies because we had worked them out ourselves, we had created them, we understood them and knew why they were there, we knew what they were based on, and we had a full description of all of the characteristics of the ingredients of hospitality at The Balsams. We were in control of it all; we delivered on all of it.

What Eloquent did was to propose to us a system that would be used by several people at the same time; that was an important ingredient. We needed to have several people dealing with the same information at the same time so there wouldn't be cross bookings and duplicate bookings as there had been before. We needed an ability to fill those one-night empty spaces. We needed to have the whole of the entire reservation staff and the front office staff dealing face-to-face or phone-to-phone with our guests. We couldn't be calling them back; we couldn't go to a larger central reservation system somewhere else. We needed to be doing it right there in Dixville Notch, and indeed, the WATS line and the other direct lines that we had were confusing to our guests. It was almost better when we didn't have them because the guests sometimes thought they weren't talking to us at the hotel.

The expertise of our management was excellent and very solid, but many of the staff were new and to deliver that expertise to them was almost impossible. We had all of these rules of thumb and kernels of wisdom, but they were in the person of Jerry Owen, the reservations manager. Jerry, therefore, was working 70-hour weeks and being called at home as much as six times a day. Eloquent promised to deliver consistently what management's goals and wishes and dreams were for the place. They said to us that a conventional computer would be able to handle a number of the individual benefits that we were going to get from their system, but it wouldn't be able to handle it all at once.

We had been unwilling to go with a database system because we had the knowledge to run it and we didn't want to translate it. We wanted something that was unique to the Balsams and not standard. We wanted something that was dynamic and was able to be changed to meet our changing circumstances, both seasonal and unplanned changes, instead of a static system which required calling in a reprogrammer to make these changes. We wanted it to be a people system. We wanted it to stand beside us and not between us and our guests, and that's what was created.

The Eloquent Systems engineers never once talked gobbledy-gook to us. The people there now are the same people who were there four years ago. They are themselves inspired by the technology. They are themselves thoroughly committed to what they've done for us. We have no financial interest in that company whatsoever. We don't get a commission, we don't own stock, but a partnership was formed there with them, and I have a great deal of respect for them. They are very ethical people. I just heard a story the other day which I thought was appropriate. It was that a young person didn't understand what the word "ethics" meant, so he asked his father, the shopkeeper, and his father said, "Well, it's like this. If someone comes into the shop and buys merchandise and overpays by $5, it's a matter of ethics as to whether or not I tell my partner." So, ethically speaking, I'm telling you that Eloquent was a first-rate company for us.

We have a system that employs 8 Macintosh computers, personal computers, several printers—a dot matrix printer for printing our own forms, two impact printers to do letters so that they look like typed letters, and a laser printer for other kinds of projects. We do not use labels; everything is typed. All of these separate pieces of equipment are connected to a Texas Instruments Explorer, a Visual Intelligence Computer, and enough disk storage for a million guest histories.

We have rapid, online access to this information; it comes right up. We don't wait for it; it's there. We can carry on a phone conversation with someone we're supposed to know, someone who has been coming for four years but whom we can't remember personally. By the time we have that person's name typed into the system, if that's the only name like it we have, the information on that person is there. If it's a name like others, by the time we hear what town he is from or whatever, we know who he is. We know what rooms he had in the past, what rates he paid, what the furniture arrangements were, what the starting times were, what tables he had in the dining room. We know what we're supposed to know when we remember our friends. And that impresses the hell out of them, I'll tell you. I talked with a fellow yesterday, or two days ago, who had never himself been to the hotel but who had made inquiries two years before and whose parents had come. His parents have the same name as his; he's an undersecretary for HUD in Washington. And he said the reason he came was that when he called again two years later, we knew about his parents and remembered that he had called two years before; that's why. And we write to all those who make inquiries; those who don't come, we write—8,000 of them this summer season, 8,000 inquiries from the previous summer season.

We are in the past-guest business. We spent a lot of time talking with Eloquent. We had formal sessions during which we told them the life story of reservations and the front office. They recorded all of this material on videotape with notes and came back with a system. They even copied our form. Our reservation form was a pink sheet, so in the computer it's called a pink sheet. They had desktop publishing so that one could move and shuffle papers right within the computer just as the staff had always done on their own desks.

It was a wonderful arrangement, just as it has always been. Only now there was no noise; now there were no files; now there was no competition on the tape chart. There were no double bookings and no holes. When we make a request for a space and we find out all the things that our guest wants—a room with a view, double beds, this and that—we ask the computer to tell us what rooms are available during the time period. The computer doesn't tell us rooms that are available for one night only. It won't offer that to our reservationist. We'll tell that guest, "Sorry, Sir; we don't have anything in that category for those dates. Would you like to change category or change dates? If you come in a day earlier or a day later, we can have something for you." Since this is usually two months in advance, the guest can adjust. Instead of our adjusting to them and being left with 500 empty-room nights, they adjust to us as recommended by the computer that viewed every room and availability for the dates requested.

The first year we had eight additional guests a day. The occupancy level increased another 3 percent that first year at an average income of $150 per guest day. We put the system in piecemeal. When last year it was fully installed, we had 20 extra guests a day. This was in a hotel that was already full, but we managed to eliminate most one-night vacancies. And, indeed, we register people who play golf and don't stay at the hotel. There are a few people who will come just for the use of the facilities. There are a few people who will come and ski for the day who are not season ticket holders. We register them as guests, get their name and address, write them, tell them about our specials. We do the same thing when a person comes for lunch or dinner at the hotel. Many people who live 50 miles away hold their anniversary party at The Balsams, paying $150 for 4 of them to have dinner, and go home afterward. We get their names and addresses, and we write to these people. We want to know every person who loves The Balsams, and we want to call them from our system by name when it's convenient to us and tell them what we've got going. We do it, and it works.

Indeed, the process has been wonderful because it's led us to understand our operating philosophy so much more. We've made policy changes that have improved reservations and maybe contributed a little to the increased sales that I reported. We no longer have anywhere near the catastrophe that had gone on there. In fact, it was reported by a person knowledgeable both about artificial intelligence and the hospitality industry who had come to see the system that it was the quietest reservations office that he'd ever been to. People are very happy there; the staff stays longer. We pay them more. We make our living on guests and only on guests, so the more guests we have, the better living we make for our staff and for us. We've never missed a past guest. Sometimes Housekeeping forgets to put the bottle of syrup in the room, but it's not because they weren't told. The arrival and departure sheets are now 100 percent accurate. Instead of its being a 4-hour process to figure out on the tape chart who's coming in today, looking it up in the file and all the rest. We now have a wonderful ability to make our projections. For example, on the 15th of May we can ask the computer what the third week of August looks like. How many reservations are there? How many guest nights are there? How many were there last year as of the same time on the 15th of May? When we know that we're doing better than we did last year by 22%, we can cut out the $5,000 ad in the *New York Times*, and we can reschedule it for a time that would be more appropriate for us.

We are now making marketing decisions months in advance. Before we never knew. I would go in and say to Jerry, the guru, "How's it look; how's the chart look?" He would say, "Well, it looks pretty good. You know, I think we're just as busy, but who knows? Right?" But we know now; we know definitely how we compare with the same period last year, and we can go in and find those guests. We can find out whether we're drawing the same from the Boston market or from the Montreal market because the reservationists can't process any reservation unless they ask the question, "How did you happen to hear of The Balsams?" They have to ask that as the very first question after they find out to whom they're talking. And they can't open the system to begin to process it until that answer has been put in there. So we now have very accurate codings.

Author Index

Subject Index